The Global Energy Challenge

Also by the authors:

Andreas Goldthau and Nick Sitter (2015). *A Liberal Actor in a Realist World*: *The EU Regulatory State and the Global Political Economy of Energy*

Caroline Kuzemko (2013). *The Energy Security–Climate Nexus: Institutional Change in the UK and Beyond*

Andreas Goldthau (ed.) (2013). *Handbook of Global Energy Policy*

Caroline Kuzemko, Andrei Belyi, Andreas Goldthau and Michael F. Keating (eds.) (2012). *Dynamics of Energy Governance in Europe and Russia*

Andreas Goldthau and Jan Martin Witte (eds.) (2010). *Global Energy Governance*: *The New Rules of the Game*

The Global Energy Challenge

Environment, Development and Security

Caroline Kuzemko
Michael F. Keating
Andreas Goldthau

First published 2016 by
PALGRAVE

Palgrave in the UK is an imprint of Macmillan Publishers Limited, registered in England, company number 785998, of 4 Crinan Street, London, N1 9XW.

Palgrave Macmillan in the US is a division of St Martin's Press LLC, 175 Fifth Avenue, New York, NY 10010.

Palgrave is a global imprint of the above companies and is represented throughout the world.

Palgrave® and Macmillan® are registered trademarks in the United States, the United Kingdom, Europe and other countries.

ISBN 978-1-137-41007-8   ISBN 978-1-137-41008-5 (eBook)

DOI 10.1007/978-1-137-41008-5

This book is printed on paper suitable for recycling and made from fully managed and sustained forest sources. Logging, pulping and manufacturing processes are expected to conform to the environmental regulations of the country of origin.

A catalogue record for this book is available from the British Library.

A catalog record for this book is available from the Library of Congress.

Contents

List of Figures/Boxes

Figures

Boxes

List of Acronyms

ACER	Agency for the Cooperation of Energy Regulators (EU)
ADB	Asian Development Bank
API	American Petroleum Institute
ASCOPE	ASEAN Council on Petroleum
ASEAN	Association of Southeast Asian Nations
bcm	billion cubic metres
BNDES	Banco Nacional de Desenvolvimento Econômico e Social
BP	British Petroleum
BRICS	Brazil, Russia, India, China, South Africa (bloc of rapidly industrialising countries)
CAFE	corporate average fuel efficiency
CAHOSCC	Conference of African Heads of States on Climate Change
CCGT	combined-cycle gas turbine
CCS	carbon capture and storage
CDM	Clean Development Mechanism
CNOOC	China National Offshore Oil Company
CHP	combined heat and power
CNPC	China National Petroleum Company
CO2	carbon dioxide
COP	Conference of Parties
CRC	carbon reduction commitment
DECC	Department of Energy and Climate Change (UK)
DfID	Department for International Development (UK)
DG CLIMA	Directorate General for Climate Change (EU)
DG ENER	Directorate General for Energy (EU)
DII	Desertec Industrial Initiative
DoD	Department of Defense (USA)
DRC	Democratic Republic of Congo
ECSC	European Coal and Steel Community
ECSEE	Energy Community of South East Europe
ECT	Energy Charter Treaty
EDF	Electricité de France
EERA	European Energy Research Alliance
EEU	Eurasian Economic Union
EIA	Energy Information Agency (USA)
EITI	Extractive Industries Transparency Initiative
EPA	Environmental Protection Agency (USA)
ETS	Emissions Trading System
EU	European Union

EUROMED	Euro-Mediterranean Partnership
FAO	Food and Agriculture Organization (United Nations)
FDI	Foreign Direct Investment
FiTs	feed-in-tariffs
FT	*Financial Times* (newspaper)
G7	Group of Seven
G8	Group of Eight
G20	Group of Twenty
G77	Group of Seventy-seven
GATT	General Agreement on Tariffs and Trade
GDL	global division of labour
GDP	gross domestic product
GECF	Gas Exporting Countries Forum
GHGs	greenhouse gases
GIZ	Deutsche Gesellschaft für Internationale Zusammenarbeit GmbH (Germany)
GW	gigawatts
HDI	Human Development Index
IADB	Inter-American Development Bank
IAEA	International Atomic Energy Agency
ICT	information & communication technologies
IEA	International Energy Agency
IEF	International Energy Forum
IGO	inter-governmental organisation
IMF	International Monetary Fund
IOC	international oil company
IO	international organisation
IPCC	Intergovernmental Panel on Climate Change
IPE	international political economy
IPPs	independent power producers
IR	international relations
IRENA	International Renewable Energy Agency
JODI	Joint Organisations Data Initiative
kWh	kilowatt-hour
LNG	liquefied natural gas
LPG	liquid petroleum gas
LTC	long-term contract
mbd	million barrels per day
MDGs	Millennium Development Goals
MEND	Movement for the Emancipation of the Niger Delta
MNC	multinational corporation
Mtoe	Million tonnes of oil equivalent
NAFTA	North American Free Trade Agreement
NAMA	nationally appropriate mitigation actions
NEA	Nuclear Energy Agency
NBP	(British) National Balance Point

NGO	non-governmental organisation
NIEO	New International Economic Order
NIS	national innovation systems
NOC	national oil company
NYMEX	New York Mercantile Exchange
OECD	Organisation for Economic Cooperation and Development
OPEC	Organization of Petroleum Exporting Countries
PdVSA	Petroleos de Venezuela S.A.
PPA	power purchasing agreement
PPP	public–private partnerships
PV	photovoltaic (solar)
R&D	research and development
REEEP	Renewable Energy and Energy Efficiency Partnership
SAARC	South Asian Association for Regional Cooperation
SALs	structural adjustment loans
SAPP	Southern African Power Pool
SCO	Shanghai Cooperation Organization
SE4ALL	Sustainable Energy for All
SMEs	small and medium-sized enterprises
SOEs	state owned enterprises
SWFs	sovereign wealth funds
tcm	trillion cubic metres
TPED	total primary energy demand
TPES	total primary energy supply
TTF	(Dutch) Title Transfer Facility
TWh	terawatt hours
UK	United Kingdom
UAE	United Arab Emirates
UN	United Nations
UNCED	United Nations Conference on Environment and Development
UNCHE	United Nations Conference on Human Environment
UNCLOS	United Nations Convention on the Law of the Sea
UNDP	United Nations Development Programme
UNEP	United Nations Environmental Programme
UNFCCC	United Nations Framework Convention on Climate Change
USA	United States of America
USAID	United States Agency for International Development
USSR	Union of Soviet Socialist Republics
WB	World Bank
WHO	World Health Organization
WMO	World Meteorological Organization
WTI	West Texas Intermediate (crude oil)
WTO	World Trade Organization
YPF	Yacimientos Petroliferos Fiscales (Argentine oil and gas company)

Acknowledgements

This textbook has been a truly collaborative effort. We have all benefited from advice and support from colleagues, friends and family over the course of the years that it took us to complete it. In particular we would like to thank Steven Kennedy from Palgrave for always guiding and encouraging us through the writing process. We would also like to sincerely thank colleagues, students and friends from the Political Economy of Energy in Europe and Russia (PEEER) network, from Politics and International Studies (PaIS), University of Warwick; the Energy Policy Group, University of Exeter; Richmond, the American International University in London; the Central European University and Harvard Belfer's Geopolitics of Energy Project for enlightening and inspiring debates about energy.

Finally, this book is dedicated to Isobel, Penelope, Ignatz and Jakob, in the hope that political and economic groups all over the world can work more successfully towards resolving the many complex energy challenges around the globe.

Introduction: The Global Energy Challenge

Since the industrial revolution, greenhouse gases (GHGs) in the atmosphere have progressively increased because of human processes, many of which are energy related. Consensus exists that if the climate system warms to more than 2 °C above pre-industrial levels, the implications for our environment and for humankind will be increasingly severe. At the same time, around 1.3 billion people (predominantly in developing states) today live without access to modern energy services (IEA 2013). Energy poverty excludes people from education, health services and economic opportunities. Acknowledging the important role that energy access plays in economic development, the United Nations (UN) declared 2012 the year of 'Sustainable Energy for All'. Concerns over energy security have also made a comeback in world politics since the mid-2000s. Factors such as the rise of China as an energy consumer heavyweight, Russia's assertive energy politics, and renewed energy-related conflict have all contributed to the securitisation of energy across the globe. In short, the world faces a triple global energy challenge: the current, fossil fuel – based energy system is environmentally unsustainable; rapid economic transformation in the developing world fuels steeply rising energy consumption; and finite resources trigger concerns over the security of supply and demand.

This set of three different global energy challenges – a 'trilemma', if you will – contains within it highly complex inter-linkages. Fossil fuel usage impacts not only on our climate, but also on other aspects of our environment, as well as on international energy politics, investments and markets. The necessity for climate change mitigation, in turn, infers the need for new sources of energy, increased efficiency of use as well as a reduction in demand for many countries. Yet, the need to rapidly expand electricity access to millions of households around the world is clearly in tension with such energy policy objectives. Any trade-off that exists between energy-intensive growth strategies and their negative environmental side-effects must be carefully managed. However, if this implies the development of alternative supplies, new technologies, and infrastructures, then synergies with environmental policy objectives may in fact exist. Yet concerns over energy security, including for the stability of supply systems, create difficulties with precisely this strategy. The highly intertwined nature of the elements of the energy trilemma has, consequently, contributed to the fact that domestic energy politics is increasingly (and deeply) embedded within regional and international contexts. In other words, markets, actors and national and international energy policy agendas can no longer be meaningfully separated. The question of what states do and where investment capital goes with regard to the energy sector are fundamentally interlinked.

In recognising these complexities, this book aims to provide substantial explanations and analysis of the global energy challenge. Its focus on the energy trilemma sets it apart from other approaches to the study of energy in the social sciences, which typically adapt a single focus (usually either security or climate), and thereby miss much of the nuance and complexity involved in the study of global energy as a whole. Furthermore, such studies often remain embedded within disciplinary boundaries. By conceptualising energy as increasingly inter-linked with, and important to, other subject areas such as politics, economics, development studies and environmental studies, this book is by necessity much broader in scope. This allows us to identify and explain some of the overlaps and tensions between different issue areas, as well as different approaches to these energy challenges, whilst at the same time offering rich empirical insights into key trends in global energy.

The approach of this book

This book begins with the premise that addressing the global energy challenge requires these complexities to be acknowledged. Different approaches to the study of global energy phenomena are therefore set out in a multi-disciplinary context. The primary focus is on international relations, development studies, economics, environmental studies and political science, along with public policy, sociology, technology studies, business and legal approaches where relevant. The emphasis is not only on demonstrating the inter-connectedness of energy issues, but also on engaging with the actors and processes that are driving world energy patterns and transformations, and key policy decisions. This book does not set out to dismiss or detract from any particular approach, but rather to explain their differences, and to demonstrate how an appreciation of the diversity of these approaches can lead to a fuller understanding of the subject matter. For this purpose, selected analytical 'perspectives' are introduced in the beginning of the book, in order to allow the reader to link these to the empirical evidence and cases that are provided throughout. We seek to highlight how different frameworks are used to interpret what are fundamental aspects of the global energy challenge. Rather than taking sides in the disputes that result, this book aims to present and evaluate different positions: non-polemic attention to the academic scholarship and intellectual debates in global energy is the key pedagogical objective.

This book also provides an overview of some of the most important and topical energy-specific debates concerning environment, development and security. The rise of energy geopolitics with its concerns for 'energy weapons' and the 'race for resources' is addressed, as are debates over the appropriate role of markets – debates that divide advocates of free market solutions to energy problems from their critics. The prospects for a low-carbon transition are considered in the context of energy system inertia, and of debates over the role of technology and innovation in solving energy problems. We engage with shifts in global energy governance – including the emergence of new global institutions – while also considering the role of non-state actors, including business interests.

Rather than providing a detailed overview of the energy politics and policies of particular states or regions, this book will enable the reader to apply a range of conceptual and analytical frameworks to case studies in which they are interested. Case studies, conceptual interventions and empirical pointers are found throughout the book, to help the reader to contextualise the material and make better theoretical sense of it. Boxes and figures are used to highlight such material where relevant.

The structure of this book

This book features nine substantive chapters as well as an introduction and a conclusion. These are: Perspectives on the Global Energy Challenge; Evolution and Dynamics of the World Energy System; The Political Economy of Energy; Actors and Institutions; Environment and Climate Change; Energy for Development; Energy Security and Conflict; Transit and Infrastructure; and Technology and Innovation.

Chapter 1, **Perspectives on the Global Energy Challenge**, places the energy trilemma within the context of four broadly defined 'perspectives': political, economic, environmental and technological. These perspectives provide an analytical 'toolbox' with which we can begin to interpret the empirical phenomena discussed in subsequent chapters. Derived from the different disciplines discussed above, the discussion of these perspectives on the global energy challenge serves as heuristic lenses and reference points for the discussion of energy events, and for reflections on the synergies and conflicts that emerge from attempts to address the energy trilemma.

Chapter 2, **Evolution and Dynamics of the World Energy System**, provides an overview of the global energy system. It explains the importance of energy in fuelling modern economies and explores the emergence of the contemporary energy world from rural societies, through industrialisation, up until today. We explore the sources and geographical distribution of global energy, and discuss how global supply and demand patterns and the energy mix as a whole are set to change in the decades ahead. Specific fuels are dissected in terms of how they are produced, distributed, consumed, priced and traded. The chapter also sheds light on the technologies and infrastructures needed to produce and trade energy.

Chapter 3, **The Political Economy of Energy**, discusses how state and market actors interact with one another in global energy. Energy challenges are placed in the context of the changing constellations of state and market actors, and of important international landmark 'events', such as the rise of the

Seven Sisters oil cartel, the 1970s oil crises, and the emergence of new energy consumers such as China. The chapter also outlines various paradigm shifts within energy governance, notably with regard to the rise of neo-liberalism and the more recent return of state involvement in energy affairs.

Chapter 4, **Actors and Institutions**, provides an overview of the governance of the contemporary global energy system. It explains the complex institutional architecture in global energy, with regard to its multilateral (GATT/ WTO) and regional dimensions (NAFTA, EU, Asian organisations). The chapter discusses the important role played in global energy policy by international organisations such as OPEC, the IEA, national and international oil companies, as well as emerging governance institutions. It also examines how current energy trends might affect the incumbent system of global energy governance, and possibly fragment it further.

Chapter 5, **Energy, Climate Change and the Environment**, assesses the energy–climate nexus and the politics of low-carbon transition. It examines the governance institutions that are most actively involved in climate mitigation, as well as the greenhouse gas emission reduction policy initiatives that are found on global, regional, national and sub-national levels. Particular emphasis is placed on the tools and mechanisms used at different levels, including binding international agreements, such as the expiring Kyoto Protocol, regional carbon trading systems (ETS), and national feed-in-tariffs (FITs). The chapter also emphasises the variety of actors involved in climate governance, ranging from multilateral lending organisations such as the World Bank to civil society networks.

Chapter 6, **Energy for Development**, addresses the energy–poverty nexus, the challenge of sustainable development in the developing world, and issues of energy and inequality. Empirical examples centre on cookstoves and unimproved fuel use, on reform strategies in the electricity sector, on rural electrification strategies and on international development aid targeting domestic energy sector modernisation. The chapter also discusses the 'resource curse' and development challenges relating to large energy endowments. Different aspects of the resource curse phenomenon are critically addressed, along with different strategies for improving energy resource management in the developing world.

Chapter 7, **Energy Security**, critically reflects on different definitions of energy security before exploring various global energy security problems. These problems are seen to arise from political events, market developments, technical failures or emerging non-traditional security threats. Particular focus is placed on contemporary security challenges, including geopolitical events surrounding Chinese energy diplomacy, problems emerging from developing states (both highly indebted poor countries (HIPCs) and emerging economies), and climate-related aspects of energy security. The chapter examines institutional energy security approaches – balancing an exporter's perspective (Russia) with an importer's perspective (the EU).

Chapter 8, **Transit and Infrastructure**, explains the crucial role transit and infrastructure play in the global energy challenge. It discusses sea-borne and network-based transit issues, notably with regard to choke points such as the Strait of Hormuz and large-scale pipelines such as Keystone XL, Nord Stream and South Stream. It also assesses the security dimension of energy transit and infrastructure and looks specifically at the Caspian Basin and the Persian Gulf. Cross-border and cooperative infrastructure issues are addressed, notably with regard to the role of electricity networks and regional grids in the context of low-carbon energy transitions.

Chapter 9, **Technology and Innovation**, accounts for the role that technology and innovation play in driving change in the energy sector. It discusses the role of markets and states in driving energy innovation, and distinguishes between sequential and disruptive effects on energy systems. The chapter emphasises the significance of energy innovation as part of the rise of 'knowledge economies' and within the context of the global division of labour, and assesses the role played by state R&D in this regard. Empirical cases used to support the analysis include photovoltaic systems in Germany, shale gas drilling technology, the electric car and the role of the US 'military industrial complex' in energy innovation. The chapter also discusses the prospects of energy technology transfer toward developing states as an option for both promoting global energy innovation and enabling new, low-carbon development strategies.

In the final section, **Conclusion: Synergies, Conflicts and Energy Futures**, we return to the question of complexity and inter-connections between the energy issues that previous chapters have covered. Synergies and conflicts in meeting the varying policy objectives of the different dimensions of the energy trilemma are discussed, with particular reference to 'energy independence', 'climate security', and poverty and equity issues. We finish with a look at 'scenario planning' – attempts to map out the future of energy systems so as to construct better business and policy strategies to meet the global energy challenges of environment, development and security.

Chapter 1

Perspectives on the Global Energy Challenge

Understandings of world energy systems and the challenges they face necessarily reflect particular perspectives. Perspectives are systems of ideas and beliefs through which people understand and explain the operation of their social world. In energy, analysts, engineers, scientists and corporate executives use these perspectives to help frame the issues, identify problems and suggest solutions. Energy governance decisions then reflect the perspectives that have been used to inform decision-making. Each perspective casts light on different aspects of the global energy challenge, but in focusing analysis on some variables this necessarily excludes others. Given the range of different perspectives available, there can be a broad variety of different policy agendas in the energy sector, and different justifications used even for the same set of policy measures. Indeed, perspectives are more than just worldviews – they are also the practical actions that derive from a particular worldview.

It is important to comprehend the scope of the different perspectives that actors are adopting with regard to energy. While individual actors or groups may adopt just one perspective, no single perspective – whatever its strengths – can provide a complete understanding of the subject. For example, analysis may focus on technology as a driver of energy system change, whilst ignoring the economic and political context within which energy, and energy technology, is produced. Alternatively, analysis might focus on the geographic location of energy resources and how this drives international conflict, whilst underemphasising the possibilities for inter-state cooperation.

It is therefore important to map the different ways in which energy challenges are analysed, and the different perspectives which actors and policy-makers adopt to make sense of these challenges. Consequently, this chapter proceeds by outlining four broad perspectives on energy. Although there are many overlaps, each perspective provides different sets of ideas about what energy is for, and how energy should be governed. Through this approach, the complex, inter-dependent and changing world of energy can be better understood, and the variety of both contemporary and historical energy interests, agendas and governance structures can be better explained. These perspectives constitute an analytical 'toolbox' that this textbook will use to address particular aspects of the global energy challenges. In this way, the different interpretations of, and policy priorities towards, the environmental, development and security aspects of energy issues will become clearer.

Perspectives on energy

Some of the different perspectives on energy issues have long intellectual and/or practical histories, and within them a number of different and even contradictory approaches can often be identified. Particular states or groups of states may have historically emphasised particular perspectives, but ultimately these approaches to energy must be seen as dynamic – constantly changing and adapting as ideas and social values change along with global, regional and national political and economic conditions. Different perspectives compete with one another over time, providing contrasting explanations of problems as well as solutions, different ideas about the goals to which state policy should be directed, and various views on the appropriate relationship between states and markets (Strange 1988: 16). One has only to look at the competing ideologies of the Cold War to realise the extent to which these perspectives can influence the structure of global politics and economics.

In the disciplines of international relations (IR) and international political economy (IPE), the dominant perspectives are liberalism, realism/mercantilism and Marxism (Gilpin 1987). An overview of these perspectives, along with emerging perspectives such as environmentalism, is provided here. However, this textbook takes a slightly different approach to the structure of discussion. As a result of the focus on global energy challenges, four sets of perspectives are overviewed: *political, economic, environmental* and *technical.* This will not amount to an exhaustive list of the ways in which energy can be interpreted, but will cover the most common perspectives taken by academics or used by policy-makers or other actors. Given the similarities and overlaps, as well as frankly porous boundaries between the approaches covered here, they must be understood as 'ideal types'. It helps to reflect upon this four-point typology by reminding ourselves of some of the theoretical claims of contemporary IPE.

IPE as a contemporary discipline makes five core propositions (see Keating *et al.,* 2012: 4).

1. An interdisciplinary approach is necessary.
2. A multiplicity of actors and institutions must be recognised.
3. Domestic, regional and global 'levels' are systematically interdependent.
4. Analysis must be open to a broad range of methods and normative concerns.
5. Policy areas are interlinked rather than discrete.

The first proposition is crucial – analysing energy 'economics', for example, without understanding how it relates to energy 'politics', would exclude significant social factors as well as power relations. It is important therefore that these energy perspectives are not simply set out: they are also critiqued, so as to identify where they constrain energy analysis as well as where they further it. Analysis of global energy challenges clearly needs to engage with other disciplines beyond politics and economics, including public international law, human geography, environmental studies and development studies.

The four other propositions are also followed closely in this book. Different actors, institutions and governance arrangements are explicitly focused on, and while the subject at hand is the global energy challenge, linkages to regional, national and even local levels are strongly emphasised throughout. Normative issues – particularly those relating to environment and development concerns – constitute one of the central concern of this textbook. Furthermore, despite the explicit focus on energy issues, these are not regarded as existing in isolation from other policy areas or from broader trends in political economy. A consistent effort is made to explain the context in which energy decisions are made by the many actors involved.

Political perspectives

The first perspectives discussed here are broadly termed 'political'. Although there are many political ideologies in the world today, the focus here is on realism, liberalism and socialism, discussing their main analytical focal points as well as their implications for policy agendas and governance arrangements. One particularly important theme in these political perspectives is the understanding of *sovereignty*; that is, of the state, and how political perspectives on energy are reflected in prospects for international conflict and cooperation between states.

Realism

Realism, which focuses on state security, has historically been the dominant perspective in international relations (see Box 1.1). Realist analysis has also predominated over international energy relations, particularly in the 20th century, given the significance of oil as a resource. Energy security, for realists, implies either security of supply (in consumer states) or demand (in producer states). For consumer states, control over, and access to, energy resources – by any means necessary – becomes a central policy priority. As President Richard Nixon put it in 1974:

> Security and economic considerations are inevitably linked and energy cannot be separated from either. (Nixon quoted in Strange 1988)

These assumptions lead to a singular conclusion: states are driven to maximise their security but have no guarantees about the actions of other states. Consequently, they seek to enhance security by maximising their power – including military power. Perversely, these military build-ups make states even more insecure. However, if warfare is necessary to achieve state goals, then for realists it should be pursued. War is simply an aggressive form of diplomacy, 'the continuation of politics by other means' (Clausewitz 1832).

Neo-realists are prepared to relax some of classical realism's assumptions. They accept that while states remain the dominant actors in world politics,

Box 1.1 Classical and structural realism

Realism has long historical antecedents, including Thucydides (413 BCE), Nicòlo Machiavelli (1532) and Thomas Hobbes (1651). Classical realism viewed human nature as self-interested, egotistical, and prone to conflict – at least in the absence of a power able to enforce cooperation through sanctions. Twentieth-century realists focused more on the structural characteristics of international politics (see Waltz 1959). The key assumptions of *structural* realism are:

- Domestic politics and international politics are two separate 'levels of analysis'.
- States are the only actors of significance in world politics.
- States are centralised, unitary and rational actors that act in their national self-interest.
- The international system is in a condition of anarchy (insecurity).
- Power is a *zero-sum game* – if one state gains, then other states are losing in relative terms.

there are patterns in the international system that cannot be explained simply with reference to inter-state power struggles. With regard to energy, this has led neo-realists to think about the role of energy *regimes*, which are forms of limited cooperation between states in the international system. Neo-realists argue that cooperation between states is most likely to occur under conditions of hegemony. In effect, a dominant world power can create and enforce rules for energy governance (see Gilpin 1987).

Geopolitical/economic realism

International energy relations are clearly complicated by geographical factors, such as the distribution of natural resources and the location of oceans and continents. This has given rise to *geopolitics*, a term coined by Rudolf Kjellén and popularised by Halford Mackinder in the early 20th century (see Mackinder 1919). Geopolitics matters, not simply because crucial resources tend to be territorially fixed and finite, but because they are bound within national borders – sovereign state territory. Consequently, energy access rights have, since the emergence of the European states system and following the period of colonisation, been controlled by states to the exclusion of all other bodies. Geopolitical realism therefore emphasises the international role of the state in energy in terms of securing supply, engaging in strategic alliances, and exercising military power, with access to energy resources seen as a zero-sum game. Evidence of the salience of geopolitical factors would include China's move into African energy markets, and the Russia–Ukraine gas disputes of 2006 and 2009.

As Michael Klare argues in *Rising Powers, Shrinking Planet* (2008), a 'new international order is emerging' which divides states with energy resources from those without. In this view, conflict over access to these resources will come to dominate international relations. States certainly have growing concerns over energy security – and are increasingly focused on 'energy independence', and on promoting the influence of their national oil companies (NOCs). States dependent on the export of energy sources have once again begun to rely on protectionism to secure their national energy industries. Consequently, a shift towards *mercantilist* behaviour in international energy relations may be seen to be emerging.

Mercantilism is economic realism, the IPE version of realism, focusing on how state power is underpinned by economic policy and international economic relations. Early mercantilists viewed trade as a form of undeclared warfare, the objective of which was to sell your goods on the markets of rival states without reciprocity. They advocated protectionism, in the form of tariff barriers, to exclude foreign products from domestic markets. In this game of 'beggar-thy-neighbour', economic relations are a zero-sum game: states must produce economic surpluses at all costs, with deficits a sign of national impoverishment. The objective is to create a trade imbalance, accumulate stockpiles of gold and silver bullion, and use this war chest to support military success (in an era of mercenary armies).

The ideas of mercantilism were restated by Friedrich List in *The National System of Political Economy* (1841), based in part on Alexander Hamilton's *Report on the Subject of Manufactures* (1791). List advocated protectionism for a very specific reason: to promote industrialisation. Industrialisation, not wealth per se, underpinned national economic and military capacity, and hence national security. 'Late industrialising' countries closely followed List's mercantilist policy prescriptions. List pointed to the significance of large national private companies or industrial 'conglomerates' to act as 'national champions' – ensuring sufficient production in key industrial sectors (such as steel) and supplies of essential resources such as coal and oil. This strategy was central to the German and Japanese success story. The USA, meanwhile, featured the highest levels of protectionism in the global economy until 1945.

Political liberalism

The main challenge to realist perspectives has come from liberalism. While classical realists saw states as incapable of cooperation even if this was in their long-term interests, classical liberal scholars believed otherwise (see Box 1.2). This is because for liberals, states are made up of individuals, and individuals are capable of seeing their 'enlightened' self-interest. Consequently, they can cooperate in their long-term interests. Politics is seen by liberals as a *positive-sum game* where everyone can benefit – in stark contrast to realism.

Democracy is important to liberalism in part due to the *democratic peace thesis*: the argument that democracies do not go to war, so by promoting democracy, international relations can be stabilised. It is held that in democracies, electorates do not support war against the citizens of other democracies because

Box 1.2 Classical liberalism

Liberalism has been an enormously influential perspective, particularly in the 19th and 20th centuries. Liberal philosophers such as John Locke (1689) and John Stuart Mill (1859) fought against feudal social organisation, where individual rights were determined by accidents of birth. Liberalism features a strong sense of human individuality, equality and freedom. Core liberal beliefs include:

- The individual is rational and cooperative, and is the main actor in politics.
- Individual rights to life, liberty and property
- Limited government
- The importance of democratic systems of government
- Equality of opportunity and equality before the law

of a shared political ideology – other democracies are allies, not enemies. Political leaders, directly responsible to the electorate, must pay a political cost for pursuing 'illegitimate wars' (i.e. against other democracies), and so they prefer negotiated solutions to international disputes. Unlike realist approaches, liberalism therefore addresses inter-state relations (including explanations for the outbreak of war) with reference to the internal organisation of states.

Political liberalism also emphasises the rights of individuals to freely trade in the marketplace, in part due to the corollary *economic peace thesis*. According to this thesis – attributable to Immanuel Kant, among others – market relations between states were held to reduce the incentives for international conflict. This is because of the resulting higher levels of economic growth, which reduces the potential relative gains from warfare, and because such relations increase the economic costs of warfare, which disrupts trading systems.

Liberal institutionalism is the main form of political liberalism in modern international relations. While accepting much of neo-realism, such as the continuing centrality of the state, this perspective directly addresses prospects for cooperation in the international system. The primary mechanism in this regard is multilateralism, in the form of international treaties, international law and inter-governmental organisations (IGOs) (sometimes called international organisations). Key examples include the United Nations (UN) and various UN agencies such as the International Atomic Energy Agency (IAEA) and UN-Energy. Liberal institutionalism also identifies the possibility of more informal channels of cooperation, in the form of international regimes. Through such mechanisms, liberal institutionalists believe that states can collectively manage their energy relations and security concerns.

Regimes are usually defined as 'implicit or explicit principles, norms, rules and decision-making procedures around which actors' expectations converge in a given area of international relations' (Krasner 1983). They take the form of specialised international arrangements through which states can cooperate to address specific international policy problems. They are usually multilateral and state-driven, and based on shared norms. When informal practices become semi-institutionalised, a regime can be said to emerge. As noted above, neo-realists (such as Krasner) accept the role of regimes in international relations – but view them as the product of a hegemonic state, and limited in their ability to promote cooperation. The role of normative values in driving international energy cooperation is therefore crucial. Norms are defined as implicit or explicit expectations that derive from and operationalise shared social and political ideals. Norms are in effect informal rules: they prescribe certain behaviour or actions, but lack formal, legal status.

For liberal institutionalists, crucially, states can learn from cooperation, which leads to further cooperation. Regimes can therefore develop into formalised international organisations. For example, based on the shared *norm* that nuclear technology should be restricted to civil use, a set of *rules* emerged in the form of the nuclear Non-Proliferation Treaty, a regime which sought to prohibit the trade of nuclear material and technology with non-members. The IAEA was then established as an *international organisation*, charged with guarding these norms and rules.

Norms are also linked to *international law*. Legally embedding norms makes them harder to ignore or overturn, and provides for an enforcement mechanism. Public international law governs the relationship between states and international organisations, while international private law is primarily about determining which jurisdiction is responsible for dealing with specific international legal conflicts. This might pertain to extraction, trade and investment issues in energy. Cross-border pipelines or joint-venture resource extraction might necessitate such rulings if cooperation breaks down.

Two of the most important scholars of liberal institutionalism are Robert Keohane and Joseph Nye Jr. In *Power and Interdependence* (1977), in stark contrast to realist scholarship, they portrayed a world of 'complex interdependence' characterised by the breakdown of the domestic–international dichotomy, the growing significance of non-state actors, the absence of a hierarchy of issues (security, in effect, is losing its relative importance), and the obsolescence of warfare. International relations, consequently, is characterised by growing interdependence between actors – including states. States cooperate because they are unable to pursue their self-interest through unilateral measures. From this perspective, international energy challenges strongly lend themselves to cooperative (including institutional) solutions. Indeed, a complex web of international energy interdependency has emerged that links consumer and producer states together in mutual self-interest.

Socialism

Socialist perspectives are similar to realist and mercantilist perspectives in emphasising the need for considerable state capacity and state economic activity. The goals, however, are egalitarian, rather than power maximisation.

Socialist thinking has however always been divided between revolutionary and reformist approaches. This led to very different strategies between communist states, such as in the Soviet Bloc, and socialist parties in Western democracies.

Two of the most important socialist thinkers, Karl Marx and Friedrich Engels, argued that the revolutionary overthrow of capitalism was both necessary and inevitable (see Box 1.3). This view was shared by Lenin (1917), Trotsky (1930), and the other Russian revolutionaries. This model of revolutionary socialism, however, stood in direct contrast to earlier socialist reformers, such as Robert Owen. Owen (1813-16) argued that healthy, educated workers liberated from the cruelties of the factory system would be more efficient – hence, reformed capitalist enterprises would out-compete exploitative ones. Later socialist reformists, such as Eduard Bernstein (1899), argued that the only ethical acts that socialism could condone were those that reduced the misery of the workers, even if this delayed the revolutionary overthrow of capitalism (perhaps permanently). Reformist socialists were crucial to the Western European labour movements, which formed socialist parties that pursued the *parliamentary route to socialism*. These social democratic parties competed in elections as the franchise expanded to the growing

---

Box 1.3 Marxism

In works such as *The Communist Manifesto* (1848) and *Capital* (1867), the core theoretical concepts of a Marxist socialist perspective are set out by Karl Marx and Friedrich Engels. These thinkers viewed capitalism as a dynamic, progressive force which had increased levels of technology at 'hitherto unimaginable rates' while creating enormous wealth. However, capitalism had a dark side, in the form of exploitation of the workers through wage-slavery, and the alienation of these workers in an oppressive and dehumanising factory system. This was caused by the class struggle between the workers (proletariat) and the wealthy owners of capital (bourgeoisie), which was the central aspect of international politics (rather than the state or the individual). The primary strategic objective of socialism was the revolutionary capture of the state and overthrow of the capitalist system. This outcome was, however, assured, as capitalists could only maintain the rate of profit by lowering wages and causing the further immiseration of – and revolutionising of – the workers (according to the labour theory of value). More than any other thinkers, Marx and Engels are responsible for the core claims and values of socialism, which while similar to liberalism, are interpreted differently:

- Liberty – understood as freedom from exploitation, alienation, class oppression, and the outcomes of a cold and impersonal market system
- Equality – understood in an egalitarian sense, as equality of outcome, and the abolition of structural inequalities such as social class
- Fraternity – understood as solidarity, where the basic social rights are those of collective bargaining and to pursue collective solutions

working classes, and were elected to power in most Western democracies in the first few decades of the 20th century. In the West, particularly after World War II, they built welfare states to provide social support and protection, underpinned by taxation and wealth redistribution.

Socialist perspectives focus on two inter-related tasks of the state. The first is to ensure greater *equity* in the distribution of wealth, whether through direct fiscal transfers or through the 'social wage' (the public provision of goods). It is important, for example, that the price of electricity should be affordable to all households. Consequently, many countries have tended to subsidise, regulate or control energy prices. The socialist agenda also included preventing wealthy elites from developing monopolies in the energy sector, and using this to engage in 'rent seeking' behaviour. The objective of creating profitable businesses in the energy sector is secondary to the well-being of the population at large. Technological progress has also been mediated by equity objectives. As new technologies have emerged (for example electricity in the early part of the 20th century), states sought to promote their diffusion – and so distribute the benefits – across society (Perez 2002).

The second task is to ensure greater fairness in *access* to social or private goods. In energy, this could mean policies designed to increase the number of people with access to electricity, or subsidising modern energy systems and appliances (particularly stoves). Universal access to modern energy services continues to be a central objective of socialist parties and governments. Indeed, within the socialist perspective, energy has been understood to play an important distributional role in society – particularly as an input into social welfare in the form of 'food, clothing, heating, health and shelter' (Helm et al. 1989: 56–7). Given the heavy and long-term costs involved in building the large-scale electricity infrastructure necessary to support such universality, state ownership and intervention has been widespread.

Indeed, *public ownership* has been the primary historical strategy of socialism, across a wide range of industries and economic sectors. The more important or strategic the sector was deemed to be, the more nationalisation was deemed necessary, as it was too risky to leave crucial economic outcomes to the vagaries of the market. Energy utilities, therefore, were in most states nationalised and monolithic in form, with energy for consumers heavily subsidised. Indeed, in Western Europe, the energy sector was one of the strategic sectors of the economy in which social democratic parties had been able to establish nationalisation. Most developing states also followed this approach. Nationalisation of energy assets was also common for large energy producers. While from the 1980s onwards state ownership ceased to be a strong feature of the policies of social democratic parties around the world, regulations designed to promote access and address equity issues remained central to their energy policy and economic policies more generally. However, there has been extensive criticism of these socialist strategies, addressed in the next section, which concerns economic perspectives.

Economic perspectives

While socialism and mercantilism have clear economic policy agendas, these are designed to serve political ends. Liberalism sees economics more as an end in itself. Consequently, economic perspectives are primarily debates between different strands of economic liberalism. At the centre of liberal economic thought are found both the market and the individual. The individuals are *Homo Economicus* – rational, egoistic, self-interested and consumer-oriented. Markets, following Gilpin (1987), feature three central elements: the critical role of the price mechanism (the laws of supply and demand) upon the exchange of goods and services; the centrality of competition in determining the behaviour of actors; and the role of efficiency in determining whether individuals and companies can survive in this context.

For economic liberals, markets are certainly the key to energy issues, as they drive investment decisions, business practices and sector innovations. Competitive markets determine energy prices, which in turn provide information about whether energy assets are making an acceptable return, and whether new energy technologies or processes are cost-competitive and so worth investing in. Markets also channel private capital into the energy sector, or withhold such investment. While liberal economic perspectives on global energy challenges focus on the role of markets, there is considerable dissension between perspectives that broadly favour free markets (neo-classical economics and neo-liberalism), and those that favour regulated markets (particularly Keynesians).

Free market economics

Free market perspectives hold that markets, once free from government intervention, are inherently efficient. This approach dominated international economic thinking from the middle of the 19th century until the 1930s (albeit interrupted by World War I), in the form of economic *laissez-faire*, and again from the 1980s onwards in the form of neo-liberalism. Advocates of this perspective argue that unfettered market relations between consumers and producers generate an optimal allocation of economic resources. This, in turn, leads to maximum aggregate levels of global economic wealth. Government intervention is unnecessary because the system is self-regulating: competition between producers and consumers ensures that appropriate prices for goods result. Efficient producers are rewarded with profits, while inefficient producers go out of business in cycles of 'creative destruction' (Schumpeter 1942). This faith in the positive effects of the price mechanism is grounded in classical liberal political economy (see Box 1.4).

However, while free market economic perspectives rose to dominance in the 1980s, this was largely in the form of neo-liberalism. Neo-liberal approaches were synonymous in this period with the policies of Ronald Reagan (US President 1981–1989) and Margaret Thatcher (British Prime Minister 1979–1990). Neo-liberalism also became central to the

Box 1.4 Classical liberal political economy

Adam Smith's *The Wealth of Nations* (1776), one of the most influential books ever written, sought to explain the rise and operation of the capitalist system, and in so doing provided some of the central concepts of economic perspectives. Smith asserted that people pursuing their own self-interest will make society better off, as their self-interest is regulated by competition in the marketplace. Smith pointed out that prices were determined by impersonal forces of 'supply' and 'demand' in a competitive market, and this fundamental principle of market operations became the *price mechanism*. Smith also argued that in the absence of government intervention, overall economic wealth will be increased if people specialise and trade. This is because only free trading relations are by definition welfare-improving (otherwise people simply wouldn't trade). Smith called for a 'Night Watchman State', providing security and enforcing property rights and contracts, and otherwise keeping out of the economy.

David Ricardo, in *On the Principles of Political Economy and Taxation* (1817), developed the concept of *comparative advantage*, which is a crucial adjunct to Smith's ideas. Ricardo argues that what is rational for individuals is also rational for states: countries should specialise in what they are good at and trade with other countries. Like Smith, Ricardo believed that free trade would maximise global economic wealth, a position with obvious implications for international energy relations.

Neo-classical economics is the mainstream approach within the contemporary discipline of economics. Neo-classical economics reflects the failure of classical liberal economics to respond to the Great Depression of the 1930s. While free markets are seen as maximising wealth, there is a clear role for the state in this economic perspective: to correct *market failures*. Market failure analysis certainly applies to the energy sector, and a range of government actions designed to make energy markets function more effectively can be identified. However, global market failures related to climate change or oil cartels, for example, pose more fundamental problems. Here, an international free rider problem exists, with no global authority able to sanction non-cooperative states. Despite this, it is important to introduce some of the most important neo-classical market failures that apply to energy issues:

- *Information asymmetry* occurs when market actors lack perfect information. In the case of global energy, there is widespread uncertainty regarding prices, supply channels, and the behaviour of various energy actors – all of which serve as a disincentive to investment. In response, states have cooperated to create international institutions explicitly designed to promote energy sector transparency and market information – most obviously, the International Energy Agency (IEA).
- *Incomplete markets* are a significant cause of market failure in the developing world. Lack of insurance companies, distressed debt agencies, stock markets and financial lending facilities create numerous problems for business, including in the energy sector. Much greater reliance on the state follows from the lack of a fully functioning modern capitalist system.

$\rightarrow$

$\rightarrow$

- *Monopolies* are a serious market failure, as they can lead to price fixing. A small number of producers can form an *oligopoly*, reproducing monopoly market conditions. Given the large investments and infrastructure management issues associated with electricity sectors, electricity utilities were historically considered 'natural monopolies'. Consequently, the state often took ownership and control of the energy sector.
- *Externalities* occur when the full cost of the production of the good is not included in the price. For example, coal-fired electricity generation facilities can pump pollution into the atmosphere, causing health costs that are picked up neither by the electricity producers or consumers. 'Third parties' to the transaction mean that markets are functioning inefficiently – which leads to resource under-pricing and over-consumption. Externalities need to be 'internalised' through state action – ensuring that the market price for electricity also reflects the clean-up costs of pollution.
- *Public goods* are products and services that the market struggles to provide. They may be 'non-excludable' (you can't prevent people from using the good) and/or 'non-rival' (one person's use of the good doesn't preclude someone else from using the good). A public goods perspective sees energy as more than just a commodity to be freely bought and sold in a market. It focuses on the broader role that energy plays in economic development, equity and security. Free rider problems emerge because individuals may not be willing to pay for these social benefits if they accrue to everyone.

development aid loan conditions of the 1980s and 1990s in what is termed the 'Washington Consensus'. The primary objective of neo-liberalism in this period was to reduce the role of the state in the market, and to extend the reach of the market into more aspects of social life. Neo-liberalism also viewed politicians as inherently self-interested. As a result, government economic decision-making is 'politicised', usually in the context of election cycles, leading to inflationary economic consequences. Neo-liberalism also responded to the neo-classical take on market failures with a simple political mantra: government failure is always worse than market failure. Consequently, no matter how extreme or difficult market failures may appear, government intervention is never justified.

There are a number of government failures which apply to the energy sector. *Bureaucratic expansionism* saw sprawling, inefficient and overemploying government energy utilities run up enormous losses – demonstrating that private monopolies or competitive market structures would deliver better outcomes. State ownership also generated 'crowding out' effects, as the private sector avoids competing with government energy companies that could be subsidised from a central budget – crucial investment capital is driven away. Government bail-outs for state or even private sector energy actors create *moral hazards*, undermining incentives to be efficient. Government regulations ('red tape'), price-fixing and subsidies (i.e. for fossil fuel production, clean energy, industry, and household consumers) lead to *distortions of the price mechanism*. This causes misallocations of investment or underinvestment. Due to *information failure*, where governments lack access to market price signals, state investment results in unnecessary 'white elephants': large infrastructure projects that are massively underutilised and run huge losses. The growing costs of government failure don't go away – they accrue to the government, and so to taxpayers.

Neo-liberal strategies to reduce state intervention in the economy included privatisation, trade and financial liberalisation, deregulation, reducing the influence of the unions, and tax cuts – particularly for the productive, wealth-generating business sector (the rich). Neo-liberal governments were scathing towards the welfare state, which was seen to entrench, rather than reduce, poverty, and sought to significantly scale back government spending. While 'public goods', socialist or mercantilist arguments led to energy sector assets being nationalised in the 'national interest', in practice for neo-liberals this simply enabled political elites to exert and maintain power, including through the pursuit of narrow, geopolitical objectives. Neo-liberals sought to privatise energy sector assets and make the energy sector reflect market relations: and by facilitating greater wealth generation, make a better contribution to the public good. The neo-liberal policy agenda particularly reflected the views of the Milton Friedman and Friedrich von Hayek (see Box 1.5).

Neo-liberalism greatly influenced energy sector governance and organisation. From a neo-liberal perspective, energy is indeed a commodity – a tradable and

---

Box 1.5 Friedrich von Hayek and Milton Friedman

Friedrich von Hayek, in *The Road to Serfdom* (1944) argued that state intervention in the economy, even when explicitly designed to promote economic security, was doomed to have the opposite effect. This is because markets operate through decentralised information available only to consumers and producers. State planners, lacking access to these crucial price signals, can only ever make second-best decisions, inevitably producing a sub-optimal allocation of economic resources. Even worse, once governments accumulate economic power, this increases their political power and leads to totalitarianism. Milton Friedman, in *Capitalism and Freedom* (1962) focuses more on the 'magic of the market' – what the free market price mechanism can achieve when liberated from government intervention. For both Hayek and Friedman, political freedom is inextricably linked to the economic freedom that can only be provided by a free market economy. Both Thatcher and Reagan explicitly cited these thinkers as inspirations for their neo-liberal policy agenda.

substitutable private good – rather than a strategic asset or a public good. Supply and demand should therefore be determined by the mechanisms of the market. In the 1980s and 1990s, many Western states not only enacted large-scale privatisation programmes but also liberalised and deregulated the energy industry so as to foster competition and consumer choice. The UK and the USA were at the forefront of this trend. Other key institutions that promoted neo-liberal energy sector reform included the Organisation for Economic Cooperation and Development (OECD) and the European Union (both within the EU and to external states), and the proponents of the Washington Consensus – the World Bank and the International Monetary Fund (IMF).

1980s neo-liberalism, clearly, was relentlessly anti-state, with government activity being seen as the cause of all problems – including those of poor developing states. However, precisely because neo-liberalism was so influential on policy-making in the 1980s, the limitations of neo-liberal policy strategies in achieving their goals were readily apparent by the end of this decade. The IMF and the World Bank's implementation of neo-liberal economic policies in the developing world through the mechanism of structural adjustment loans (SALs) was disastrous, particularly in Latin America and sub-Saharan Africa. In order to explain the failure of market economics in the 1980s, neo-liberalism adopted the view that the state in these regions lacked the capacity – the 'good governance' – to manage a transition to free market capitalism. Corrupt, unaccountable and undemocratic regimes ('poor governance') held back market-led development. Neo-liberalism therefore shifted from the view that the state was the problem, to the position that the state – a small, efficient, particularly neo-liberal state – was necessary to 'lock-in' free market capitalism.

The case for regulated markets

Alternative economic perspectives, however, are much more sceptical of the operation of the market mechanism, and of capitalism more generally. These perspectives share a broader conception of market failure, and of the ability of markets – particularly unregulated markets – to deliver socially acceptable outcomes. Indeed, it was precisely the consequences of unregulated market activity that exacerbated social inequality in the socialist perspective.

Indeed, socialist critics viewed capitalism as a system of cyclical economic crises. Marx, for structural reasons, argued that the only solution was to abolish the market. Later Marxists such as Lenin and Trotsky argued that capitalism was a system that promoted 'uneven and combined development' (see Trotsky 1930); that is, it also drove inequality between states, creating tensions between them. Capitalism, therefore, was even more unstable than Marx had believed. The theory of Imperialism (see Lenin 1917) held that states responded to these tensions through a kind of expansionist mercantilism: first seeking access to foreign markets (the Great Powers' 'race to the colonies' of the late 19th century), and then engaging in military conflict over these colonies (World War I). The link between inter-state rivalry, military conflict and the drive for resources is even more evident during World War II, where lack of access to oil was a serious issue for both Germany and Japan. Indeed, German desperation led to the mass production of 'Jerry Cans' (with 'Jerry' common slang for the German soldiers used in World War I) – small oil containers carried by soldiers to be used for siphoning petrol.

However, socialists in the reformist camp saw capitalism's tendency to collapse as policy-based. Capitalism could in fact be regulated and controlled through judicious state action. 'Market socialism', welfare capitalism, social democracy and other varieties of state-managed capitalism would result in a more stable and socially progressive system. One key thinker in this socialist perspective is Karl Polanyi, author of *The Great Transformation* (1944). For Polanyi, the problem is not markets, but the *market utopia* of unfettered, unregulated free markets that *laissez-faire* (and neo-liberalism) represents. With proper – and democratic – control of the economy, government regulation could ensure socially progressive outcomes for ordinary people as well as for the environment. Hence, a regulated market economy, linked to democratic systems of accountability, was socialism by definition. The attempt to 'free' markets through liberalisation and deregulation, however, created both economic and social instability, and resulted in economic crises. These led inexorably to societies moving back towards statist economic management.

In the West, however, one economic perspective that advocated regulated markets was far more influential than all others: Keynesianism (see Box 1.6). Keynes offered a 'third way', a state-managed form of capitalism that would enable liberal democracies to survive in the face of the two less appealing choices that arose in the 1930s: fascism and communism. This call for government intervention to manage, stabilise and restore to growth the capitalist economies fell on receptive ears, and Keynesianism was so successful it effectively replaced classical economics as the standard approach followed by government policy-makers in non-communist countries.

The Keynesian plan for 'managed capitalism' overlapped to some extent with the reformist traditions of the socialist perspective. Indeed, for many social democratic parties, the practical policies with which they sought to reform capitalism came straight out of the Keynesian toolbox. A mix of Keynesian economic policies and socialist nationalisation strategies therefore characterised the energy sector in many post-war social democratic states. The Keynesian approach justified widespread state intervention, particularly in strategic economic sectors which underpinned employment, as well as calling for redistributive welfare spending. This also carried implications for the energy sector, which served as an input to all other segments of the economy: the state could not afford to let the market decide economic outcomes in this case. Prices for end-consumers were also managed to ensure economic stability. Keynesian deficit spending, aimed at 'pump-priming' the economy, focused on large infrastructure sectors – of which energy was a significant

Box 1.6 Keynes's general theory on employment, interest and money (1936)

The Great Depression of the 1930s seriously undermined classical liberal economic theory, which argued that recessions and structural unemployment were impossibilities. In the *General Theory*, Keynes dismissed 'Say's Law', demonstrating that recessions could happen, and argued that it was possible for economies to reach 'underemployment' equilibrium – featuring long-term, stable unemployment. The classical solution to the Great Depression, furthermore, was to do nothing: governments, like households, should operate within their budget. Keynes freed economics from these constraints, not only enabling governments to try and kick-start the economy ('stimulating aggregate demand') through deficit spending, but arguing for the necessity of this demand management. Part of the problem was that individuals tended to act *pro-cyclically*, hoarding money and reducing expenditure in response to an economic recession precisely at the time when spending was most needed. Only states had the power to act *counter-cyclically*, and bring economies out of recession. Large public works and infrastructure building projects were therefore deemed necessary, though it was the even greater increase in government spending caused by World War II that ultimately lifted the West out of depression – and into two decades of strong economic growth under conditions of full employment. Indeed the 1950s and 1960s, the 'golden age of capitalism', occurred under the 'Keynesian consensus' on economic policy.

beneficiary. For example, in the USA Roosevelt's 'New Deal' featured strong investments in hydro-electric dam projects.

This predominance of Keynesianism as an economic perspective lasted until the 1970s, when new forms of economic crisis caused Keynes's ideas to be thrown into question. By the 1980s, neo-liberalism had emerged as the economic perspective that policy-makers adhered to, and deregulation of the energy sector was widely pursued. Nevertheless, in the wake of the global economic crisis (2007 onwards) – a crisis of neo-liberalism – Keynesian ideas underwent something of a revival. Yet, the sovereign debt crisis (2010 onwards) that resulted from the global economic crisis has led to *laissez-faire* style 'austerity' approaches. In the contemporary world, economic perspectives are clearly in flux. By extension, energy policy is also in a deep state of uncertainty – uncertainty that is only exacerbated by concerns with, and debates over, climate change.

Environmental perspectives

Economic and political perspectives can all be deemed *anthropocentric*: they focus on humans and human institutions. They lack a well-developed conception of the relationship between humanity and nature – a gap which environmental perspectives seek to fill. Environmental perspectives have a long history (see Sørensen 2012), but only began to penetrate into broader social debates in the 1970s (see Box 1.7).

The modern environmental movement that emerged from the 1970s began to develop broad critiques of consumer capitalism. While communist states had worse environmental records, in Western countries where interest in the environment was flourishing markets were seen as putting short-term individual self-interest above environmental concerns. Similarly,

Box 1.7 The modern environmental movement

Post-war environmentalism developed out of historical concerns with conservation into a broader critique of human society, particularly in economic terms. The green movement emerged out of other movements, such as the civil rights, peace and anti-nuclear movements. One key early work is Rachel Carson's *Silent Spring* (1962), which detailed the imminent threat to nature and wildlife posed by the widespread use of pesticides. This book was instrumental in the banning of DDT in the USA, and in the formation of the Environmental Protection Agency (EPA).

The 1970s was the key period in the emergence of the environmental movement: Greenpeace was formed in 1971, and the United Nations held its first environmental conference in 1972. Herman Daly, author of *Towards a Steady State Economy* (1973), founded the sub-discipline of ecological economics. Daly's influential work argued that economic growth led directly to environmental collapse. Only a radical restructuring of the global economy away from growth could help. Daly also worked as a Senior Economist at the World Bank – evidence of how environmental perspectives started to impact on mainstream political and economic debates. 1972 saw the publication of the Club of Rome's controversial *The Limits to Growth* (Meadows et al.). This report used computer simulations to show how the combination of finite planetary resources, world population growth, industrialisation and pollution was placing insurmountable pressures on planet Earth. Drastic measures for environmental protection were required. Reflecting the growth of the environment as an issue, *The Limits to Growth* was translated into 37 different languages, and over 12 million copies were distributed.

Although there are clearly different positions within the modern environmental movement, the core values, ideas and principles of an environmental perspective can be identified as follows:

- Planet Earth is an inter-connected biosphere on which humans depend.
- Human activity (particularly economic) is disrupting the ecological balance.
- Humans should live in positive co-existence with nature – not seek to dominate it.
- Humans must take responsibility for limiting the environmental damage they cause.

states prioritised a range of 'national-interests' over environmental concerns. Therefore aspects of both political and economic perspectives were understood to lead to a range of negative impacts of human activity on the environment. As we will see below, the medium and long-term consequences of this were understood to be significant.

Environmental perspectives, however, have tended to come and go in public discourse. As early as 1972, Anthony Downs published 'Up and Down with Ecology: The Issue Attention Cycle', which used environmental concerns as a key example of how issues rise to public prominence and then fade away again. Certainly, economic recessions tend to push environmental issues out of the spotlight, as problems with unemployment and business collapses take precedence. In better economic times, however, people reflect the kinds of 'post-material values' (Inglehart 1981) that enable growing public support for environmental issues.

Environmental concerns and activity have often been highly localised, focusing on the storage of nuclear waste, local air or water pollution, land degradation, urban hazards or toxic spills. The environmental perspective, however, is also concerned with environmental problems at a global level. Indeed, the concept of the *global commons* is highly significant to environmental perspectives. The existence of such commons enables the environmental perspective to move beyond local and national issues, and provide a critical perspective on international politics and economics. The term 'global' has begun to replace the term 'international', in part as a reflection of the growing significance of non-state actors to world politics. The term 'commons' refers to a resource to which no single decision-making unit holds exclusive title, the origins of which lie in medieval times, when pasture and woodland were by custom set aside for the joint use of villagers.

The global commons are understood as areas beyond sovereign state jurisdiction that no one individual or group of individuals can lay claim to. Examples include Antarctica, the deep seabed, space and the atmospheric commons. They belong to us all equally, and no one has the right to do anything that might damage these common goods. From this position, many environmentalists advocate that we 'think global, act local' to ensure a better environmental future (see Schumacher 1973). However, managing global commons is in effect a global public goods problem. As neo-classical economics suggests, no one wants to pay to maintain global commons that others will exploit, and no authority exists that is able to punish those that do damage these commons. Some attempts, however, are made on an international scale to protect aspects of the global environment – such as the Kyoto Protocol of the United Nations Framework Convention on Climate Change (UNFCCC).

Today, environmental perspectives propose a broad range of solutions to various environmental governance issues, including different conceptions of the relationship between humankind and nature. They can, however, be grouped into two broad camps. Radical environmentalism works in the anti-growth traditions of Daly, and argues for significant changes to human relations with the environment. Mainstream environmentalism, which is reformist and pro-growth, emerged in the late 1980s, in part due to its less adversarial view of the political and economic perspectives has become increasingly influential.

Radical versus mainstream environmentalism

Radical environmental perspectives emphasise the non-hierarchical inter-relationship between humans and nature, and view the environment holistically. Economic growth – the primary objective of almost every country in the world – is seen as the major cause of environmental stress. In energy terms, radical environmentalism is historically strongly anti-nuclear, and highly critical of carbon-intensive and polluting modern energy systems. This approach is shared by a number of 'Green' political parties around the world, global environmental non-governmental organisations (NGOs), and environmental scientists. The deep structural changes that need to take place in social, political and economic systems imply that we should slow growth, consume less and conserve more. Radical lifestyle changes are mandated, shifting towards localised production and consumption, eating seasonal and regional foods, travelling less and consuming only that which can be reproduced without detrimental effects on nature.

In the 1980s, broad social support for environmental positions began to be seen around the industrialised world. A string of environmental problems became big news in this decade, increasing the pressure on states to formulate a response. First, the hole in the ozone layer not only demonstrated that industrial and commercial chemicals used by humans damaged the environment, but also that states could, through multilateral cooperation, address these issues (in the form of the Montreal Protocol). Second, sulphur emissions from industrial production began to fall back down to Earth in the form of sulphuric acid. Acid rain caused widespread demands for pollution controls, particularly in Germany where serious damage was done to the Black Forest (the *Schwarzwald*). Third, the 1986 Chernobyl disaster – the ongoing costs of which are measured in hundreds of billions of US dollars – massively raised awareness of the limits of human capacity to control environmental risks posed by technologies, as well as of the obvious problems with nuclear energy. Finally, as addressed in detail below, the global scientific community reached a consensus on the role of greenhouse gas emissions from human sources in causing global climate change.

However, the response to these issues was characterised more by the mainstream environmental perspective than by the radical one. Given the extent of environmental problems, constructing a society wherein humankind could live in an environmentally sustainable way according to the radical approach implies revolutionary rather than evolutionary change. Consequently, while the concerns of radical environmental perspectives were recognised, their solutions constituted too much of a challenge to current world systems, markets and values, and so they remained on the fringes of political debate. Mainstream or reformist environmentalism, by contrast, was human-centred and informed by liberal economic perspectives. In this view, environmental protection was primarily for the benefit of humankind, and furthermore, could be incorporated within the political and economic structures of modern society without undermining economic growth models, material prosperity or liberal democracy. Improving natural resource allocation and environmental quality through market processes is a core strategy for these moderate environmental perspectives (see Anderson and Leal 1991). Moderate environmentalists also tend to put faith in the ability of science and technology to solve environmental problems without fundamentally challenging our institutional and value systems.

More moderate forms of environmentalism therefore can be explained as a response to both the seriousness of the environmental issues that emerged in the 1980s as well as to the power of the critique of global political and economic structures that radicals such as Daly had provided. States simply could not envisage moving away from economic growth, which continued to underpin social welfare (both directly by creating employment, and indirectly through taxation and redistributive welfare spending). A way of addressing global environmental challenges that did not rest on radical environmental perspectives was needed, and in 1987 this was provided in the form of sustainable development. As Box 1.8 details, this concept was developed under the auspices of the United Nations Conference on Environment and Development (UNCED), in a document titled *Our Common Future* (the Brundtland Report).

Sustainable development, however, has been widely criticised as a concept. Setting aside debates over the use of market mechanisms to solve environmental problems, the precautionary principle is decidedly ambiguous: it isn't clear why environmental risks should be prioritised over economic ones. States have demonstrated only a limited ability to negotiate workable multilateral environmental treaties, and have struggled to provide equity while engaging in environmental reforms even within a single generation. Nevertheless, sustainable development provided moderate environmentalism with a theoretical framework through which the movement could gain better access to government policy-making channels, and garner the support of business interests. It helps to think of sustainable development as a pragmatic or flexible concept, within which different interest groups can move towards a better relationship with the environment at their own pace, and through a range of different strategies and approaches. From the radical environmental perspective, it is questionable whether sustainable development reforms are occurring fast enough to make a significant impact given the scale of environmental problems faced. The kinds of environmental policies and governance reforms that states have pursued – including regulations directed at energy producers – are largely seen as post-hoc sticking plasters. Of course one environmental threat currently outweighs all others: climate change – a problem so vast it almost constitutes an environmental perspective in its own right.

Box 1.8 The concept of sustainable development

Sustainable development is defined by the Brundtland Report as 'forms of pro-gress which meet the needs of the present without compromising the ability of future generations to meet their needs'. The core finding of this UNCED report was that all over the world economic development was taking place in an envi-ronmentally unsustainable manner. However, strong links between environ-mental damage and poverty were also identified. Consequently, the Brundtland Report concluded that rather than *reduce* economic growth and development, it was necessary to *accelerate* it. To square this conclusion with the evidence that economic growth had caused natural resource depletion and other environmen-tal problems, it was argued that the nature of economic growth needed to change to become more sustainable. The debate shifted, in effect, from pro- or anti-growth, to the 'quality of growth'. The Brundtland Report led directly to the Rio conference on sustainable development in 1992, which in turn resulted in the Earth Charter, Rio Declaration, and Agenda 21 (Blueprint for the 21st Century).

Five core principles of sustainable development can be identified:

1. *Integration* – economic goals and environmental goals need to be integrated in decision-making
2. *Market mechanisms* – based on principles of polluter pays and user pays, and on internalising externalities (see neo-classical economics above), mar-kets can be used to resolve environmental problems
3. *Inter-generational equity* – meeting the needs of future generations as well as providing equity within current generations
4. *The precautionary principle* – a call for environmental 'risk management': 'Environmental measures must anticipate, prevent and attack the causes of environmental degradation'
5. *The global dimension* – environmental problems transcend national bounda-ries and so require multilateral solutions

Climate change

By taking human interaction with nature as a central concern, recent scholar-ship (emanating originally from within environmental communities) has come to focus increasingly on climate change. Scientific studies have provided mounting evidence that humankind is having a serious detrimental impact on our planet by exacerbating climate change. The long history of planet Earth has seen many different climates – from ice ages to more tropical times – but what climate scientists argue is that humans are causing a vastly accelerated turn towards tropical times. This is primarily due to the release of high levels of greenhouse gases (GHGs). The greenhouse gases covered by UNFCCC and EU targets are: carbon dioxide, methane, nitrous oxide and fluorinated gases such as hydrofluorocarbons, perfluorocarbons, sulphur hexafluoride and nitrogen trifluoride (see European Commission 2015). Much of this scientific thought is based on earlier discoveries about how energy reaches the Earth from the sun, how it is then absorbed and radiated back into space, as well as how some gases in our atmosphere act. Like the glass in a greenhouse, the Earth's atmosphere traps some of the solar energy – causing surface temperatures to rise (Garner 2011: 2). The more such gases become trapped, the greater the rise in surface (including ocean) temperatures.

Over the past 150 years greenhouse gas concentration in the atmosphere has increased markedly, and continues to do so (IPCC 2013: 4). This reflects the transformation of human economic activity following from industrialisation, including in energy consumption and land use. These activities result in greenhouse gases being emitted more quickly than they can be absorbed by natural processes (for example the conversion of carbon dioxide into organic matter through photosynthesis). A broad consensus also exists that if the global climate system warms more than 2 °C above pre-industrial levels (1850–1900), then the implications for the environment, and for humankind, will be increasingly severe. Consequently, keeping climate change to below a 2 °C increase is the primary objective from a climate change perspective.

For the many politicians and activists who accept the new scientific consensus on anthropogenic climate change, finding solutions has proven highly problematic. This is in part because of continuous challenge from climate change sceptics, but primarily due to disagreement on exactly how to mitigate climate change. One key split is of course between moderate environmental perspectives, which view the problem as relating to how energy is produced, and radical approaches that see the problem as caused by humankind's broader relationship to the environment, by current social, political and cultural practices, and by the limits to, or undesirability of, economic growth. Responses to climate change therefore reflect the choice of environmental perspectives.

It is fair to state that the reformist environmental perspective has been the most significant with regard to climate change. Reformists have certainly been more influential amongst the political elites that promote climate mitigation policies within various governments and international institutions. For example, several NGOs (including the Global Green Growth Institute for example) along with a number of academics (such as Michael Jacobs) have promoted a 'green growth' model of addressing climate change concerns that has been picked up by these elites. Creating 'green jobs' while addressing climate change, and continuing with rapid economic growth while promoting innovation and new business opportunities, is obviously an appealing scenario for certain political and economic perspectives (IRENA 2014). In this view, society also benefits from the infrastructure and technology spending associated with establishing new energy systems. Such arguments are used by those looking to boost support for both state and private sector investment in renewable and energy efficiency innovations, as well as in new technologies. Indeed, a recent report by Pricewaterhousecoopers (2013), in their capacity as advisor to the European Climate Foundation, shows that four of the five countries covered in the report managed to expand their economies whilst decreasing greenhouse gas emissions. The low-carbon and environmental sector of the global economy is now valued at around US$5 trillion, and clearly some companies and states perceive a need to be a part of this rapid growth. For mainstream environmental perspectives, while the economic costs of a low-carbon transition must be acknowledged, the economic costs of not taking action are viewed as far higher (see the 2006 'Stern Review').

There are, however, complications even here, which reflect the main economic perspectives. Some reformist environmentalists argue that the market should be the principal agent in climate change mitigation, while others call for a much greater degree of state intervention – particularly in driving technological change and renewables investment. Further complications come from developing states, particular large ones such as India and China. They may not disagree with the emerging scientific, economic and political consensus on climate change, but they have argued that in the specific context of development, rapid economic growth must be prioritised. They have argued that climate change mitigation strategies must be left to – and paid for by – advanced industrial countries. Addressing environmental problems clearly requires consideration of political and economic perspectives as well as environmental ones.

Technological perspectives

Addressing climate change is also a matter of how optimistic one is with regard to technological solutions to environmental problems. Technology is a crucial mediator between energy and environment, and so technological perspectives may be able to provide alternative insights into complex energy challenges. These perspectives are able to reflect on how technology has evolved over time, as well as on prospects for energy innovations. There are a range of different views on how new energy systems emerge, reflecting, for example, the varied disciplines that contribute to the leaps of technology that underpin new energy systems – engineering, chemistry and physics to name a few.

Ideas about how to produce, distribute and transport different sources and forms of energy are important to understanding global energy challenges. They focus analysis on the fundamental and complex question of what energy is, and how it is produced. It is also important to understand the quite intricate mechanisms involved in transporting, storing and using various different types of energy once it has been produced – as well as how these mechanisms have changed over time and might be improved in future. As concerns with the governance of energy systems shifted in the 1980s towards a focus on markets, questions of how to provide energy services and how to promote energy sector innovation were largely left to market actors. Technological perspectives, as a consequence, were somewhat downplayed. However, as global energy challenges have become more pressing – and so have risen up the agenda of national policy-makers – questions of energy technology and energy sector technological advancement are becoming more critical.

Technology and energy systems

New ideas and discoveries about how energy can be produced and used have underpinned radical and profound changes in the history of modern life. The discovery that energy could be produced not just by animals (i.e. muscle power) but also from inanimate sources (i.e. coal) was a core driver of the industrial revolution. Discoveries regarding the many uses of oil (from illumination to plastics to the powering of modern militaries) transformed both national economies, and ultimately, international relations. Understanding how these historical energy transitions evolved, and how they impacted upon society and politics, requires some knowledge of energy technologies. Advances in energy technologies enabled modern lifestyles – in effect, the emergence of such technologies has changed human social, political, economic and cultural practices. More problematically, they have also changed the environment in which we live.

From a technological perspective, energy can be shown as crucial to almost all contemporary human needs and wants. Energy is the key input for food production and preparation, heating, lighting, health care provision, and powering the various technological devices that we depend upon for transport, communication, processing and accessing information, as well as entertainment (see Schobart 2014). If energy inputs are to be provided through modern energy services, then their provision depends upon complex technical systems and processes that have evolved over time. Technicians, engineers, and others who adopt a technological perspective often bemoan the fact that, although it is ubiquitous in our lives, we tend to take energy for granted. As inventions such as electricity and combustion engines became commonplace, questions about the incredibly complex processes that deliver useable energy to us have ceased to be asked. But these details are necessary if the security and affordability of energy systems are to be maintained – and even more necessary if we are seeking to redesign these systems to deliver a more sustainable future.

In practice, energy is provided in many different ways. There are numerous sources, and different processes through which these energy sources can be converted into consumable forms. Each process is, in turn, supported by complex infrastructures and production chains. This is because the most common sources of energy – oil, gas, coal, hydro and nuclear – must be processed before they can be turned into practical services such as electricity generation or transportation (see Box 1.9). For example, the process through which petroleum becomes useable for transport begins with exploration, then moves through production (drilling and extraction), transport, and refining stages, then storage, and finally transport to petrol stations. By comparison, coal for electricity needs to be mined, transported and converted into usable energy by being burnt in power plants, so that the energy end products (heat and electricity) can be distributed to houses, industrial plants and electricity consuming appliances.

To achieve these energy production processes requires a range of technologies and infrastructures, multiple inter-related companies, enforceable corporate contracts and legal and regulatory frameworks, and varying sets of government

---

Box 1.9 Producing energy sources

The technological aspects of energy systems can be illustrated simply by focusing on the narrow question of how different types of energy are produced. Energy services, such as electricity or transportation, depend upon suitable inputs that result from the processing of primary energy sources. As these energy sources have different characteristics (such as being finite or renewable), the production processes that convert them into end-use energy vary in complexity.

Finite energy sources that require production processes to manufacture:

- Oil: Largely used for transport but also as an input into fertilisers and chemical processes
- Gas: Often used for heating and cooking, but also to generate electricity
- Coal: Mostly used for electricity generation – but also for district heating

Finite energy sources that require production processes to manufacture and decommission:

- Nuclear: Derived from uranium. Used for electricity – but also for military purposes

Renewable energy sources that do not need production processes to manufacture:

- Wind/solar/wave: Used for electricity production

Renewable energy sources that require new infrastructures to be put in place to produce:

- Hydro-power: Used for electricity generation. Can require river rerouting and/or land clearance before dams are constructed

---

policy measures. Infrastructure in particular can be highly expensive, with complex and diverse forms often needed – some of which can create serious 'visual pollution' effects on otherwise picturesque landscapes. And of course, teams of people are needed to ensure that supplies are not interrupted due to infrastructure breakdown or other failures of technology. All of these systems, practices and economic relations imply both *sunk costs* and *vested interests*. Consequently, radical changes to energy systems (such as a low-carbon transition) are a considerable political challenge, while the potential backlash against attempts to disturb existing energy systems can have implications for the security of supply.

The production of electricity from gas is a good example of how many different specific processes must take place for energy to be delivered to end consumers. Once again, a range of different companies and a host of experts on the technological requirements of production processes are required for the smooth running of the involved energy systems. Gas needs to be extracted from the ground through exploration and production – usually by specialist oil and gas companies. Captured gas is then sold, often through specialist gas traders or brokers. The transportation phase – from production sites to market – often crosses multiple state boundaries and sometimes seas. This may occur through pipelines (that may be owned by private or nationalised pipeline companies), or in the case of liquefied natural gas (LNG), by ship following liquefaction, and then regasification, once target markets are reached. Once the gas reaches generation plants electricity is produced – possibly by separate generation companies. Transmission companies must then transmit this electricity through transmission grids (across wires and pylons) to distribution points. From the distribution point electricity is then distributed via even smaller circuits to individual households and businesses, this time by distribution companies. Finally, the electricity must be measured by electricity meters at the point of usage so that electricity distribution companies know how much to charge particular end-consumers.

There are, however, other aspects of electricity production that need to be considered. There are questions regarding efficiency: of different energy sources and the processes by which they become useable; of different energy systems; and of different end-uses. Further questions concern the economics of energy at each of these junctures. Electricity is produced from a wide range of sources, but at any given point of technology some are going to be more efficient than others: more electricity is produced per cost unit of raw material (and perhaps fewer greenhouse gases). Yet while technology advances, infrastructure decisions linger, creating 'path dependency' that will eventually reflect outmoded technologies.

For example, in most developed countries, electricity systems are centralised (i.e. through a national grid), as this strategy reflected technological capacity and economic efficiency measures for most of the post-war era. In these centralised systems, electricity tends to be generated at scale in large plants, which then require huge transmission and distribution networks to deliver the electricity to where it is consumed. The least efficient part of current electricity systems (where the largest technical losses of electricity occur) is, consequently, during the transmission and distribution phases. Crucially, in recent decades, technological advances have largely been in small-scale energy generation and in distributed energy systems (decentralised or localised alternatives to the grid). It is possible, therefore, that the entire energy systems of, for example, OECD states reflect past technological and economic calculations. Moving beyond these established systems, however, invariably comes up against sunk costs and vested interests.

Technological perspectives, therefore, provide us with important information about how our various energy systems evolved, how they operate in practice, and how complex and socially, politically and economically embedded they are. Consequently, these perspectives provide some insight into the challenges that are faced in keeping our energy system secure, efficient, cost-effective and sustainable. Crucially, looking at energy from a technological standpoint can also provide us with innovative ideas about how we can produce and use energy in better ways. Pure technological perspectives, that focus on the functionalities of each form of energy and the complex ways in which they work, are therefore clearly useful in addressing global energy challenges. However, other emerging technological perspectives are able to link technological change to changing human social practices.

Socio-technical transitions

The socio-technical transitions approach is an example of this broader technological perspective. The socio-technical transitions literature brings insights from sociology and economics into technology studies. As a result, it can be understood that energy technology is relevant precisely because of its ability to provide human services, such as light, heating, cooking, transport and electricity. History is well supplied with energy transitions, where one dominant form of energy is replaced by another (for example the shift from coal to oil), but each transition has also resulted in increased reliance of human beings on these energy sources. Security of energy supply, by extension, has become more critical with each jump in energy technology. It is humankind's heavy reliance on energy services that renders them so crucial – which is why, from a radical environmental perspective seeking to address climate change concerns, one solution is to simply consume (and hence produce) less energy, to reduce dependency on energy services.

The socio-technical transitions perspective reveals further complexities, dynamic inter-connections and path dependencies in energy systems – which are re-cast in this approach as energy regimes. These regimes are characterised not only by specific energy innovations, infrastructures and technologies, but also by their inter-relations with other systems across industry, businesses, transport and other political and social institutions. For example, the fossil fuel and transport systems have become intrinsically inter-linked, and practices in each area tend to both influence and support certain practices (mainly carbon-intensive) in the other. These systems can be understood as having co-evolved, and when taken together, constitute an energy regime – a regime which is the source of powerful path-dependencies (Unruh 2000).

Indeed, fossil-fuel energy regimes as a rule demonstrate very fixed patterns of inter-connections, and are particularly heavy in terms of sunk costs – the massive investments that private companies have already made, and upon which they expect a significant return. This includes generation facilities, transmission and distribution infrastructure networks, and pipelines and LNG facilities (including ports) that together, in wealthier countries at least, have been able in a reasonably secure manner to provide modern energy services such as universal access to electricity. Political capital has also been invested into fossil fuel regimes: lobbying governments, making campaign contributions, providing testimony and 'expert' opinions to legislatures and regulatory agencies as well as advertising campaigns designed to influence public opinion (including demonstrating the environmental credentials of the fossil fuel industry). The fossil fuel energy regime is so entrenched that some scholars refer to a 'carbon lock-in' situation. Understanding patterns of energy reliance and their social and technological consequences therefore helps to explain some of the resistance to a low-carbon transition and, particularly, the existence of powerful actors and interest groups that oppose climate change mitigation measures. The political and economic difficulties associated with profound change to energy regimes should not be underestimated (see Box 1.10).

Technological perspectives – even the socio-technical transitions approach – may therefore place too little emphasis on the economic and political context in which climate mitigation happens. Important questions of the affordability of climate change mitigation and of building political support (particularly of key social coalitions) for environmental measures can be downplayed, as are other drivers of change to energy regimes such as geopolitical security concerns. Yet, it is precisely the problem of how to manage the costs of a low-carbon transition, and determining how these costs are to be distributed across socio-economic groups and industry sectors, that constitute the barriers to technological solutions. Building broad social coalitions of support for technological change is a problem of political economy, not a technical issue.

Furthermore, the focus on fostering technological innovations and bringing them to market rests on the assumption that climate change will primarily be addressed through technological means once political and economic (cost) barriers to new technologies can be overcome. The implicit and rather strong claim here is that everything is ultimately fixable with new material inventions. Alternative strategies – such as fundamental changes to human lifestyles, moving away from mass consumption – based social models and radically reducing levels of energy usage – are, by extension, negated. Furthermore, if all that is needed to solve incredibly complex climate change problems is new technologies, then wider societal groups become absolved from responsibility for both the causes of environmental problems (bad or old technology) and for generating solutions to them (a task delegated to inventors and entrepreneurs). This has been disparagingly referred to as the politics of 'catalytic converters, power station scrubbers and bottle banks' (Garner 2011: 8). From a radical environmental perspective, the solutions that technological perspectives provide may in some respects only serve to reinforce broader political, social and economic structures.

Box 1.10 The limits of technological perspectives

Those who argue that as a general principle environmental problems generate incentives for innovation that result in technological solutions are termed Prometheans. However, emphasising technological solutions (for example to climate change problems), including through energy system transitions, might be considered to be falling into the 'technicist fallacy' (Leftwich 2000) – believing that complex problems of political economy have 'technical' solutions. In practice, any change in the use of resources creates winners and losers – even if only in relative terms – and so needs to be managed politically.

Despite these concerns, it cannot be forgotten that currently embedded energy regimes were themselves the product of technological changes with profound social consequences. New technologies, therefore, can – and certainly will eventually – overturn existing energy systems, creating new patterns of social life and generating a redistribution of (or new distributive possibilities for) social and economic wealth. If one thing is clear about energy systems, it is that they change over time despite their apparent inertia – as demonstrated during the industrial revolution, in the rise of mass electrification, and the switch from coal to oil.

Socio-technical transitions perspectives, therefore, can help explain in a broader, non-technical sense how energy innovation occurs, and the likely impacts of this on existing energy regimes. Through this approach, analysis can focus on the social, political and economic mechanisms and policy constellations necessary to nurture new technologies and innovations – and help them in their own transition from the laboratory, research centre or workshop to success in the marketplace. Clearly, not all innovations (or energy innovations) make it this far, but an improved rate of alternative energy technology innovation might be achieved with appropriate support mechanisms. This is a defensible focus even if technological change is only one of a set of different solutions to climate change problems, and if innovations can in fact also enable a reduction in demand for energy services. As many societies are attempting to shift to more sustainable energy production and consumption patterns, it is necessary to build a better understanding of how alternative, low-carbon technologies and innovations can be supported and their widespread dissemination enabled.

Conclusion

This first chapter sought to place the trilemma of global energy challenges (environment, development and security) within the context of four different 'perspectives': political, economic, environmental and technological. The analytical toolbox this provides serves as an introduction to the academic and political debates concerning the global energy challenge, as well as enabling the reader to more coherently engage with the real-world empirical problems that are addressed in the rest of the book. Understanding the different approaches taken by different disciplines is an end in itself; however, it is also a means of providing the reader with a broader framework through which to critically assess and examine the key events and ongoing tensions and dilemmas in the world energy system. To complement this, the following chapter directly addresses the evolution of this system, strengthening our historical understanding of global energy challenges, and providing empirical detail, in particular, on the changing energy mix and the dynamics of global energy markets.

Chapter 2

Evolution and Dynamics of the World Energy System

Energy has often been referred to as the 'lifeblood of modern society'. Energy input makes economies run, and without modern fuels such as oil, gas or electricity societies would find it hard to develop economically, or to maintain adequate levels of welfare or economic output. The energy industry has also become a key economic factor in some countries. Russia's majority state-owned gas company Gazprom accounts for an estimated 10 percent of total Russian gross domestic product (GDP), and 25 percent of state revenues. In Saudi Arabia, oil and oil products generate an estimated 90 percent of all export revenues, more than 70 percent of state income, and 45 percent of the country's GDP. The energy sector can also underpin significant employment levels. China National Petroleum Company (CNPC), the Chinese national oil company (NOC), is said to employ more than a million people. The German coal sector (until the 1980s at least) provided jobs for a million people and represented the backbone of the country's steel industry. Indeed, in the post–World War II era, the size and economic impact of coal within the domestic economy gave this industry significant political power as well. Petroleus de Venezuela S.A. (PdVSA), the Venezuelan NOC, became both the largest employer in the country and the main source of funds for social welfare programmes. Given this, it is hardly surprising that governments have sought to protect or even control the energy sector.

This chapter seeks to build an understanding of today's energy system through exploring its evolution and changing role in society. A key aspect of energy that will be emphasised here is the intense degree to which energy has become critical to modern culture, welfare, industry and business. To understand today's Global Energy Challenge, it is necessary to look at energy's history. At the same time, it is also crucial to understand the nature of energy fuels, and their technicalities and specificities. Oil has different characteristics than gas or coal, and fossil fuels differ from renewable sources of energy. To understand the dynamics of the world energy system, it is essential to 'unpack' the various types of fuels, and to assess the way they are produced, distributed, consumed and traded.

In light of this, the chapter first assesses the substantial role of energy in modern economies and, in particular, how this has evolved over time. The switch to machine-based energy production in the 19th century, and changing preferences over supply fuels over time (that is, coal, oil and gas), have had far-reaching international political and economic consequences.

The chapter then looks further into the economics of energy markets, and explains how the 'lifeblood' of modern societies is produced, traded and priced. It also sheds light on the sources and geographical distribution of global energy, and the technologies and infrastructures needed to produce and trade energy.

The evolution of the energy mix: From rural societies to industrialisation

Energy and energy use is deeply intertwined with humankind's evolution from rural societies to complex post-industrialised ones. Each of the major leaps in economic production, particularly through phases of industrialisation (and possibly further into a post-carbon world) is flanked by major shifts in energy supply and use: in other words an energy transition.

There are two important characteristics of energy that help to explain why humankind switched from biomass in the pre-industrial era to coal, and then later to oil: energy density and energy quality. In a nutshell, energy density depicts the amount of energy contained in a unit of fuel. Energy quality, in turn, refers to the ability of a unit of energy to produce goods and services for people. Fossil fuels such as coal or oil have much higher energy densities than biomass, i.e. wood or dung. Hence they are much easier to transport or store. High-quality primary fuels also allow for the generation of convenient secondary energy sources (such as electricity or refined energy products), as well as fuelling industrial production processes, computers or cars (see Box 2.1). In short, fossil fuels gave a competitive edge to the societies that embraced them, and allowed them to enhance their quality and scale of economic activity, expand production from agricultural produce to higher value-added products, and so increase their level of economic development.

Box 2.1 Primary and secondary energy fuels

A fuel is any material that allows storing energy for later conversion into other forms of energy such as mechanical energy or heat. Primary fuels constitute the source of energy that, once converted, is typically used for appliances and end uses (such as engines or electric devices). Typical examples of primary fuels are hydrocarbons, such as coal, oil or gas. Petrol or electricity, by contrast constitute secondary fuels, as they represent forms of energy derived by converting primary sources. In the case of petrol, the conversion process is refining, and in the case of electricity it is burning coal or gas in power plants.

Closely correlated with a transition from low-quality energy to high-quality energy fuels is the switch to different and more powerful 'prime movers', i.e. devices that help to transport cargo across geographical distances. The more powerful prime movers are, the better they facilitate (international) trade and thus economic specialisation. As Vaclav Smil (2010) reminds us, technological progress enabled societies to switch from draft animals (i.e. horse power) to steam machines, combustion engines and eventually gas turbines. This switch to different prime movers not only resulted in deep shifts in energy consumption – notably towards higher-quality fuels such as diesel and engine fuel – but also constituted a precondition for the most recent step in humankind's economic evolution: globalisation. As a result, the world saw a remarkable shift from biomass (representing around 85 percent of total primary energy supply – or TPES – in 1850) to fossil fuels (around 85 percent of TPES today).

Needless to say this evolution also correlated with a global (re-)distribution of political and military power. Making their way up the energy quality ladder, industrialising economies became economically dominant. They also tended to use their economic supremacy for political purposes, for the conquest and colonisation of other world regions, primarily to ensure the supply of crucial raw materials and to create markets for their products. A case in point is the British Empire, the power it derived from coal in the 19th century and its expansion across the rest of the world. In turn, nations like China that had dominated the world for centuries lost out as European nations began to dictate terms of trade with the Middle Kingdom. This, in turn, tells us something about how important international trade was even in this period of history.

In all, as this brief introductory discussion reveals, energy has been crucial for modernising societies, as has been the ability to replace lower-quality with higher-quality fuels. It has been widely understood that failing to do so puts economic development and welfare in danger; impacts on a country's ability to effectively participate in the global economy; and might have negative repercussions on national security and sovereignty. This is the reason why energy has for centuries been such a strongly contested and politicised policy field. No modern society and sovereign country can afford *not* to deal with it. Put simply, the degree to which people have been able to access, control and distribute sources of energy lies at the heart of understanding the changing place of energy in world politics.

Industrialisation: From biomass to coal

For most of its history, humanity has needed energy to enable daily existence – to gather, hunt and provide shelter. For the vast majority of our history this energy has been produced through the simple conversion of chemical energy, or calories, into muscle and brain power. Unsurprisingly, human power has been crudely associated with physical strength for thousands of years. As the centuries progressed, however, humankind learnt to harness other groups of biological converters, such as draft animals. But energy still largely came from muscle power. This underpinned persisting limits on the manufacture and transport of goods, and in part explains why rates of economic growth remained relatively low until the 19th century (it is estimated that global GDP grew over 600 percent between 1800 and 1900). The crucial change that came with the industrial revolution was the way in which energy was converted. The 'scientific revolution' which began during the Enlightenment provided conceptual tools that ultimately allowed people to master new sources of energy. This meant that energy came to be produced on vastly greater scales, through mechanical means. As noted by Carlo M. Cipolla, economist and author of *The Economic History of World Population* (1964), energy production shifted from biological converters to inanimate means.

The key to the industrial revolution was an invention by Scottish engineer James Watt in 1765: the coal-fired steam engine, a new prime mover. Steam power soon became the primary means not only of mining coal, but also of enabling the transportation of coal at an enormously accelerated rate. Coal-powered machinery made it possible to produce coal in sufficient quantities to support other emerging aspects of industrialisation. In 1800, world production of coal was 15 million tons per annum. By 1860 this had expanded to 132 million tons, with an energy equivalent of about 1,057 million megawatt-hours, and by 1900, it was 701 million tons with an energy equivalent of about 5,606 million megawatt-hours. Although it took more than 20 years for steam to start being used commercially, rapidly growing steam engine capacity, increasingly efficient engines, and ever new appliances offered opportunities for entrepreneurs. The technology spread from mining to textiles, the metallurgical industry and other sectors, eventually industrialising much of the economy. The production of goods became organised in factories, railways connected growing cities, and steamboats opened up new sea routes for shipping goods as the cost of energy steadily fell. The process of industrialisation continued to diffuse rapidly across Western societies, emanating from England but spreading quickly across Europe and the USA. The European continent entered a phase of sustained economic growth. In short, the industrial revolution was a period of major political, economic and social change underpinned by changes in energy production, trade and usage.

Whilst innovations in technology and new knowledge were arguably crucial in facilitating the industrial revolution, there were a number of other important factors. First, as industrialisation went hand-in-hand with the rise of capitalism, there was sufficient capital and entrepreneurial interest available to enable emergent technologies to move towards commercialisation and widespread deployment. Second, timber (one of the more traditional sources of energy) was in short supply, creating an opportunity for a higher quality fuel-like coal to achieve economies of scale and eventually overtake timber as a fuel source. Third, the new steam technology enabled the conversion of coal into both energy and transportation, facilitating large-scale production and associated reductions in cost. These three factors seem to characterise major energy transitions in more general terms. It is also worth noting with regard to today's global energy challenges that major energy transitions have usually occurred with a gap of as much as 150 years between the discovery of new ways of utilising a fuel source, and their widespread dispersion.

Interestingly, the 18th and 19th century energy transition reveals emergent features of foreign policy that would become more prominent in the 20th century with the rise of oil. As Western economies rapidly industrialised, coal became geopolitically significant – a 'strategic resource' or asset. This is because of the growing reliance on coal of numerous sectors of the economy and of society, from the steel, textile and mining industries to railway transportation as well as for the domestic production of heat and light. By the advent of World War I, states had also come to recognise the importance of energy, specifically coal supplies, for their national security. As such, the possession of or access to coal became a major objective of foreign policy. This was so much the case that in 1919 negotiations over access to Europe's coal came close to breaking the Paris Peace Conference apart, as European nations sought to redraw national boundaries so as to capture major coalfields.

There are many more examples linking energy resources to foreign policy when considering the Industrial Revolution. Crucially, geographical patterns of industrialisation came to coincide with the geological distribution of coal beneath the ground. Industry emerged in the Midlands and North of England where there was plenty of coal, rather than the South. France and Germany possessed good reserves of coal, but Italy, which had led Europe in technology and wealth in the 15th century, was now handicapped by its lack of this increasingly fundamental resource. As a result, in Italy as well as Greece industrialisation was largely delayed until after World War I. Great Britain's period of empire and world leadership (hegemony in IPE parlance) in the 18th and 19th centuries can therefore be linked to its national possession of large quantities of coal, in the same way that US hegemony (and grand strategy) can be linked to its access to large quantities of oil in the late 19th and early 20th centuries.

The century of oil

By the early 20th century, oil started to rival coal in key economic sectors and began to gain military significance. This reflected the discovery of large quantities of oil in the United States and elsewhere at the end of the 19th century. Furthermore, emerging technologies allowed for the extended usage of oil, notably the combustion engines invented by Rudolf Diesel and the four-stroke and petrol-fuelled Otto engine. A key turning point in the history of oil was Winston Churchill's decision as First Lord of the British Admiralty, on the eve of World War I, to convert the British Navy to oil for its power source instead of coal. As British vessels switched to a higher density and quality fuel, they had higher speeds and a greater range of operations, increasing

Britain's military might on the high seas. With Britain having taken the lead, oil began to overtake coal as the main power source for military activity, as it already had for domestic light and heat.

Nevertheless, the extent of the current global reliance on oil really originates in the United States of America. Daniel Yergin, in *The Prize* (1990), provides a detailed description of the evolution of oil. 'Rock' or 'seneca' oil as it was initially known had been used since the early 19th century in America as a folk medicine. In 1854 a scientist, Benjamin Silliman Jr., was employed by industrialist George Bissell to prove that rock oil could be used as financially competitive lighting fuel alternative to the more commonly used whale oil or vegetable fat. Around the same time, Edwin Laurentine Drake successfully drilled the first 'modern' oil well in the US. Both events are widely regarded as kick-starting what would later become a multi-billion dollar global industry. In the early 1860s, the new sector experienced something of a 'gold rush', followed by a period of boom and bust (typical for commodities). Oil also became subject to fierce struggles over market shares and dominance. Towards the end of the 19th century, Rockefeller's Standard Oil Company, known for its organisational qualities as well as its innovations, proved successful in cementing a strong domestic and international trade in the new lighting fuel. The quality of light this fuel produced was comparable with the clear, strong brilliance of sunlight. By that time, and against the backdrop of a rapidly growing domestic market for oil products, the USA overtook Imperial Russia in crude oil output to become the world's number one oil producer.

Cheap and plentiful supplies of oil meant that as the 20th century progressed America became, more than any other nation, reliant on oil across both commercial and domestic sectors. As other industries began to take advantage of its wide and varied uses, oil become less associated with its early role as a lighting fuel. The rapid growth of the automobile industry, which played a crucial role in US economic growth between the 1920s and 1960s, was facilitated by both easy access to oil and quickly advancing engine technology. Because oil was highly fungible and had twice the thermal content of coal, oil or oil products such as petrol and diesel became the fuel of choice in land and sea transport, as well as the only fuel for air transport. Oil was also crucial to the modernisation of the agricultural sector, not only as farms became mechanised, but also because it was an important feedstock for fertilisers, petrochemicals and pesticides. It also continued, though to a lesser extent, to play an important role in heating and electricity generation. By 1950, oil had come to represent 38 percent of TPES in the USA, and globally about a quarter of TPES.

In the first half of the 20th century the United States continued to dominate world oil production despite intermittent competition from Russia/the USSR. US oil fields accounted for more than 70 percent of world oil production in 1925, and although this overwhelming dominance was in decline they still produced over 50 percent of world oil in 1950. Moreover, five of the seven major oil companies (see Chapter 3 for details on the 'Seven Sisters') that dominated the international oil industry until the 1970s were American. This mattered, as whoever controlled output was also in a position to cash in on the huge economic rents to which direct and easy access to oil gave rise. It also mattered from a geopolitical perspective as whoever controlled output was also in a position to starve their enemies of this vital resource (a significant factor in the outcome of World War II). There are, therefore, both economic and geopolitical arguments behind the notion that US hegemony in the 20th century was built on abundant supply, and easy access, to the world's premier energy resource.

However, large oil discoveries in the Arab regions challenged the dominant producer position of the USA, and indeed, in the 1950s and 1960s US (and OECD) oil production began to decline. Nevertheless, the exploitation of Arab oil assets relied to a large extent on the capital and know-how of the established Western oil companies. A series of contracts and alliances were established between Arab ruling dynasties and these international oil companies (IOCs) during the first half of the 20th century – though the terms were largely unfavourable to these regimes. These terms were redressed in the late 1960s and early 1970s, primarily through the auspices of the Organization of Petroleum Exporting Countries (OPEC). This, in turn led to fears in the West of dependence on 'politically unstable' oil suppliers, fears that were realised during the oil crises of the 1970s (see Chapter 3 for details).

Given the strategic nature of oil, now a vital resource for fuelling modern economies, consumer nations sought to reduce import dependency, in part by flattening out demand. The introduction of corporate average fuel efficiency (CAFE) standards, for example, significantly increased the mileage of the US car fleet. Imports were also replaced by indigenous oil supplies where feasible. Explorations by a number of Western nations, including the UK, the Netherlands and Norway, also led to the development of North Sea oil in the 1970s. New energy institutions were created, the most significant of which was the International Energy Agency (IEA). Established by OECD countries, the IEA's role in part was to manage strategic petroleum reserves to buffer against supply shocks.

Many countries also sought to switch to alternative fuels for certain services such as electricity production. Nuclear energy in particular came to the fore. Many changes in energy production and usage ensued: France decided to rely on nuclear energy for most of its power production, Denmark took the global lead in wind power generation, and Japan became the world's most energy-efficient industrialised nation. Natural gas, now used for generating heating and electricity, emerged as an important fuel in the energy mix. This was, of course, bad news for oil producers. However, even at the peak of oil dependency, many energy-rich countries had paradoxically failed to achieve economic development, despite (or perhaps because of) their energy endowment. This 'resource curse' question is discussed in detail in Chapter 6.

By the end of the 20th century, oil made up for 37 percent of TPES, followed by coal (25 percent), natural gas (19 percent), traditional and modern biomass (10 percent) and nuclear (6 percent). Oil had emerged as the backbone of key economic sectors, including the chemical and fertiliser industries, in addition to creating entirely new (and important) markets such as for refined oil products. Oil also, as noted above, dominated transport on land, sea and air. Oil was unrivalled in fuelling individual mobility and aviation. Coal, natural gas or nuclear were rival fuels, but really only to each other, and then only in electricity production and heating.

By the end of the 'century of oil' most production took place in the non-OECD world, primarily in OPEC countries, but also in Latin America and Africa. By contrast, most demand was located in the industrialised world, such that sites of production of oil were increasingly geographically separated from the major sites of consumption. A vast fleet of 'Ultra Large Crude Carriers', able to ship more than 320,000 deadweight tons, was now necessary to physically carry oil from major sites of production (such as the Persian Gulf) to key consumers (notably Europe and the USA). Sea lanes and canals emerged as crucial geographic focal points of the international trade of oil, including the Straits of Hormuz and Malacca and the Suez Canal (see Chapter 8). A dense pipeline network linked up oil fields, refineries and consumer markets, sometimes covering distances of several thousand kilometres as in the case of West Siberian oil supplied to Western Europe. Elaborate distribution infrastructure was needed to ensure access to oil and oil products within a country or a region. In all, oil had not only gained a dominant position in the global energy mix; it had also come to represent the biggest and most international of all world commodity markets. This reflected both its high energy density and quality, and its highly fungible nature.

Energy in the 21st century: The rise of new consumers

Since the start of the 21st century the energy world has taken yet another turn. Three important factors have come to shape global energy debates and politics: the rise of new – Asian – energy consumer heavyweights, notably China and India; political awareness of rising energy poverty; and the need to mitigate for climate change. Whilst the first factor comes with implications for market power and design, the second and third are about charging the energy sector with new policy agendas (covered in detail in Chapters 5 and 6 of this book).

The emergence of Asian economies in the post-war era, and particularly the rise of India and China in the first decade of the 21st century, has exerted an increasingly visible impact on the global energy balance. Fast economic growth rates, soaring industrial output and rapid population growth significantly increased overall energy demand. During the global economic crisis that began in 2007, global energy consumption did take a hit, but rebounded heavily in 2010 as global energy consumption grew by 5.6 percent, the highest rate since 1973. In 2011 and 2012, energy consumption growth was around 1.2 percent. While non-OECD consumption has grown significantly since 2000, energy consumption in OECD countries was in overall terms flat during the first decade of the new millennium.

World primary energy demand is expected to rise by a total of 35 percent between 2010 and 2035 (1.2 percent per annum). This growth trend comes against the backdrop of continuing flat-lined OECD energy demand growth. According to IEA statistics, the rich world's energy consumption will peak by 2020. As a corollary, 96 percent of the estimated increment in world primary energy demand until 2035 will stem from non-OECD countries, which will then constitute 65 percent of world demand (for details see Box 2.2). In short, the centre of gravity of global energy consumption is shifting away from incumbent OECD countries towards Asia.

This shift has so far been accompanied by a return of the classic security of supply agenda (see Chapter 3 for more details). Although China has large coal reserves its rate of growth demands imports of coal, oil and gas. The import–export situation has been exacerbated strongly in the aftermath of the Fukushima crisis given Japan's need to import more alternative sources of energy to replace nuclear production. Consequently, China (amongst other Asian countries) nurtures NOCs as part of their strategy to secure supplies in producer regions. Asian nations in general seem to be strengthening dip-

---

Box 2.2 The rise of Asia in global energy demand

The rate and scale of Chinese, Indian, and more generally Asian demand growth for oil and gas, and the economic and political methods these states have used to secure supplies, have shaken up the political economy of energy. The IEA projects that China's energy demand alone will grow by 60 percent between 2010 and 2035, which will make China by far the world's largest energy consumer, dwarfing the second placed USA by a 77 percent higher rate of consumption. India's energy consumption will come third after China and the US, making the largest contribution to demand growth after China. China's crude consumption is expected to almost double to more than 15 million barrels per day (mbd), and will account for half the net global increment in consumption until 2035. India's oil consumption will grow steeply as well, reaching 7.5 mbd, up from 3.0 mbd in 2010. Total non-OECD demand overtook OECD oil consumption in 2014. In natural gas, developing Asia represents 43 percent of demand increases until 2035, and in coal China and India make up some 75 percent of non-OECD growth, with India doubling its share of global demand to 16 percent. Overall, this means that the OECD will represent only some 35 percent of global total primary energy demand (TPED) in 2035, in a major shift of the centre of global energy gravity towards emerging economies in Asia.

Sources: (BP 2013; IEA 2012)

lomatic ties with energy-rich countries (see below). OECD member South Korea has for instance sought to foster economic relations and establish an 'energy cooperation belt' with Russia and Central Asian countries as well as with oil producers in Latin America.

And whilst new energy producers emerge – notably Brazil as a global biofuels producer, and the USA as a major producer of unconventional oil and gas – the Persian Gulf and former Soviet states retain their importance and strategic role as exporters of fossil fuels. Asian NOCs, notably the China National Offshore Oil Corporation (CNOOC) and its subsidiary PetroChina have therefore been keen to engage directly in producer countries, and have become investors in upstream fossil fuel projects as well as in resources more generally. Some observers have invoked the idea of 'resource wars', reflecting the re-emergence of geopolitical perspectives with the eastward shift in energy demand.

Before we discuss the security, sustainability and development challenges related to this eastward shift in subsequent chapters, we will look closer at the fundamentals of production, consumption, trade and pricing of energy.

The economics of energy markets

The economics of energy markets very much depend on how fungible specific fuels are, whether they are traded domestically, regionally or globally, and to what extent they are subject to market forces or political influence. In this chapter we focus on primary energy sources, i.e. oil, gas, coal, nuclear and renewables. The challenges facing the electricity sector and secondary energy sources are dealt with in subsequent chapters.

Oil

Reserves, production and trade
Oil is the world's most important fuel and at present accounts for 32 percent of total primary energy supply. Conventional crude oil reserves are famously concentrated in relatively few world regions. According to statistics by the global energy company British Petroleum (BP), the Middle East is home to some 48 percent of known conventional oil reserves. The remainder is found in The Americas (33 percent), Africa (8 percent), the Former Soviet Union (7 percent) and the Asia-Pacific region (2.5 percent). The EU, the world's largest economy, owns only 0.4 percent of global oil reserves. Importantly, OPEC, the oil producer club, controls some 86 percent. The largest reserve holding countries are Venezuela (279 billion barrels or 17.8 percent of global reserves), Saudi Arabia (265.9 billion barrels/ 16 percent), Canada (173.9 billion barrels/ 10.4 percent), Iraq (157 billion barrels/ 9.4 percent) and Iran (150 billion barrels/ 9 percent). The largest markets for oil are the US (18.5 million barrels of consumption per day), the EU-28 (12.8 mbd), China (11.3 mbd), Russia (3.1 mbd), and Brazil (3.0 mbd) (see Figure 2.1). Overall, the world consumes around 87 million barrels per day.

Figure 2.1 *Global distribution of conventional oil reserves*

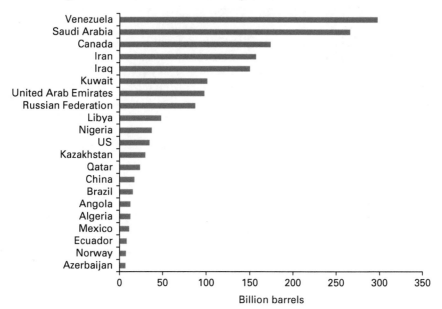

Billion barrels

Not all reserve holders produce oil, or at least not at equal quantity or pace. In terms of production, Saudi Arabia has the world's largest crude oil output, at 11.5 mbd in 2012. Russia remains the second largest producer for the time being (10.6 mbd), closely followed by the USA (9 mbd). The USA is likely to overtake Russia as the world's second largest producer of oil given surging unconventional oil production. Other major producers include Canada (3.7 mbd), Iran (3.7 mbd), Iraq (3.1 mbd), Kuwait (3.1 mbd), Venezuela (2.7 mbd) and Nigeria (2.4 mbd). Oil production, particularly in non-OPEC countries, has gradually moved into technically more demanding offshore areas, including very deep-sea wells in the Gulf of Mexico and offshore Brazil, and potentially into Arctic sites. Major new finds of the past years, such as the Libra field off the Brazilian coast or Norway's Johan Sverdrup field in the North Sea were predominantly offshore and have therefore been interpreted as signs of peaking global reserves (see Box 2.3). Production costs of offshore and deep-sea oil tend to be significantly higher and are regarded as one of the drivers of rising oil prices in recent years.

More recently, however, unconventional oil production techniques, notably hydraulic fracturing (see Box 2.4), have promised to make vast additional reserves available for production. The US has led the way with new technologies, and has seen a surge in domestic supply from the Bakken formation in North Dakota, the Eagle Ford formation in Southern Texas, and soon the giant Spraberry Wolfcamp shale area (unconventional gas is discussed below). In addition, the high price of oil has rendered the production of bituminous sands

---

Box 2.3 The 'peak oil' debate

'Peak oil' refers to a theoretical point in time when global oil production reaches a maximum, and thereafter declines. It is based on the idea that natural resources are finite and that geology will eventually put a limit to extracting further growing volumes of crude oil. The peak oil theory was developed by Marion King Hubbert, a Shell geologist, in the 1950s and has received widespread attention among politicians and security scholars. Recent progress in extraction techniques, the development of unconventional oil reserves as well as the fact that the global oil market tends to grow rather than contract have however put in question the validity of a purely geological perspective on oil production. The latter seems to be better described as a function of the price and technological innovation rather than pure geology. Still, the idea of peak oil is gaining academic and political momentum at the moment. Climate change groups also cite 'peak oil' as another urgent reason the world needs to push forward with investment in alternative and sustainable energy sources.

(also called tar sands or oil sands) economical. The world's largest tar sand reserves are found in Canada, Kazakhstan and Russia, although only Canada has so far developed a sizeable commercial tar sands industry. The production of tar sands is frequently criticised because of its environmental impact – land use, water use and heavy metals use during the extraction process. As the IEA estimates, a total of US$10.2 trillion or US$430 billion per year need to be invested worldwide in the oil sector by 2035 to meet growing world demand.

A fungible commodity, oil is traded globally. Oil is transported by tankers and pipelines but also vehicles and trains. In terms of dollar volumes, the oil market is the largest commodity market in the world. More recently, the oil market has become increasingly subject to (private) financial investment and speculation. As a result, the growing trade in oil futures (aka 'paper oil') has become somewhat decoupled from physical transactions.

Pricing
Since it is a globally traded commodity, the price of crude oil is principally a function of global supply and demand. It therefore strongly reflects the state of the global economy and the general macroeconomic conditions characterising major consuming nations. However, too high an oil price can negatively impact on these macroeconomic conditions. While a fully exchangeable commodity (a substitute good) in theory, in practice different types of crude exist, with varying value on the market. Groups of crudes differ by 'API gravity' (ranging from heavy / 22° to light /above 33°, as defined by the American Petroleum Institute – API) and sulphur content (oil with less than 0.5 percent of sulphur content is called 'sweet' and with more than 1.5 percent 'sour'). For each of those groups a benchmark, or 'marker', signals the price. 'Sweet' (low sulphur content) and light (high score on API gravity) crudes (such as North Sea Brent oil) tend to be high priced, whereas

heavy and sour crudes (such as Venezuelan oil) typically come with discounts. Leading markers on global oil markets include the West Texas Intermediate (WTI), Brent Blend, Dubai, Tapis, and the OPEC basket. The standard unit for trading oil is a barrel (159 litres), and crude is typically priced in US dollars.

As a commodity, crude oil leads global markets in terms of trade activity as well as in terms of volumes. Crude oil futures have replaced spot as the global standard for oil trading, and as a corollary, commodity futures exchanges such as the New York Mercantile Exchange (NYMEX) have become the place for setting the oil price. Crude oil futures have now become the world's largest market for futures on a physical commodity. It would however not be accurate to argue that oil pricing is a function of market dynamics alone. In fact, historical oil price developments reveal a very strong correlation between political events and oil price movements (see Figure 2.2). This reflects the important role that oil plays in modern societies, fuelling the world's major economies. At the same time, this correlation reminds us that while oil may be traded and priced on a global scale, it remains a strategic commodity and crucial to national welfare and security concerns. The price of oil has not only seen great volatility in the past two decades, but also a constant overall rise in absolute terms. The longer-term target price for oil, according to OPEC statements, is now around US$100 per barrel, which compares to a price of below US$10 per barrel in 1998. Too high an oil price endangers economic activity and welfare as much as insecure physical supply. In this, oil is a private good whose reliable and affordable provision has strong public goods characteristics (see Chapter 3 for further discussion of this).

Figure 2.2   *Oil price movements and political events*

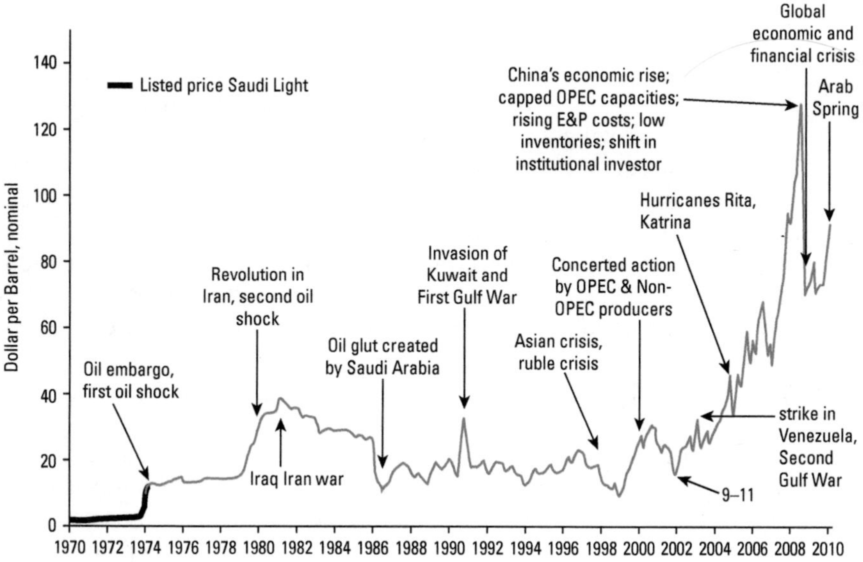

Source: adapted from EIA

Natural gas

Reserves, production and trade

Natural gas has emerged as an important fuel in the global energy mix and at present accounts for 22 percent of total primary energy supply. Given its comparably light carbon footprint amongst established fossil fuels, this share is set to grow significantly in the future. Some refer to natural gas as the 'bridge fuel' between the current fossil fuel economy and a low-carbon future. Natural gas reserves can be found across the world but are unevenly distributed. BP statistics suggest that the Middle East is home to some 43 percent of known conventional gas reserves, followed by the former Soviet Union (30 percent). The Americas holds around 10 percent, and Africa and the Asia-Pacific 8 percent each. The largest reserve holding countries are Iran (33.6 trillion cubic metres or 18 percent of global reserves), Russia (32.9 trillion cubic metres /17.6 percent), Qatar (25.1 trillion cubic metres/ 13.4 percent) and Turkmenistan (17.5 trillion cubic metres/ 9.3 percent). The largest markets for gas are the USA (722 billion cubic metres—bcm—of consumption per year in 2013), the EU-27 (443.9 bcm), Russia (416 bcm), Iran (156 bcm), China (143.8 bcm) and Japan (116.7 bcm). Among the latter, the EU represents the world's largest import market, due to its small levels of indigenous production.

In terms of production, the USA, with an output of 681 bcm of gas per year, has recently overtaken Russia (at 592 bcm). Qatar is also amongst the world's largest producers with 157 bcm, along with Iran (160.5 bcm), Canada (156 bcm) and Norway (115 bcm) (which mainly sources from now declining North Sea reserves). As noted above, unconventional gas production techniques have added potentially vast volumes to existing conventional gas reserves. As the IEA estimated in a 2013 report, unconventional gas essentially doubles globally available reserves. So far, however, only the USA has become a major producer of shale gas, but despite soaring production has not as yet become a gas exporter. According to the IEA, a total of US$8.7 trillion or US$360 billion per year needs to be invested worldwide in the gas sector by 2035 to meet growing world demand.

Conventional natural gas is typically produced as an 'associated' by-product of oil production, or from natural gas fields. Once on-stream, some of these fields produce for up to 50 years. The Russian giant fields of Medvezhe, Urengoy and Yamburg have been producing since the 1970s, and at current production levels the South Pars / North Dome field – the biggest gas field in the world, shared between Qatar and Iran – is expected to produce for some 400 years into the future.

Because of its low energy density, natural gas cannot be easily stored or transported by vehicle, which makes pipelines the infrastructure of choice. As a consequence, natural gas trade is mostly restricted to regional markets. Liquefied natural gas (LNG), however, has recently emerged as a cost efficient way to transport natural gas over long distances. Gas is turned into LNG as it is cooled to −162 °C, increasing its energy density, and can then be shipped in purpose-built vessels. It is re-gasified at its destination and fed into traditional pipeline grids.

The current major LNG exporters are Qatar, Malaysia and Indonesia, but other countries are firmly determined to gain a growing stake in the LNG market, including Australia and West Africa's Nigeria and Angola. LNG already accounts for some 30 percent of internationally traded gas. Thanks to LNG, inter-regional trade is projected to expand by more than three-quarters within the next 20 years.

Pricing

With regards to gas pricing, two models largely dominate existing natural gas markets. Most international gas trade is carried out on the long-term contract (LTC) model. These are take-off agreements that tie a producer of gas (such as Russia's Gazprom) and a consumer of gas (such as a European utility) into a contractual relationship of 20 years or more. They usually define minimum volumes that a consumer has to purchase ('take off'), hence LTCs are also referred to as take-off agreements. LTCs typically peg the price of natural gas to the price of a substitute, mostly oil. LTCs have emerged because natural gas is less fungible a commodity than oil and for most of its trade is reliant on pipelines as transport infrastructure. Moreover, natural gas production projects have lead times of several years or even a decade, and are highly capital intensive. Producers therefore need to have clarity about whether there will be a market to serve upon completion of the project, and about its size, before such long-term and substantial investments are made. Consumers, on the other hand, have an interest in knowing what volumes of gas they can count on in order to develop strategies of placing that gas in the domestic market. As consumers bear the risk of having to take off a certain volume of gas, the price risk is left to the producer – hence the oil price peg. LTCs therefore allow splitting the risks related to uncertainties about the market environment before an upstream gas project is started. LTCs, and the bilateral character of gas trade that they infer, are the primary reason why natural gas markets have so far remained primarily regional in nature.

Interestingly, the growing LNG sector also tends to rely on the LTC model. This is precisely because of the capital-intensive nature of the technology and the risks associated with the long-term time horizons of the business. LNG pricing also relies on the oil-link, although possible exports from the USA and elsewhere may in the future move some markets (particularly in Asia) more towards spot markets.

Indeed, some countries and regions feature a second pricing model based on spot and futures markets. Here, prices are determined on the basis of availability and demand, not through a link to the oil price, and the natural gas market resembles the oil market or other commodity markets. It is notably in North America where gas-on-gas competition determines prices. In the USA, Henry Hub in Louisiana serves as the primary spot market and as a pricing point for futures contracts traded on the New York exchanges. In Europe, gas-on-gas competition is well established only in the UK, and emerging in the Netherlands. The British National Balance Point (NBP) and the Dutch Title Transfer Facility (TTF) represent these countries' key spot markets (see Figure 2.3). However, given the structure of the European gas market and the

Figure 2.3   *Regional gas markets and dominant contractual models*

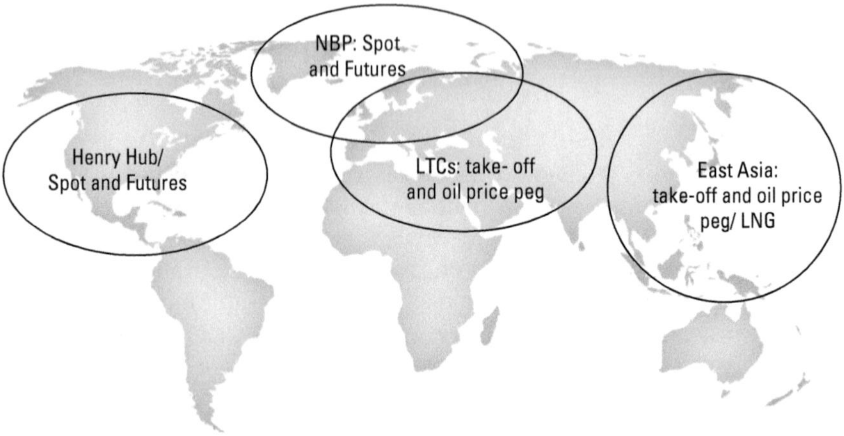

incumbency of the LTC model, it is conceivable that established pricing patterns will prevail for some time, and that the share of spot and futures traded gas will rise only gradually in Europe.

The 'shale gas revolution'
Recent progress in extraction technology – hydraulic fracturing – has allowed the exploitation of vast reserves of unconventional natural gas at economic costs (see Box 2.4). Dubbed the 'shale gas revolution', the development of the massive Marcellus, Haynesville, Barnett and Utica shale reserves has resulted in soaring production of unconventional sources of natural gas (including shale gas, coalbed methane, tight sandstones, or methane hydrates) in the United States of America. The share of shale gas in overall US gas production had by 2010 increased to 20 percent. By 2020, domestic gas production in the US is expected to outpace domestic consumption, making the US 'energy independent' in natural gas.

Developments in the US gas market have repercussions for international gas trading and pricing. Most importantly, LNG cargos destined for the USA at the end of the last decade had to find new markets, and went to Europe instead. Here, additional supply hit NBP and TTF spot markets, and put LTC pipeline gas under pricing pressure. As a consequence, European importers of LTC gas were forced to push for a change in contractual arrangements with Russia's Gazprom and/or Norway's Statoil, away from the oil price peg, and towards a larger representation of (lower) spot market prices within pricing arrangement. Some European utilities such as Ruhrgas even went out of business. Furthermore, if the USA decided to export gas in the near future, then the US shale gas revolution may have led to additional liquidity in LNG markets, strengthening their role in the overall global energy supply.

Box 2.4 Hydraulic fracturing in oil and gas

Hydraulic fracturing, or fracking, is an extraction technique used to produce oil or gas from underground rock formations. Fracking involves the high-pressure injection of water, chemicals and sand to create small fractures that release the oil from the rock formation. It is typically used in combination with horizontal drilling, to cover large underground areas with only one borehole. Fracking can also be used to stimulate the productivity of a conventional oil well once it approaches the end of its life span. The technique is typically used in areas between 1.5 km and 6 km below the Earth's surface. Although this technique has been around since the late 1940s, fracking only became a major driver of unconventional oil and gas production in the early 2000s. In the USA, the frontrunner country, 'fracked' hydrocarbons constituted 67 percent of natural gas production and 43 percent of oil production in 2013.

Fracking has, however, raised environmental concerns in the USA and elsewhere as the Oscar-nominated documentary 'Gasland' (2010) clearly illustrates. Concerns centre on potential ground water contamination, leakage of methane or other greenhouse gases, seismic disturbances, and negative impacts on water reserves. A number of US states have placed a moratorium on fracking, as have countries such as France, Bulgaria and South Africa.

Finally, net importers of natural gas such as China, the UK or Poland have started to explore shale gas reserves, and are determined to produce unconventional gas in their own domestic market or even for export. However, prospects of this in Europe look less promising than initially projected, for reasons of difficult geology as well as 'above ground' factors such as environmental movements, inappropriate regulation, lack of a service industry and missing infrastructure. Still, an overall growing unconventional gas sector may further globalise the gas trade and erode the prevalent LTC oil price peg. In this case, the three separate regional gas markets – the North American market, Europe and East Asia – may eventually see strong interregional gas trade, gas-on-gas competition and (global) gas pricing based on actual supply and demand patterns.

Coal

Reserves, production and trade

Coal remains the backbone of the world's electricity supply. As BP statistics demonstrate, coal accounts for more than 40 percent of global electricity production and 27 percent of overall global energy demand. In terms of reserves, the USA tops the list with 27.6 percent of global deposits in 2012. Russia is second with 18.2 percent, and China is third with 13.3 percent, followed by Australia (8.9 percent) and India (7 percent). The largest producer of coal is China, accounting for 46 percent, followed by the US (11.7 percent),

India (7.5 percent) and Australia (5.3 percent). The largest consumers of coal are China (50.2 percent of world demand), the USA (12.5 percent) and India (8 percent). Despite its production of 3,700 megatons of coal per year, China has emerged as the world's largest importer, followed by Japan, South Korea and India.

According to the World Coal Association, only 15 percent of the world's consumption of coal is traded. In other words, in contrast to oil or natural gas, coal is mostly consumed where it is produced. The coal trade, such as it is, is divided between the Atlantic market (covering North America and Europe) and the Pacific market (including among others Australia, China, and OECD-Asia). Following the shale gas revolution in the USA, the transatlantic coal trade has picked up, as coal is increasingly priced out of the American market and seeks margin elsewhere – notably in Europe, where despite low-carbon policies CO_2 emissions have recently grown as a result of increasing coal imports from the USA.

Pricing
The price for coal is principally set on commodity exchanges such as NYMEX (for the North American market) or ICE (mainly for the European market). Because of its importance as an input fuel for electricity production, futures have emerged as the standard contract for trading coal, thereby allowing producers and consumers to hedge the risk of adverse price movements. Coal futures are typically denominated in US$. It is however worth mentioning that not all coal is priced that way. In fact, fossil fuels are subsidised in a great many countries of the world, and this includes coal. Although G20 leaders agreed in 2009 to phase out fossil fuel subsidies, the IEA estimates that in 2011 US$523 billion was spent on artificially reducing the price of fossil fuels, up from US$401 billion in 2010. Some countries, such as Russia, sell gas domestically and internationally at subsidised rates (particularly to former communist countries). Other countries, such as the UK and Germany, continue to subsidise their coal sectors. These subsidies serve as a good introduction to the links between energy policy and domestic social demands and the degree to which nationally specific political and economic structures impact on how energy is governed.

Nuclear

Production and trade
Nuclear provided about 5.7 percent of the world's energy supply in 2012, according to IEA statistics. Its key primary fuel is uranium. The largest reserve holders of uranium are Australia (31 percent of the world total), Kazakhstan (12 percent), Canada (9 percent) and Russia (9 percent). In terms of uranium production, the World Nuclear Association lists Kazakhstan as the top producer, providing more than a third of the world's output, followed by Canada (15 percent) and Australia (12 percent). Importantly, however, uranium has to

be enriched to be of value to operators of nuclear plants, the major customer of uranium products. Yet, only a handful of countries, including the United States, France, Germany, Russia and the Netherlands have managed to build up sizeable enrichment facilities, and therefore these countries constitute an important factor in the market for uranium.

Coincidentally, and unsurprisingly, these countries also represent the largest producers of nuclear energy. In the EU, nuclear provides around 30 percent of total electricity supply, and in the US around 19 percent. A number of nations, including China, are in the process of establishing their own enrichment facilities, in order to make their nuclear power sector independent from the countries that have already mastered enrichment technology. The market for uranium, though international, does not feature mechanisms typical for commodity trading, such as elaborated spot markets or futures. Instead, uranium trade relies primarily on bilateral deals between a producer and a consumer. Most uranium traded is also subject to long-term contracts similar to the ones in natural gas. Furthermore, there are only a few experienced nuclear operators in the world, all of which feature strong involvement by their respective governments or state ownership. In light of this, and given the rather exclusive number of countries producing uranium and capable of utilising uranium in electricity production, incumbent patterns of uranium trade are not likely to change any time soon.

Pricing and financing nuclear
For a number of reasons, uranium prices have been highly volatile in recent years, with the price climbing from US$7/pound (lb) in 2001 to an all-time high of US$137/lb in 2007, down to US$40/lb in 2010 and back again to more than US$70/lb in 2011. However, the economics of nuclear do not necessarily depend on the price of uranium, which is but one cost factor. Rather, they hinge on the overall investment costs of building nuclear power facilities. A 2010 report by the IEA and the OECD's Nuclear Energy Agency stressed that (new) nuclear plants are still very high cost, as well as coming with a well-established tradition of large cost and time overruns. The investment challenges are significant. As a 2012 report by the OECD's Nuclear Energy Agency suggests, 289 of the world's 440 reactors are over 25 years old, of which 73 have reached the usual reactor life span of 60 years. A total of 160 reactors could be taken off the grid within the next ten years because they have reached retirement age. The private sector views nuclear as bound with high risk (see Box 2.5), which limits private capital investment into the sector. To help overcome this, state support is provided in terms of loan guarantees, fixed prices paid for nuclear electricity or take-over of decommissioning risks and costs in order to encourage private sector investment. Others have suggested that recent new builds, for example in the USA, have even been 100 percent state financed. It has also been argued that even in France, arguably the world's leading producer, there has been no demonstration of a nuclear learning curve, with France's last plant 3.5 times more expensive than the first, and taking

Box 2.5 The Fukushima disaster

On 11 March 2011, following an offshore earthquake, a tsunami hit Japan's Fukushima Daiichi nuclear power plant and caused the largest nuclear accident since Chernobyl in 1986. A series of cascading events led to a failure of the cooling system, a nuclear meltdown and eventually the release of nuclear material into the environment. The Fukushima accident ranks Level 7 on the International Nuclear Event Scale, the highest on the scale, and therefore is on a par with the Chernobyl disaster. Investigation concluded that the incident could not be deemed simply a natural disaster, given the poorly chosen reactor site and severe failures in safety measures.

In 2013, the Japanese government admitted that the area surrounding Fukushima may no longer be inhabitable. Severe problems persist with regards to managing the devastated plant and the consequences of the accident. Notably, the power plant continues to leak radioactive water into the Pacific Ocean. The Fukushima disaster has prompted the Japanese government to close down all nuclear power plants and to initiate safety audits on all sites. Internationally, the accident has led to a significant rethink of the role of nuclear in the energy mix. Germany decided to phase out nuclear; Belgium, Italy, Malaysia and Switzerland put a moratorium on new power plants; and even China first suspended and later slowed down nuclear development.

nearly twice as long to build. Financing nuclear and keeping the sector in the energy mix will therefore require significant government involvement, and nuclear energy is not likely to become cost covering unless certain types of risk are transferred to the state.

Renewables

Renewable sources of energy, including hydro, solar, wind, biofuels and traditional biomass, marine energy and geothermal play an important role in addressing the carbon challenge and in rendering the global energy system more sustainable in the future. In 2010, renewables accounted for some 13 percent of global TPED, according to IEA data. If planned renewable policies stay on track, the organisation estimates that renewables will see a steep growth path in the next few decades and almost double from 1,684 million tonnes of oil equivalent (Mtoe) in 2010 to 3,079 Mtoe in 2035. Importantly, this growth rate will most likely occur outside of traditional biomass (the lowest fuel in terms of energy quality and density). The reasons behind this growth path are mainly governmental policies, but also because of learning curves and economies of scale in renewable technology. Major consuming regions have set targets for the use of renewables in the energy mix. For instance, in 2009 the EU enacted the legally binding goal of raising the share of renewables to 20 percent of total consumption by 2020. The USA has put in place blending targets for biofuels, and China has adopted policies to increase the share of renewables in electricity production.

Renewable sources of energy, however, feed into the energy system in different ways. Wind power, hydro-electric power, and electricity from geo-thermal or solar all directly feed electricity generation. Biomass, by contrast, primarily fuels cars and therefore feeds into the market for liquid fuels. In other words, given the different fuels for which individual renewables are sub-stitutes, the economics of renewables may differ. In what follows, therefore, we first address renewables feeding the electricity sector, and then consider biofuels.

Production, trade and financing of wind, wave, solar, geothermal and hydro
In the electricity sector, renewables make up for 10 percent of global con-sumption, according to IEA data. Among all renewables currently feeding into the electricity sector, hydro-electric by far dominates with 3,431 terawatt hours (TWh) of consumption, followed by wind (342 TWh) and solar (32 TWh). At the same time, wind and solar have the highest growth potential, with hydro remaining stable. This reflects the likely continuance of the steep growth trajectory that wind and solar have been on since 2000, growing by a yearly average of 27 percent and 42 percent respectively. Obviously, there are great differences across regions. BP statistics reveal that 93 percent of all consumption of solar energy was in the OECD, and 76 percent of the total in the EU. Here, frontrunners Germany (30 percent of the world's total), Italy (20 percent) and Spain (13 percent) represent the bulk of solar electricity use. Germany also leads in terms of installed capacity (33 percent of world's total), followed by Italy (16 percent), China (8 percent) and the USA (7 percent). In wind, the USA leads both in consumption and installed capacity (27 percent and 21 percent respectively), followed by China (19 percent/26 percent), Germany (9 percent/ 11 percent) and Spain (9 percent/ 8 percent). Overall, there are 284 gigawatts (GW) of installed capacity in wind and 100 GW in solar (photovoltaic).

With regard to trade, and except for some (limited) cross-border trade between neighbouring countries, electricity generated from renewables is largely consumed in the market in which it is produced. The only region that fosters international trade of electricity (generated both from renewables and fossil fuels) is the European Union, but here the electricity market also remains far from fully integrated.

With regard to pricing, renewables generally remain uncompetitive against their fossil fuel competitors. Therefore, they need to be pushed into the market through various forms of state support. Supporting policy tools include man-dated targets, feed-in-tariffs, direct subsidies or regulation that favours less polluting fuels over carbon intensive ones. The IEA estimates that in 2011 renewable energy subsidies stood at US$88 billion, a figure that is set to grow to some US$240 billion per year by 2035 in order to implement policies and targets that governments have committed to. It is, however, important to note that renewables continue to fight an uphill battle, as subsidies to renewables are dwarfed by the financial support for fossil fuels – explaining in part their continued competitiveness. As indicated above, global fossil fuel subsidies were US$523 billion in 2011, six times the amount for renewables.

Production, trade and pricing of biofuels

Biofuels are primarily used for fuelling the vehicle fleet where they are blended into, or may even replace, traditional gasoline. Bioethanol, which is the most common biofuel, is typically generated from corn, sugar cane or wheat. Biodiesel, mostly used in Europe where it is blended into regular diesel, is produced from vegetable oils such as palm oil but also soy or sunflower. The main consumers of biofuels in 2011 were the USA (49 percent of global consumption), Brazil (20 percent) and Europe (19 percent) according to the US Energy Information Agency. Coincidentally, the main producers also feature the USA (45 percent of world production), Brazil (27 percent) and the EU (16 percent). According to IEA data, total world production of biofuels amounted to the equivalent of 1.3 million barrels of oil equivalent per day in 2012.

Estimates are that global demand for biofuels is set to triple within the next 20 years. This is because of ambitious government policies to push biofuels into the transport sector. The US has adopted the Renewable Fuel Standard, stipulating that 136 billion litres of biofuels be used in the transportation sector by 2022, and has set in place tax incentives for using biodiesel and bioethanol. The EU, in turn, has set the above-mentioned 20-20-20 goals, featuring biofuels within the 20 percent target on renewables. The EU's Renewable Energy Directive also sets a 10 percent target for renewable energy in transport fuels by the year 2020. Brazil, a traditional biofuel producer where all light vehicles now run either on ethanol or ethanol blends, has made biofuels an explicit focus of its renewable energy policy, and will continue fostering biofuels as a transport fuel. Japan also aims at increasing the share of biofuels to some 10 percent of domestic gasoline consumption.

Biofuels are a globally traded commodity. A 2010 OECD/FAO report suggests that for the coming years, around 7 percent of global production will be subject to international trade. An agricultural product, biofuels are frequently subject to trade disputes, most recently between Brazil and the EU. As the IEA projects, biofuel consumption notably in the EU and Japan but also other countries will soon exceed domestic production. This implies that international biofuel trade is likely to pick up further in the next few years.

In terms of pricing, biofuels such as bioethanol are subject to spot and futures trading on commodity exchanges such as the London-based ICE Futures. In addition to changes in the commodity market biofuel pricing seems to follow price developments in the oil market, which can be explained by the fact that biofuels have become a direct substitute for gasoline – a key petroleum product.

Conclusion

This chapter sought to provide an overview of the global energy system, explaining how important energy is to economics, politics and livelihoods in modern economies, as well as how the way in which societies provision themselves with energy has changed over time. In exploring the geographical distribution of energy supply and demand, the geopolitics of energy become clearer, along with the fractures and points of tension in world energy. The focus on changing patterns of supply and demand was supplemented with empirical detail on specific fuels, exploring how the most important sources of energy are produced, distributed, consumed, priced and traded in global energy markets, as well the kinds of technologies and infrastructure necessary to underpin this process. To complement this, the following chapter looks at the politics of these changing global energy markets, and the changing role of the state in relation to energy markets and energy sources – adding further levels of sophistication to our understanding of global energy challenges.

Chapter 3

The Political Economy of Energy

The political economy of energy – what states do, and what markets do, and the relations between states and markets – is important to understanding contemporary global energy challenges. States are legal entities often referred to as nations, nation-states or countries. They are most famously defined by Weber in 1919 as having 'the *monopoly of the legitimate use of physical force within a given territory*' (Weber 2009). Within this territory, states have legal and judicial power, military and police enforcement capability, and the ability to set both economic and political rules and regulations. States can, in effect, command and control. Legitimacy may be derived from a popular mandate, as in a democratic state, or in non-democratic states from coercion, historical tradition, patrimonialism, or the delivery of economic goods and resources. States interact with other states through foreign policy, including foreign economic policy.

States are certainly constitutive of energy governance. By deciding what states will own, operate and control and what is left to competitive markets, states set the broad *rules of the game*. States are also players in the game: they formulate specific rules and regulations that affect non-state actors as well as influencing energy sector outcomes and development. However, energy is a game mostly played on the international level. While some states may be powerful enough to take unilateral action on energy issues, most states are required to cooperate with one another on either a bilateral or multilateral basis in order to establish enforceable rules of the global energy game, or at least to generate norms of energy-based interaction. The practical outcomes of these moves to generate international energy governance systems are explored in more detail in Chapter 4.

Markets operate through the price mechanism, following the laws of supply and demand. Markets enable investments to be allocated, and determine wealth generation and distribution. In practice, states may regulate and intervene in markets in a range of different ways, which affects market outcomes to varying extents. Whether energy markets can become internationalised depends on infrastructure, resource availability, relations between energy consumers and producers, geopolitical realities, and of course the broader stability of the international system: during both world wars, international energy markets either ceased to function or were co-opted for war efforts. The international political economy of energy, then, concerns the changing balance of state and market activities in the governance of energy issues. The example of the world wars is representative of the bigger picture: broader

58

changes in and crises of the international system affect energy; energy, in turn, can disrupt, or at least contribute to the instability of, the world order.

This chapter seeks to address this changing balance in the political economy of energy through the concept of *paradigms*. Both political paradigms (in particular the dominance of the West) and economic paradigms (in particular the dominance of the market as a mode of organisation) are explained with reference to the changing international political economy (IPE) and of course to energy in particular. The chapter then overviews three historical periods or 'eras' in the IPE of energy: the era of the Seven Sisters, the era of OPEC, and the era of neo-liberalism. Finally, the chapter looks at the prospects for an emerging fourth, post-neo-liberal era in the IPE of energy. Following Chapter 1, we keep in mind that how relations between states and markets are understood is as much a question of perspective as it is of empirical evidence.

Economic and political paradigms in international energy

The term *paradigm* is defined by Thomas Kuhn (1962) as a set of ideas, shared amongst practitioners, academic and policy-makers, which provide both 'problems and solutions'. *Paradigm shift* occurs when the dominant paradigm, unable to continue to explain empirical reality ('facts') is challenged by an alternative set of ideas (the new paradigm) that are better able to do so. Paradigms therefore are not completely dominant – they are always challenged, and may be incomplete in their ability to drive solutions for policy-makers. The work of Hall (1993) is crucial here, because it adapts Kuhn's paradigm approach to policy-making. Policy paradigms are important because ideas influence both behaviour and interests – policy-makers are likely to respond to new challenges through the embedded approach to problem solving that has worked well for previous sets of problems.

For the IPE of energy, the different paradigms produce very different analyses of global energy problems, and so very different solutions. Policy-makers, in turn, are likely to operate within the framework of a particular policy paradigm. As Keynes (1936) put it, 'Practical men, who believe themselves to be quite exempt from any intellectual influence, are usually the slaves of some defunct economist'. It is crucial to realise that relations between states and markets in energy take place within a broader political-economic context, and policy paradigms are a key part of this. Two core paradigms that are crucial to understanding the political economy of energy are here identified. First, there is an *economic paradigm*, and second a *political paradigm*.

The economic paradigm influences the balance between states and markets in driving economic activity, and so has clear implications for the political economy of energy. Paradigm shifts have occurred twice in this regard. The first is the shift from the market-oriented paradigm of classical economics, also known as *laissez-faire*, to a more state interventionist paradigm often termed *Keynesianism*. This shift resulted from the failure of classical economics to account for or respond to the Great Depression in the 1930s. The second paradigm shift occurred in reaction to the failure of Keynesianism to respond to the economic crises of the 1970s. The new paradigm, *neo-liberalism*, is a return to a market-oriented approach, calling for reductions in state regulation and intervention, and for the market to set prices. Privatisation and competition were two of the key watch words of this paradigm. Questions about the continuing dominance of this paradigm are ongoing, not least owing to the global economic crisis of 2007.

As to the dominant political paradigm, it is crucial to realise that for around five centuries, the world has been characterised by Western hegemony. A *hegemon* is defined by Robert Gilpin (1987) as having a preponderance of military, political and economic power in the international system. Since industrialisation (when energy became a crucial issue for states) there have only been two hegemonic powers. Britain was the dominant world power from roughly 1688–1792, and then in a second phase from 1815 until 1914. After 1945, the USA became the world hegemon by virtue of its containing over 70 percent of the world's industrial capacity after the destruction of World War II. The USA was able to exercise a decisive influence over the design of the post-war order, and the stability of this order, furthermore, has largely been a product of continuing US economic and military predominance.

However, within Western hegemonic rule there are competing tendencies towards two political paradigms: mercantilism, characterised by the self-interested economic behaviour of states; and liberal institutionalism, which seek to build formal mechanisms for cooperation and trade between countries (see Chapter 1). Attempts to build a liberal institutionalist world order had failed after World War I, but since World War II this vision has to some extent been realised. The US and its Western allies were able to lock-in a largely free trading global economy, and have limited the extent to which interstate economic competition has managed to spill over into military conflict. A critical aspect of this hegemony in terms of energy was the USA's support for decolonisation, a process which began not long after World War II ended. The liberal institutionalist paradigm is far from complete, particularly in the energy sector, but it is clear that greater possibilities for energy cooperation exist now than prior to 1945. Furthermore, in the immediate post-war era, energy was still largely characterised by the mercantilist behaviour of the traditional great powers. A more liberal, free-trade based energy system had to wait until after decolonisation was largely completed, and after the economic crises of the 1970s. This is discussed in detail below.

Significant challenges to US hegemony are evident in a contemporary setting. The rapid economic growth of first Western Europe and then East and South East Asia meant that US economic might has already suffered enormous relative decline. The global economy has clearly become more multipolar in nature. The rise of rapidly industrialising countries such as Brazil, Russia, India, China, and South Africa (BRICS), including a resurgent Russia, implies the prospect of multiple economic, political and (least convincingly) military centres to the international system, as well as a degree of de-Westernisation. This is evident in the shift from the G7/G8 to the G20, and the economic significance of China following the global economic crisis of 2007. As Western dominance is increasingly challenged, the question arises whether a wider breakdown of the US-sponsored liberal institutionalist post-war world order will occur. However, as Keohane argued in *After Hegemony* (1984), it may be possible for a multipolar world order to exist without shaking the dominant paradigm of liberal institutionalism.

Together, the economic and political paradigms (and their challenges) provide a framework within which the political economy of energy can be explored in the increasingly dynamic and uncertain world. The significance of these paradigms for energy policy is set out below, across the different 'eras'. The final section addresses the key question of whether energy remains characterised by a compromise between liberal institutionalism and the neo-liberal market order, in the context of continuing Western dominance. Certainly, many scholars have claimed that given the contemporary global energy challenge, energy is in crisis. Crisis, in turn, is often a precursor to large-scale political change. In energy, therefore, we cannot discount the possibility that further paradigm shifts are already taking place.

Three eras in the IPE of energy

The international political economy of energy reflects shifts in paradigms and power, but is also constitutive of such shifts. States pursuing industrialisation and rapid economic growth required energy. In the 1880s, for example, the USA and Western Europe began the move towards electricity-based economic activity which would henceforth underpin their economies. Large-scale hydro-electricity plants and coal-fired power stations became the dominant form of energy generation. The link between resources, world power and state economic self-interest is clearly evident: coal, along with steel, was presented in national discourses as a strategic necessity, crucial to state survival. Control of a state's own economic resources was paramount, and protectionist economic practices were predominant.

Coal remained the key domestic product and international export until well after World War II. The centrality of coal is evident in the fact that the EU began as the European Coal and Steel Community (ECSC) in 1952. The ECSC constituted a deliberate internationalisation of energy in an attempt to reduce the chances of further European conflict (following the liberal economic peace thesis). Nevertheless, it was oil that became the world's dominant energy source in the post-war era. Petroleum output had risen drastically since the 1880s, with the USA as the main oil producer and exporter. Oil became an increasingly important battleground in contests over broader political and economic power, with the design of oil markets and the dominance of certain players within them central, and it is oil which is crucial to understanding the different eras in the IPE of energy.

To demonstrate how energy has interacted with the broader changes in IPE since industrialisation, this section details three key historical periods. The first is the era of the Seven Sisters, characterised by the dominance of private, IOCs, overtly supported by Western military-political hegemony. The second era roughly covers the 1970s, in which a wave of nationalisations enabled NOCs to predominate. Power shifted to oil producers, the most significant of which formed the OPEC club. This second period is called the era of OPEC because of the price-fixing power of this club, and the impact of their oil pricing activities on the broader global economy. The third era is that of neo-liberalism. While neo-liberal policies and politics were widely utilised in the 1980s, it was in the 1990s that the most significant changes to global energy systems took place.

The era of the Seven Sisters

The Seven Sisters were private, Western oil corporations that emerged in the early 20th century, and dominated the international oil system (outside of wartime) until 1973 (Box 3.1). They constitute a key energy sector example of how states and companies interact for mutual gain. The Sisters benefited from tax breaks, diplomatic support and military aid when necessary, from the main states that sponsored them: the US and Britain. Such support reflected the perception of shared national-corporate interests in the energy sector. The era of the Seven Sisters is also important as a backdrop to understanding how oil markets, in particular, have historically been characterised by severe market imbalances.

The Sisters were all *vertically integrated* companies, controlling all stages of the productive process for energy from well to pump. This included exploration, transportation and marketing, and to an extent technological change. The build-up to World War I, in particular the 'race to the colonies', created new international opportunities for these companies, and after the war they were able to form an international *producer cartel*. The Sisters divided up markets between them, and used LTCs to avoid price competition. In 1928, production quotas were settled in the 'Achnacarry Agreement', enabling the Sisters to effectively fix international prices. The predominant role of the Sisters in the Middle East, in particular, was crucial, as this enabled them to control around 85 percent of global oil reserves.

The post-war era began very favourably for the Sisters, as Western states and a number of developing states become significant oil importers. In order to maintain their market position, crude prices were kept high. This ensured that the downstream oil industry was relatively unprofitable, while the Sisters' control of oil refineries and transportation systems also contributed to extremely high market entry costs. Nevertheless, oil prices were not so high as to create incentives for energy consumers to move away from oil.

Box 3.1 The Seven Sisters

After a series of mergers, the Seven Sisters are now four major international oil companies. ExxonMobil, Chevron, Royal Dutch Shell and BP are all key players in oil markets today, as well as influential in global energy politics more generally. They remain crucial to exploration, technological development and downstream markets, but no longer dominate oil production.

Standard Oil of New Jersey (Esso) and *Standard Oil Company of New York* (Socony)

- These two US companies merged to form ExxonMobil
- In 2010 ExxonMobil produced around 3 percent of all world oil, and turned a profit of over US$30 billion
- ExxonMobil owned and operated the *Exxon Valdez*. When this ship sank in 1989, it caused the second largest oil spill in US history

Standard Oil of California (SoCal), *Gulf Oil* and *Texaco*

- These three US companies merged to form Chevron
- Chevron turned a profit of over US$26 billion in 2011
- Chevron's Gorgon Gas project in Australia is alone worth US$43 billion

Anglo-Persian Oil Company (British Petroleum)

- Commonly called BP, and majority owned by the British government until the election of the Thatcher Government, which completely privatised the company by 1987
- Ironically, the government of Kuwait is now the largest single shareholder
- The 2010 Deepwater Horizon oil spill was the largest maritime oil spill in history. Clean up costs amounted to US$28 billion, plus US$4.5 billion in fines and up to a possible US$18 billion in ongoing court proceedings

Royal Dutch Shell

- This joint British-Dutch company topped the Fortune 500 list of the world's largest companies in 2013
- Shell has been particularly criticised for its operations in the Niger Delta region of Nigeria
- Arctic oil exploration has also brought Shell into conflict with Greenpeace

In the aftermath of World War II, under US hegemony, a determined effort towards liberal institutionalism had resulted in the UN system. A significant part of this system – reflecting the liberal economic peace thesis – was the General Agreement on Tariffs and Trade (GATT), designed to promote and maintain free trade, thereby preventing a repeat of the disastrous slide into protectionism and rival economic blocs which had preceded both world wars. However, energy was such a contentious issue, and so close to vested national interests, that it was by necessity excluded from the GATT. Consequently states could practise protectionism in the energy sector. Of most significance however is the decision of the USA to protect its oil markets. Given the relative size and purchasing power of the US market in the post-war era, the Seven Sisters, in order to stay competitive, had to lower oil prices. Crucially, this came at the expense of oil producing nations, rather than of corporate profits.

The international political economy of oil became increasingly dynamic from the 1950s onwards, making the Sisters' cartel arrangement more difficult to maintain. Perhaps most significantly, as the USA was no longer the world's largest producer and exporter of oil, the geopolitical significance of the Middle East to the international oil system became increasingly paramount. Oil supply became increasingly internationalised, as new sites of significant production such as the Soviet Union and Venezuela came on-stream. Furthermore, the process of decolonisation increased the bargaining power of oil-rich states, which began to demand the nationalisation of oil industry assets. Middle Eastern and North African states in particular felt economically disadvantaged by the activities of the Seven Sisters.

However, in the case of conflicts with producer countries, the Sisters could rely on the support of the Western powers – which actively opposed economic nationalism. The clearest example of this is the 1951 attempt at oil nationalisation in Iran. When a boycott failed to resolve the affair in their interests the US and British governments intervened directly, overthrowing the democratically elected regime. They created a puppet government under the Shah, to the direct benefit of US oil companies. The long-term consequences of this for Western interests in the region have of course been resoundingly negative, but what this military intervention clearly demonstrated was the centrality of oil to the foreign policies of the 'Great Powers' in this period.

However, as a sign of shifting power dynamics in the region, and in the political economy of the international oil industry, five years after Iran, Britain and France failed to deter Egypt's nationalisation plans in the 1956 'Suez Crisis'. The Suez Canal is a key transit route for Middle Eastern oil coming to Europe (see Chapter 8). Through a realist lens, international oil supply constitutes a *zero-sum game*: states are required to secure finite energy assets or their competitors will – with implications for industrial production and military capacity. Unwilling to grant control of this key transit route to an emerging regional power, Britain and France launched a military expedition force: but the failure of the USA to back its European allies in this regard seriously undermined the scheme. The balance of power would continue to shift towards Middle Eastern states, until it was they – rather than the Western states and their oil companies – who would dominate the international oil industry, in the era of OPEC.

The era of OPEC

In the 1960s some of the larger oil producers, particularly Libya and Saudi Arabia, demonstrated their ability to renegotiate oil agreements to their economic advantage. Greater foreign earnings, in turn, increased the capacity of these states to manage price instability – and crucially, it encouraged cooperation between oil producers. Indeed, Iran, Iraq, Kuwait, Saudi Arabia and Venezuela formed the Organization of Petroleum Exporting Countries (OPEC) in 1960. In 1969, when Colonel Qaddaffi seized power in Libya, his strategy of threatening production strikes succeeded in extracting even more favourable prices from international oil companies. High oil demand in the West, combined with lack of domestic energy production, appears to have left the West highly vulnerable to cartel behaviour. By 1970, furthermore, OPEC membership had expanded to 13, and now represented 85 percent of world oil exports. In 1971, with the base price for oil standing at US$1.80 per barrel, the now emboldened OPEC countries were able to pressure the Seven Sisters into a five-year deal on oil prices that significantly benefited OPEC producers.

However, by the early 1970s the USA was facing serious economic problems in the form of *stagflation*: a combination of high inflation, high unemployment and low economic growth. This was caused in part by the ongoing costs of the Vietnam War, and in part by loss of economic competitiveness as the global economy had strongly recovered following World War II. In response to this situation, Richard Nixon unilaterally broke the link between the US dollar and US gold reserves, in the year 1971. In the wake of this collapse of the post-war Bretton Woods financial order (which had rested on a gold-backed US dollar), the US dollar was heavily devalued, both in 1971 and 1972 (see Gilpin 1987: 140–41). Crucially, as all oil contracts were negotiated in US dollars, this amounted to a cut in the price of oil for OPEC countries. Renegotiations with the Seven Sisters resulted in further price increases, but oil asset nationalisation was now added to the list of OPEC demands.

By 1973 oil demand was surging, but given the long-term contracts they had signed with the Seven Sisters, OPEC countries did not benefit from this. Furthermore, inflation in the Western, industrial economies had decreased the purchasing power of oil money against manufactured goods. OPEC was once again able to bring the international oil companies back to the negotiating table, but any prospective renegotiation was disrupted by the 1973 Arab–Israeli war. In response, in particular, to the perception of American support for Israel in this war, OPEC unilaterally massively increased the price of oil twice, such that by the end of 1973, prices had reached US$11.65 per barrel, a previously unthinkable level. This was the *first oil shock*.

By the 1970s OPEC had in essence replaced the Seven Sisters as a functioning producer cartel. With large oil reserves and enormous production capacity, OPEC could cooperate to manage international oil production, and thereby the price. If reduced production was needed to maintain OPEC agreed prices, then for the first five years of OPEC, Saudi Arabia alone absorbed the necessary losses. OPEC was now both able and willing to leverage its pricing power, and the consequence of this was the rapid and total nationalisation of all oil company subsidiaries and production facilities located in OPEC countries. The Seven Sisters lost their central role in oil production, while efforts by the USA to form a buyer's counter-cartel, through IEA, largely failed. As Gilpin (1987: 232) states, 'World history records few equivalent redistributions of wealth and power in such a short period'.

By 1978, oil had clearly become a sellers' market. Furthermore, the long-term consequences of the 1951 military intervention in Iran became apparent, as Iranian revolutionaries cut off oil exports as part of their attempt to overthrow the Shah. Saudi Arabia was able to increase production to compensate, but global markets responded poorly to the situation, and the fear of further oil supply problems led consumer states to begin to stockpile reserves. Consequently, oil prices escalated, with OPEC prices leaping 10 percent in December 1978. International oil companies responded to this by re-selling OPEC oil bought on lower-priced long-term contracts, on the higher-priced spot market, causing OPEC countries to contemplate breaking contract. Certainly, it was clear that Saudi Arabia could no longer unilaterally manage world oil prices, which increased rapidly throughout 1979. Furthermore, when the Iran–Iraq war broke out in 1980, both sides targeted each other's oil facilities, effectively halting their oil exports. Supply shortages became more severe, and by the end of 1980 oil had reached US$33 per barrel (US$41 in the spot market). This was the *second oil shock* (see Box 3.2).

Economic differences between OPEC members did cause tensions within the cartel. States with large oil reserves, such as Saudi Arabia, Kuwait and the United Arab Emirates (UAE), prefer high production levels and low oil prices. This is a strategy for minimising the incentive for energy consumers to move away from oil, and so ensure oil profits in the long term. Most OPEC countries, however, prefer limited production and high prices, so as to maximise short-term returns from their dwindling reserves. The OPEC cartel is a compromise between these contradictory interests, but even states with an interest in low production levels have an incentive to *free ride*. Cheating on the OPEC cartel often took the form of arguing for low quotas, and then overproducing, and became an increasing problem for the cartel in the 1980s. Key free rider states included Iran, Algeria, Libya, Nigeria, Venezuela and Kuwait.

The rise in non-OPEC oil production also made it difficult to maintain the cartel through the 1980s. New sources of international supply came on-stream in Mexico, China, Malaysia, Egypt and the USSR. In the North Sea, both Norway and the UK were producing oil at below-OPEC prices. Domestic production increased markedly in big consumers such as Brazil and India. Furthermore, oil stockpiles built up during the crisis-ridden 1970s were now pushed back onto the market. The energy mix also diversified away from oil in the 1980s. An expansion of nuclear power (particularly in Japan, France, Germany and the UK) was matched by the rising significance of gas and the re-emergence of coal, as well as by emerging technologies such as solar power

---

Box 3.2 Supply shocks and cartels

For neo-classical economics, the two oil shocks of the 1970s are examples of *adverse supply shocks*. In formal terms, 'an increase in the cost of supply of input factors increases the cost of production, and so the price of output supply also increases'. Due to the massive economic dependency on oil as an input factor, this affected the production costs of almost all industrial manufactured goods, as well as agricultural produce. Consequently, the oil shocks were highly inflationary. While in the 1970s there were some significant non-OPEC producers, it was very difficult for any state aside from Saudi Arabia to quickly and significantly *increase* levels of oil production. World oil demand, furthermore, proved *inelastic*: oil continued to be consumed at the same rates, even as the price increased.

As Gilpin (1987: 297) notes, effective cartelisation requires a large producer with excess capacity, to provide discipline. In the case of OPEC, Saudi Arabia's enormous oil reserves, production capacity, and stock of foreign currency holdings enabled it to manage supply and so minimise price variation. However, cartels can also be seen as self-defeating. Given demand inelasticity, the more successful the cartel is in cooperating to reduce production, the greater the profits will be. Yet the more profitable the cartel becomes, the greater the incentive for a market response, to move demand away from the cartelised product, or to diversify sources of supply away from the cartel – spelling trouble for OPEC in the medium term.

(Lipsey and Chrystal 2011: 170). Demand growth had also slowed, due both to the recessions that the oil shocks had caused and to new energy efficiency standards for houses and particularly cars. When oil prices began to fall in the 1980s, this was precisely because of the success of OPEC.

To maintain agreed OPEC prices, OPEC production levels had to be constantly lowered, with Kuwait, the UAE and particularly Saudi Arabia taking large hits. However, more oil-revenue dependent states such as Mexico, Nigeria and Venezuela suffered greater political consequences. Managing an uneven distribution of benefits in the 1970s had been easy: the distribution of the costs of declining oil prices between members now exacerbated political tensions within the cartel (Lipsey and Chrystal 2011: 171). Attempts by OPEC members to generate revenue in downstream markets only brought them into direct competition with each other at the point of sale, further weakening incentives for cartelistic cooperation. Free riding spiralled out of control, and by 1985 the cartel, in effect, had ceased to exist, with its members engaged in a damaging *price war*. Saudi Arabia used its capacity to massively increase oil production in an attempt to discipline OPEC members, causing prices to plummet to less than US$12/barrel by 1986. Despite this, effective cartel activity could not be restored, and for the first time since the Seven Sisters agreed to set prices, world markets took control. Oil-consuming countries were the main beneficiaries of this, as the international oil economy became the mirror image of the 1970s in many ways. Indeed, for neo-classical economics this constituted a *favourable supply shock*, which might be seen as a causal factor in the high-growth, low-inflation period in the West that followed. More importantly, the role and behaviour of OPEC in this period in part explains the shift to the era of neo-liberalism (see Box 3.3).

Box 3.3 The broader impact of the era of OPEC

The rise of OPEC impacted significantly on the broader global politics of the 1970s. By 1974, the perceived unfair *terms of trade* between goods produced by advanced, industrial economies and those produced by agriculture and other primary commodity dominated developing states had led to demands for a 'New International Economic Order' (NIEO) in the United Nations: greater developing state control over their natural resources, improved terms of trade, better regulation of foreign multinational corporations (MNCs), technology transfer, more aid and debt relief, greater market access and more influence over the institutions of global governance. This was led by the 77 poorest countries (the G77) – who then constituted a majority cluster in the UN General Assembly. However, OPEC was not prepared to link its oil cartel power to demands for structural changes to the global economy as a whole. This effectively divided developing states into two groups: those with oil, who would benefit from the OPEC-dominated system, and those without. The G77 was therefore unable to maintain a unified challenge to Western hegemony and to the rules and institutions of the global economy. Quite simply, those with oil had no interest in disrupting the system – evidence of how important energy was to the economies of states. Furthermore, the impact of high oil prices was also severe in non-oil producing developing states, who therefore were big economic and political losers from the era of OPEC.

The oil shocks also led to billions of dollars in extra revenue flow from the West to OPEC members – flows too great to be soaked up by purchasing Western industrial goods (Spero and Hart 1997). This led OPEC countries to become a new source of development aid, with the IMF and World Bank as key players in the emerging system of 'recycled petro-dollars'. Debt as a strategy for promoting development had strong support, and the result of this was a massive programme of lending. Indeed, according to Spero and Hart (1997) the debt levels of oil-importing poor countries exploded from around US$11 billion in 1973, to US$89 billion in 1980. By 1980, such states were borrowing around US$35 billion a year. However, after the second oil shock, Western states addressed their inflation problems with sharp interest rate rises, making debt repayment for developing states difficult, if not impossible. The era of OPEC therefore is also a factor in the developing state debt crisis. The Mexican default threat of 1981 led directly to the 'structural adjustment' loans (SALs) of the 1980s. Through these conditional lending programmes, the World Bank and IMF demanded economic policy changes in return for aid and debt restructuring. The economic policies advocated were those of neo-liberalism, and the period of structural adjustment is the hallmark of the rise of this new economic paradigm after the collapse of Keynesianism.

The era of neo-liberalism

The neo-liberal era can be divided into two very different phases: the 1980s and the 1990s. The 1980s saw this paradigm rise to predominance on the back of the elections, in particular, of Thatcher in the UK and Reagan in the USA. Neo-liberalism became the driving ideology of the World Bank in this decade, enforced through structural adjustment conditional lending (as noted above) – particularly in sub-Saharan Africa. The privatisation of previously state-owned assets, a basic principle of neo-liberalism, and several waves of deregulation significantly affected the energy sector in a number of domestic economies. In the 1990s, the principle of good governance partially replaced or at least complemented the deregulation agenda of the 1980s.

Under the neo-liberal paradigm, governments sought to 'de-politicise' economic decision-making through privatisation. The private sector therefore gained significant influence in the international energy trade, including with regard to investment decisions for future energy supply. Oil markets began to be transformed as price and competition controls were dismantled in OECD oil-importing countries, and a combination of growing international demand and technological advances promoted strong growth in international fossil fuel trading. Pricing significantly shifted towards spot markets, reflecting changing supply and demand, and highly specialised production chains emerged. While this process started with oil, it also included other areas, notably the electricity sector. In natural gas, 'spot' markets also began to emerge in the 1990s, given both strong demand and the rise of LNGs, but this process remained more constrained than with oil given the more regional character of the natural gas market, and the emphasis on LTCs.

Energy overall was increasingly understood as a market-based, trade-driven sector, in a world of 'complex interdependence' (Keohane and Nye 1977) between nations, corporations and societal groups. By this point, energy had lost much of its strategic character. Typically of neo-liberalism, political analyses of international energy were sidelined in favour of economistic and technicist approaches. Trade and investment in energy also became increasingly subject to the intermediary role of global financial markets. Financial sector liberalisation enabled new financial products such as futures and options to bolster the international energy trade – though they also fostered speculation.

The United Kingdom was a clear leader in the neo-liberal restructuring of energy, but similar processes are evident in numerous OECD countries. Norway's electricity sector underwent particularly rapid neo-liberal reforms, while in the developing world Chile led the way with neo-liberalism, including in the energy sector. The 1990s also saw the collapse of Communism in Europe. Russia and other 'transitional economies' switched towards a more pro-market energy model in this period, partly due to conditional loans and advice provided by the IMF. Russia is such a key energy producer that its decision to privatise and liberalise its energy industry was seen as a sign of the strength of the neo-liberal paradigm, as well as of a confirmation of the 'correctness' of the neo-liberal model at the end of the Cold War. State-oriented models were understood to have been discredited and rejected. The impact of neo-liberalism in the energy sector of developing states was also significant, as Chapter 6 details.

Yet, the outcomes of market-oriented structural adjustment policies in the 1980s were in many ways disastrous, particularly in the non-OECD world. Energy sector privatisation programmes, rather than promoting transparency and accountability, created new opportunities for nepotism and corruption. By 1989 the World Bank therefore began to prioritise 'good governance' – the importance of a functional state in enabling markets to work. Of course, the good governance state is a particularly neo-liberal state: efficient, non-corrupt, transparent and accountable, but also limited in size, intervening in the market only when required to address market failures, and building social safety nets – rather than broad social rights of the social democratic model. It is the 1990s, during the good governance phase of neo-liberalism, which is most significant for the rise of the market in the energy sector.

Neo-liberalism in the international energy system was in this period concomitant with the political paradigm of US/Western-sponsored liberal institutionalism. Neo-liberal rules, norms, and principles that already existed in other areas of trade and economic relations also began to emerge in the energy sector. In 2001, Mitchell et al. (2001: 176) stated that in international commodity markets, including those related to energy, 'competition is the rule and economics works'. Five years later, Hayes and Victor (2006: 322) held that 'almost all consuming markets have adopted plans to allow for a greater role for the "invisible hand" of the market'. Certainly, the bugbear of the 1970s – energy security – had dropped off the political agendas of many OECD countries (Mitchell et al. 2001). While these energy paradigm shifts were clearly politically driven, economic factors must also be taken into consideration: strong demand growth had been met or even outmatched by growth in supply, which had also become increasingly diversified.

Whilst neo-liberalism had come to dominate as an overall political and economic paradigm, it did not prevail across the board. In fact, promoting deregulation and good governance in the energy sector proved particularly difficult. The power sector is core to national commercial and private life, and so remained highly regulated; and the same vested interests that made deregulation a political problem also sought to limit transparency and accountability. Electricity has also remained largely domestic in character. Prospects for any international power trade were limited by a lack of infrastructure, and by the technical losses incurred in moving electricity over long distances. The European Commission, firmly rooted in the pro-market paradigm, strongly promotes the idea of an EU-wide electricity grid, as well as building connections to 'third countries' (non-EU members). Gas and electricity 'supergrids', it is argued, would diversify supply, foster competition, and reduce system vulnerability to shocks (see

Chapter 8). Still, as argued in Chapter 4, the EU has thus far struggled to complete its internal market for energy.

Competition policy in the energy sector has also lagged behind: genuinely competitive market structures were rarely the outcome of neo-liberal reforms. Furthermore, given the use of conditional loans to promote energy sector reforms, it is not clear to what extent these reforms represented voluntary policy transfer by policy-makers who shared neo-liberal ideals, as opposed to being the outcomes of external inducement or coercion – which are far less likely to be successful. Liberal internationalism therefore also displayed its limitations in the third energy era. The long slow demise of the OPEC cartel through the 1980s meant that neo-liberal reforms of the international energy system were delayed. Furthermore, as the GATT exempted 'natural resources' from its trade negotiations, states such as Russia and Saudi Arabia could join its successor institution, the World Trade Organization (WTO), while avoiding energy sector liberalisation. This is in part why the EU tried – and failed – to create its own rules-based energy trading system with Russia through the Energy Charter Treaty (ECT) (see Chapter 4). Meanwhile, resource-based warfare (such as the Gulf Wars) and conflicts (such as between Ukraine and Russia) in this period demonstrated the continued centrality of oil and oil access to foreign policy and international relations.

Global energy in the wake of economic crisis: A fourth era?

In 1999 the *Financial Times* (FT) confidently forecast average oil prices of around US$5 per barrel going forward. This was for the FT the payoff for the success of neo-liberal reforms in the energy sector. Yet, in practice, between 2000 and 2013 the average price of crude oil was over ten times this amount – around US$56 per barrel. The stark limitations of the neo-liberal paradigm lead to the possibility of a 'fourth era' in international energy – in which the state may again play a more prominent role. Such a change is foreshadowed by a confluence of three key elements. First, at least since 2007, the neo-liberal economic order (global *laissez-faire*-style finance capitalism) has been in continuing crisis, even setting aside ongoing environmental concerns. Second, the return of the state is already occurring, as is evident in the activities of the BRICS for example. Finally, the securitisation of the energy agenda has changed the priorities for states, and changed the importance of energy within state foreign policy apparatus.

The crisis of neo-liberal capitalism

Criticisms of neo-liberalism were widespread before the crisis (see for example Harvey 2005), and events in the energy sector had also suggested limits to the neo-liberal paradigm. The California electricity crisis of 2000/2001 demonstrated that the market model would struggle to deliver its promises, at least in the electricity sector, in the absence of strong regulations. Enron, which collapsed spectacularly in 2001, was one of the world's largest energy companies, and had been considered one of the most innovative players in the new global economy of neo-liberal capitalism. The collapse created long-running doubts about the stability of the neo-liberal economic model, as the scale of the speculation, greed and dishonesty involved became clear. The global economic crisis that began in 2007, however, causing economies to collapse and governments to lose power, is clearly a historical nadir for neo-liberalism. Beginning in the US sub-prime housing mortgage market in 2007, the crisis has spread to every corner of the globe. This collapse, more than any previous systemic economic crisis in the era of neo-liberalism, has cast serious doubts on the ability of neo-liberalism to deliver economic needs, including in the energy sector. This is in part because this crisis had its origins in the West, rather than more peripheral economies, but also because this crisis severely damaged the financial sector which had played such a crucial role in the era of neo-liberalism.

The tendency of the world capitalist system towards cyclical structural crises seems to have accelerated in an era of neo-liberal globalisation. As booms and busts become more severe, growing interdependence between states, and interpenetration between economies, has also massively heightened the sense of national economic vulnerability. The energy sector is not immune from the consequences of the transformation of the world economy. If the neo-liberal model is seen to have failed, then greater degrees of strategic state investment and management of the energy sector may be required, for example in regard to renewable energy.

Meanwhile, emerging economies in Asia have weathered the crisis fairly well, at least in the short to medium term. Continued (albeit slowed) economic growth in China heightens the recognition of China's centrality to the global economy, but also China's centrality to investment in renewable resources, to the production of alternative energy technologies across the supply chain, and to the carbon future of planet Earth over the coming decades. Crucially, of course, China does not follow the neo-liberal or market paradigm in any sense. The degree of state intervention is more reminiscent of East Asian development than the Anglo-American experience, and of course no re-nationalisation and re-regulation has been required in China's energy sector as liberalisation and privatisation never took place to begin with. Of course, unlike Russia, China remains a net importer of energy and energy resources: there is no Chinese 'energy weapon', and as such, as China's relative political and economic might grows, this does not necessarily forebode the collapse of energy markets and market systems – China may in fact be a key beneficiary of continued market-based energy trade.

As climate change has continued to gain traction over the last decade in the public debate – particularly in OECD countries (see Chapter 5) the lack of political progress in addressing these growing energy concerns has heightened worries about the failures of the neo-liberal energy paradigm. Through a number of policy documents, the EU has stressed the need to think holistically about energy, integrating energy security concerns with more meaningful climate action. A number of scholars have argued that current energy policies and institutions are insufficient to address climate problems, a point forcefully made in the Stern Review (Stern 2006). Others have called for greater cooperation between energy consumers and producers so as to facilitate a more rapid low-carbon transition, and to directly address the climate and security dimensions of energy policy (Claes 2001; Harks 2010; Mitchell 2005; Victor and Yueh 2010). Meanwhile, environmentalists continue to point to the failures of the neo-liberal market model in delivering sustainable outcomes (Gonzalez 2006: 12; Heynen et al. 2007). The global economic crisis of 2007 further emboldened critical perspectives on the ability of neo-liberalism to address climate change in a serious and sustained manner (see Rudd 2009).

However, since 2010, the 'sovereign debt crisis' has shifted attention away from poorly performing markets towards poorly performing states. The sheer size of the economic bail-outs required for private banks and other financial sector actors in the wake of the crisis meant that national budget deficits became a serious political issue. In an era of austerity, with a rise in Euro-scepticism, retrenchment of climate change programmes and expenditure is a serious possibility. There may be little scope or appetite for large-scale state-driven energy market intervention, even as doubts about the veracity of markets grow. And given that this newer phase of the crisis has largely affected the EU – the leader on climate change action – there are potentially serious consequences for international energy investments and policy decisions.

The return of the state

In practice, as markets have become increasingly significant in energy, so the regulatory role of the state has grown. This is the case even in the United Kingdom, previously one of the foremost advocates of the neo-liberal energy agenda. Under the leadership of Gordon Brown, the state took a more central role in energy governance through the 2008 creation of the Department of Energy and Climate Change (DECC). The formation of DECC constituted a sign of the necessity and importance of integrating climate change and energy issues in policy-making terms. As Secretary of State for Energy in this period, Ed Miliband sought to meld dynamic energy markets with a vision of a 'strategic role for government' that had been absent under neo-liberalism. DECC went on to implement the Climate Change Act, with legally binding climate targets, and has promoted energy sector reforms that require increases in state funding and state intervention. Energy policy largely continued in this mode under the Conservative-Liberal Democrat coalition government elected in 2010, despite austerity policies.

This 'strategic role for government' deserves further consideration. As with other policy areas, the required enhanced state functions may be threefold (see Keating 2012b). First, there are the enhanced regulatory functions that neo-liberalism effectively embraced during the transition to good governance in the early 1990s. Second, however, states are required to make increased financial commitments – to compensate for market failures, to supplement markets, or to create functioning markets in the first place. Private sector investment occurs with, rather than instead of, public sector investments, and public–private partnerships (PPP) continue to emerge as a viable solution to policy problems. The role of the state here is moving beyond that envisaged within neo-liberalism. The third enhanced state function pushes us even further in this direction. It is increasingly apparent that states also need to provide oversight of policy sectors, particularly so as to promote coordination – not simply between states, but between a range of state, market and civil society actors. A clear example of where this is needed is in promoting networking and coordination between universities and researchers in renewable energies, and entrepreneurs, Small and medium-sized enterprises (SMEs) and international business at the production for market end of the innovation spectrum (see Chapter 9).

It is telling that some previously strongly pro-market scholars have moderated their position on the role of the state. Daniel Yergin and Joseph Stanislaw, authors of the influential *The Commanding Heights* (1998), were amongst the most prominent of these. They worked as energy writers and consultants throughout the 1980s and 1990s, advocating neo-liberal solutions to energy security problems. Yet, only six years later, Stanislaw (2004) observed that energy policy-making overemphasised market competition. He recognised that given the different energy requirements of a wide range of individual nations, and the social, political and economic factors intertwined with these, promoting cooperation was a more significant challenge than that of promoting unilateral market rules. The market, in fact, had only addressed energy concerns in a limited manner – particularly with regard to climate change. Stanislaw concluded that 'without firm government guidance, investors and the markets cannot reconcile short-term tribulations with long term goals'. Meanwhile, in his 2008 address to the US House of Representatives Committee on Foreign Affairs, Daniel Yergin argued that energy security not only requires liberal markets, but also increased state involvement. This would underpin improved international energy relations, as well as help promote energy mix diversification and energy efficiency.

Japan provides a clear example of the growing significance of state strategic oversight in the energy sector. In 2006, in response to China's aggressive pursuit of energy resources and the resulting skyrocketing of demand, Japan devised a new National Energy Strategy. This strategy called for more direct government involvement in securing access to oil, gas and other energy sources. It also demanded an increase in energy stockpiles in case of future shortages and a strengthening of diplomatic efforts to underpin new bilateral and multilateral international agreements. Furthermore, since Fukushima, the

Japanese government has been restructuring its entire national energy system in order to facilitate a phase-out of nuclear – 35-odd years after having restructured its energy system towards nuclear in response to the 1970s oil shocks.

The return of the state to the energy sector is even more obvious when looking outside OECD countries. A global economic shift towards East and South East Asia, where state intervention is more widespread, is clearly occurring. States in this region provide numerous examples of complex state interventions in the energy sector. Furthermore, re-nationalisations of oil industry assets have been occurring in the developing world, for example in Venezuela and Argentina (which re-nationalised the Argentine oil and gas company Yacimientos Petroliferos Fiscales, or YPF, in 2012). As a consequence of this, the increasingly public character of energy assets, and the strategic position of NOCs in international energy markets must be recognised, though it can be envisaged that IOCs and NOCs will both be influential on the future world energy order. It is also the case that in the last few years the links between energy, poverty and development have begun to be taken seriously by the donor community (see Chapter 6). This may lead to more strategic state intervention in the name of poverty reduction in the energy sectors of even the world's poorest states.

However, it is the rise of a bloc of rapidly industrialising countries known as the BRICS (Brazil, Russia, India, China and South Africa) which is central to the contemporary return of the state in the energy sector. In the 2000s, Russia and China overtly pursued statist energy policies. Russia, somewhat shockingly to the West, rejected the path of liberalisation and privatisation it had pursued in the 1990s, and led the way in regard to the re-nationalisation of oil assets. China and India in particular have emerged as key energy consumers, but as late entrants to global energy markets they have pursued more mercantilist approaches. This involves nurturing 'national champions', in the form of state-owned national oil companies (NOCs) that have caused particular controversy with their activities on the African continent. With a preference for bilateral agreements, such states have been able to bypass global markets and its associated norms and rules, and are seen to directly threaten the multilateral approaches that the liberal internationalist paradigm rests upon.

The rise of the BRICS constitutes an economic and political challenge to US hegemony. The West has clearly undergone relative economic decline in relation to the BRICS and East/South East Asia as trade and financial interdependence has significantly increased. This was demonstrated by the 2007 global economic crisis and the various responses to it, perhaps most overtly in the change from a G8 to a BRICS-inclusive G20. The 'big picture' question for international relations, of course, remains whether post-hegemonic stability is at all possible (see Keohane 1984; Cohen 2008); but in energy the question is slightly smaller – whether liberal institutionalism will continue to be the dominant paradigm for addressing energy issues, or whether bilateralism and mercantilism, and indeed realism (in the form of resource nationalism), will once again become a significant factor in the international political economy of energy.

The securitisation of energy

The final factor which is pushing international energy out of the era of neo-liberalism is securitisation and its consequences. This is dealt with in detail in Chapter 7, but it is worth providing an initial overview of the issues here. By 2006, energy security was again clearly visible at the top of the agenda of G8 summits and EU meetings. The wider political context within which energy was understood had changed – beginning with the 9/11 terrorist attack on the Twin Towers. The resulting 'War on Terror' crossed over with energy issues in a number of ways – most obviously in Iraq. US foreign policy became dominated by neo-conservatives, who set a more 'assertive realist' tone. The Obama administration has largely pursued a continuation of Bush-era foreign policy strategies, though greater emphasis on active government decision-making in energy is evident in response to both environmental and energy security concerns. Former Secretary of State Hilary Clinton appointed David Goldwyn as Coordinator for International Energy Affairs, with the responsibility of 'elevating energy diplomacy as a key function of the State Department through coordinating a Department-wide approach to traditional, new and nuclear energy security'.

Of course, the more security-oriented scholars of international energy have long stressed that energy is not 'just another commodity': it is both a means and an end of statecraft (O'Sullivan 2013). Michael Klare, in *Rising Powers, Shrinking Planet* (2008), has taken the view that the era of neo-liberalism has proved insufficient to enable a low-carbon transition, and built upon this observation new dimensions of concern with regard for energy security. Klare argues that lack of climate change action has become a key driver of geo-strategic risk. More mercantilist behaviour by states may become evident as a result. If this leads to a rise in resource nationalism, then the potential for disputes over energy resources to spill over into open conflict becomes far greater. Within this security-focused analysis, the conclusions are very similar to many of the environmental critics of neo-liberalism: greater focus is needed on foreign policy and on the promotion of international cooperation, and much less on domestic policies and on the creation/promotion of markets and market actors.

Realist scholars in particular see global energy as returning to an era of self-interested great powers engaged in implacable economic, if not military, competition. In this narrative, the market liberal order is being overturned, as energy security again becomes central to state policy. In its more extreme forms, realist analyses see energy-producing countries with significant reserves or geo-strategic location as able to leverage their 'energy weapons' for political or economic gain. It is evident that the energy literature is increasingly influenced by this view, as measured through references to 'locking up' energy reserves, the need for 'energy independence', and the 'race' to secure natural resources (see Goldthau and Witte 2009).

The Russia–Ukraine 'gas wars' of 2006 and 2009 were taken by realists as a sign of things to come in the 21st century. This view is reinforced by the fact that energy has also emerged as a more prominent foreign policy instrument of Western states. The energy sanctions imposed by Western countries after Russia's annexation of Crimea in 2014 target Moscow's primary source of state revenue: the oil sector. Recognising the central role the extractive sector plays in the Russian economy, sanctions are designed to gradually increase Moscow's costs for failing to comply with Western political demands. The ability of fossil fuel exporters or importers to affect the world political agenda simply because they own or control resources may have a limited shelf life, but nevertheless the re-emergence of energy geopolitics, with its emphasis on sovereignty and control, fundamentally challenges liberal institutionalism in its assumptions about the benefits of economic interdependence and the positive spill-over effects of this on international cooperation. Resource nationalism, furthermore, challenges the direction of international trade towards ever more open and free markets. To add to this, the challenge liberal institutionalists have faced over the least two decades – to build an alternative international system for energy cooperation and governance – has clearly not been achieved. Even with US support, the lack of which was seen as hampering Kyoto, the Copenhagen summit of December 2009 could not secure adequate shared climate change action commitments from OECD countries, the BRICS and other developing states.

The political economy of energy therefore clearly remains in flux. The GDP, trade, defence and energy patterns currently observed can change rapidly, while trends in Great Power rivalry, regionalism, bilateralism, multilateralism, economic development, the significance of corporate and other non-state actors and the unfolding effects of the 2007 global economic crisis interact in unpredictable ways. The uncertainty that this creates is of course a fundamental and ongoing problem for both private and public investment. While demand growth projections look extremely strong, investment levels in energy supply are certainly insufficient, and investment in renewable technologies is falling massively short of socially optimal levels. Meanwhile, fossil fuel supply is concentrated in increasingly unstable states, particularly after the Arab Spring, or in highly problematic locations such as below the Arctic, or at the bottom of the ocean (with Deepwater Horizon as a case in point for the potential consequences of this).

While the rise of energy security can be clearly explained, it is also of itself a cause for concern. Just as in the era of neo-liberalism analysts focused on the market at the expense of all other factors, so as geopolitical issues become the centre of attention, the need to find global institutional and cooperative solutions to energy challenges may again be de-emphasised (Goldthau and Witte 2009). More optimistically, as we move out of the era of neo-liberalism and into a period of uncertainty, policy-makers may find themselves able to pragmatically 'pick and mix' solutions from a range of different political and economic paradigms. If energy debates could become less ideologically charged, policy-makers might find more space for reflective policy learning, learning by doing, and the decentralised development of localised governance responses to energy issues from which shared knowledge could be derived. Of course, in places like the USA and Australia, the opposite appears to be happening: climate change debates are becoming even more politicised. Furthermore, pragmatic policy space may not deliver the kinds of radical changes that many analysts fear are required. But one thing is certain: while we cannot predict how the international political economy of energy will unfold over the coming decades, the global energy system will certainly be very different from the inadequate and crisis-ridden situation we find ourselves in today.

Conclusion

This chapter provided a chronological overview of the changing political economy of energy, covering three key 'eras': that of the Seven Sisters, OPEC, and neo-liberalism, with an emphasis on political and economic 'paradigm shifts'. Discussion then moved to the flux and uncertainty of the contemporary era, particularly in the wake of the global economic crisis that began in 2007. Clearly, the balance between states and markets remains a key theme in responding to global energy challenges, while the limits of attempts to build a liberal institutionalist world energy order since 1945 are a key stumbling block for multilateral solutions moving forward. Nevertheless, it is important to address the structures, institutions and practices – as well as the limitations – of current global energy governance in more detail, and this is where the following chapter builds upon the understanding of the political economy of energy presented here.

Chapter 4

Actors and Institutions

Energy, like any other good or sector, is governed by a set of rules, institutions and policies. By definition, crucial policy choices, such as those relating to the energy mix, market design, or energy infrastructure have to be made on a national level and are hence left to nation-states. Governments, therefore, play an important role in today's energy governance. At the same time, however, a number of energy challenges exceed the regulatory capacity of national governments and transcend the nation-state. Most energy commodities are traded and transported across national jurisdictions. Individual importing nations of oil and gas cannot unilaterally ensure that their own supply of energy will be reliable, nor can they effectively address market imbalances such as cartels. Negative externalities such as carbon emissions ignore national borders. Fighting energy poverty and providing access to modern energy services for the 'energy poor' is also a task that clearly exceeds the capacity of countries aspiring to catch up with industrialised nations. In short, global energy challenges require both national and global answers. Consequently, a multilayered, somewhat fragmented and complex architecture of international institutions and organisations has emerged to deal with these and related challenges. They include clubs of states (such as oil producers and consumers), international agreements (such as the Energy Charter Treaty) or agencies (such as the International Renewable Energy Agency, or IRENA and IAEA), in addition to important regional arrangements (such as in the EU). Deeply intertwined with these institutional arrangements are actors in global energy – private companies (IOCs), state-owned corporations (NOCs) and organisations representing special interests (e.g. global civil society such as NGOs).

This chapter seeks to build an understanding of the actors and institutions governing the contemporary global energy system. It discusses the nature and functioning of the international energy architecture and explains the various forces that have led to its establishment. It also examines how current supply and demand trends likely affect the current system of global energy governance. The chapter begins with a discussion of the evolution of the global energy architecture, explaining its fragmented nature. Particular light is shed on the legal and multilateral dimensions of global energy governance, arguing that the current shift in the centre of global economic gravity towards Asia fundamentally challenges the dominance of OECD countries in governing global energy. After discussing the limits of a multilateral approach, which are primarily rooted in limited enforcement capacity and dispersed interests, the chapter moves on to focusing on the main actors in global energy. It concludes with a discussion of the regional dimension of global energy governance.

Who governs energy, and how?

Energy governance is not 'value free'. By contrast, it is a function of interests, normative (economic) models and power distributions. The evolution of the institutional architecture of global energy vividly demonstrates the struggles between different ideological concepts (neo-liberal/pro-market versus 'public interest'); the material interest of key actors that shape energy governance (e.g. private corporations and state agents; exporters and importers); and the different and sometimes contradictory policy goals of states (e.g. 'energy independence' versus free trade). It is therefore no surprise that global energy governance has so far remained fragmented, complex and often one-sided.

As the previous chapter detailed, international agreements and institutions in energy historically emerged in the context of the conflicting interests of oil producers and exporters. Both Middle Eastern producer states and Western (net) importer states founded 'clubs' representing their respective interests. In the 1960s OPEC broke the cartel of Western companies (the Seven Sisters) on global oil production and sales, resulting in a larger share of oil revenues for reserve-holding nations. The IEA, in turn, was established in 1974 as a reaction to the 1973 oil shock, when OPEC threatened oil supplies to key OECD nations. In the face of what importing nations perceived as a national security threat, they sought to coordinate strategic oil stocks through the IEA, and established joint procedures for managing future supply shocks. Other exclusive institutions, such as the G7, were also in part established to help powerful industrialised states to address their energy security and energy-related economic policy interests collectively.

By the 1980s and 1990s, however, a more pro-market energy agenda had emerged in response to changing international patterns of energy supply and demand. Existing Western energy institutions were recalibrated towards fostering the market-making agenda and the facilitation of international energy trade, while state interference in energy affairs was reduced. This neo-liberalisation of world energy, enabled by entrenched post-war institutions of free trade, such as GATT, gained further momentum due to the collapse of the planned economies at the end of the Cold War. It also coincided with the rise of a neo-liberal policy agenda in the main institutions of international development, the IMF and the World Bank, which began to promote energy sector liberalisation, privatisation and deregulation (see Chapter 6 for more detail).

The policies and institutions of global, Western-dominated energy governance were consequently geared towards establishing an international energy order based on legal rules and aimed at fostering principles of free trade, economic interdependence and investment. The 1994 Energy Charter Treaty, discussed in further detail below, clearly represents a legalistic and rule-based approach towards energy governance. It also demonstrates the importance of rule-setting power in international energy affairs: the Western world and its economic model dominated global affairs in the aftermath of the Cold War, which allowed leading OECD nations such as the US to shape the rules and institutions governing energy production and trade according to their interests and blueprints. Just as importantly, energy players such as the EU modelled their energy governance systems on the liberal market model, thereby pushing this model to the global level in order to give 'their' companies – ExxonMobil, BP or Shell – a competitive edge in oil production and trade. This shaped oil markets as they are found today – pricing based on demand and supply, production chains being highly specialised, and trading being subject to a complex interplay between financial market actors, physical traders and oil companies.

Recent challenges to the liberal market model include the emergence of significant new consumers such as India and China. As non-OECD countries, they cannot join the IEA's club of oil consuming nations, and as developing states they do not see their interests as being fully represented by existing institutional arrangements in any case. Moreover, being latecomers to established global markets, they feel disadvantaged vis-à-vis established players, not least because they were effectively excluded from the setting of global rules and norms. Newly created platforms that are more inclusive, aimed at bridging existing divides between producers, consumers and established versus emerging energy players (such as the International Energy Forum, or IEF) have so far remained largely inconsequential. Mercantilist models have therefore begun to predominate: these states have nurtured their own national champions to engage in upstream production across the globe, and have ventured into bilateral contracts with oil and gas producers, bypassing international markets whose rules and institutions they cannot fully control or influence. The 'China goes to Africa' model of energy access is the most well cited example of this. Moreover, NOCs are once again challenging the dominance of Western private IOCs.

The rising economic significance of the developing world has also led to energy access becoming a significant focus for policy makers. As Chapter 6 details, some 1.3 billion people lack access to modern forms of energy, with a significant share of these living in developing Asia. Particularly for high growth countries such as China, Brazil and India, it is of utmost importance to make higher quality fuels available to their population for fostering economic development and increasing welfare. In this context, energy is conceptualised as being subject to the 'public interest', and across-the-board or nationwide coverage of energy services becomes a public policy imperative. The rise of Asia and other developing economies therefore not only comes with challenges to the existing institutions in global energy governance; it also implies new agendas and institutional arrangements, notably in the context of the global fight against poverty. The United Nations has recently acknowledged the important role that energy access plays in economic development and put a focus on energy in the context of the Millennium Development Goals, declaring 2012 the year of 'Sustainable Energy for All'.

Pushing the evolution of global energy governance in entirely new direction, the climate change challenge has recently triggered a set of institutional developments in global energy. Climate change is now overwhelmingly viewed as being rooted in existing patterns of energy production and use, warranting a fundamental decarbonisation of the global energy system. Fighting climate change has therefore become deeply entrenched in the energy agenda. As discussed in more detail in Chapter 5, the United Nations Framework Convention on Climate Change (UNFCCC) and its Conference of Parties (COP) process have been established in order to stabilise and reduce greenhouse gas emissions. They have produced a number of international mechanisms and agreements, notably the (now expired) Kyoto Protocol, which have influenced the establishment of new arrangements (such as the EU's 20-20-20 Goals and its Emissions Trading System), and partially are at odds with the goals of established fossil fuel institutions (such as OPEC). Moreover, the carbon challenge has triggered the establishment of new organisations such as IRENA, specialised in fostering the development and deployment of alternative fuels.

In economic terms, the climate challenge very much concerns the question of energy finance, that is, the mechanisms governing the sources, channels and instruments of (clean) energy investment. Multilateral agencies such as the World Bank, the IMF and the regional development banks have come to play a central role in mobilising public and private funds. This makes them key actors in the global (and regional) governance of energy finance, a role which builds on their state-backed mandates, their ability to leverage (public) funds and their strong institutional capacity (Newell 2011). In addition, a plethora of mechanisms govern private finance flows in the energy sector. These include international public – private partnership (IPPP) agreements, such as the Renewable Energy and Energy Efficiency Partnership (REEEP), to promote and fund clean energy investment. They also include instruments such as the Climatescope index, sponsored by the UK Department for International Development (DfID), the US Agency for International Development (USAID) and the Inter-American Development Bank (IADB), which aims at encouraging governments to improve investment conditions in clean energy, as well as the United Nations Environmental Programme (UNEP) Finance Initiative, established to support sustainable banking, insurance and investment. In addition, various international civil society actors are active in this and related policy fields (see Box 4.1). Unsurprisingly, the governance of (low-carbon) energy finance appears as fragmented as the global energy governance architecture in general terms (Newell 2011).

Finally, despite the global nature of key energy challenges, it has become increasingly evident that energy remains very much a regional affair. In fact, as we shall discuss in more detail below, regional governance arrangements have gained importance in the last years. This reflects, amongst other things, the fact that regions come with different resource endowments, economic structures, and exposure to energy-related risks, all of which require regional answers to rather global problems. The EU, for instance, being heavily dependent on imports of natural gas (mainly from Russia) as well as oil, and having experienced several 'gas cut-offs' in the 2000s, has adopted policies aimed at

Box 4.1 Civil and uncivil society in world energy

Civil society can be defined as private, voluntary, not-for-profit organisations that operate between the state and the market. They can be divided into the formal civil society sector, primarily NGOs, and the informal sector, usually social movements. Though they are typically domestic in character, there has been strong growth in international civil society since the end of World War I. These actors may be minor players in international energy compared to states, multilateral organisations and market actors (such as NOCs and IOCs, financial markets, and credit ratings agencies), but nonetheless their impact cannot be ignored. It is also important to note that the energy sector creates space for 'uncivil society'. Here, social movements, perhaps finding that mainstream insider (lobbying or advertising) and outsider (marches, protests, sit-ins) strategies are not getting results, move into criminal, military or terrorist activities.

Three examples of energy sector NGOs:

- *Ceres* was formed in 1989 to promote corporate social responsibility with particular regard to environmental issues. It has been at the forefront of promoting corporate environmental transparency through the Global Reporting Initiative, and in providing a forum through which corporations can provide support for calls for radical climate change action.
- *Greenpeace* is at the forefront of a range of environmental NGOs which engage in campaign, lobbying and public advertising activities. In 2012, Greenpeace published the fifth of its Energy [R]evolution Scenario documents, which includes demands for the phasing out of subsidies for non-renewables, and higher mandatory targets for energy efficiency and renewable energy production.
- *Oilwatch* is a network of NGOs, social movements and individuals engaged in 'resistance to oil activities'. It functions as a forum for exchanging information and tactics with the objectives of preventing oil companies from extracting oil in developing states, protecting the collective rights of local populations, and defending biodiversity in tropical rainforests. It also provides support for people or groups negatively affected by oil exploration activities.

Three examples of energy sector social movements:

- The *Transition Towns Movement* has its origins in the UK in 2006, and seeks to promote the environmental restructuring of urban forms. The pathway towards sustainability that the movement seeks to promote includes an emphasis on local energy independence, and on a shift in transport infrastructure to move away from dependence upon oil.
- The *Narmada Bachao Andolan* (Save Narmada Movement) is an Indian social movement that engaged in extensive protests against the Sardar Sarovar dam – also known as the Narmada dam. It is one of the largest dams in the world, and the protests by largely local subsistence farmers faced with losing their land attracted international attention. The movement was partly responsible for the World Bank withdrawing its financial support for the

→

> $\rightarrow$
>
> dam in 1994 – thereby providing encouragement to other anti-dam protest movements from around the world.
> * *Movement for the Emancipation of the Niger Delta* (MEND) is one of a number of groups in Nigeria that have become militarised in their long-standing conflict with the Nigerian government and the Western IOCs that operate in the Delta. MEND has been linked to the kidnapping of foreign workers, acts of sabotage on oil infrastructure, and guerilla attacks on oil production sites.

decreasing its exposure and vulnerability towards supply shocks in natural gas. It has also sponsored arrangements such as the Energy Community of South East Europe (ECSEE) to project its own rule-based (liberal market) model towards 'third countries', in the hope of stabilising crucial transit routes. By contrast, Petrocaribe, a Venezuela-sponsored regional oil club linking countries in Central America and the Caribbean uses energy wealth to foster development and regional integration, albeit under the clear leadership of Caracas. Regionalism, while not entirely at odds with a global multilateral approach, at least questions the effectiveness and 'reach' of global arrangements. As we will discuss in more detail below, global multilateral approaches to energy governance also face clear limits because key players, including many Western institutions and actors (including the EU) either don't fully comply with their own international commitments, or lack the tools to enforce them.

The question of who governs energy, and how, therefore becomes one of governance 'for what'. This relates directly to the 'trilemma' of global energy challenges: environment, development and security. As energy policy agendas have changed and refocused, so the tools and governance arrangements shift as well. The initial energy security agenda of the 1970s has clearly been complemented by an energy access and low-carbon agenda. At the same time, the liberal paradigm dominant in the 1980s and 1990s has revealed evident limitations in its delivery of these (and related) energy policy goals. Liberalisation and privatisation are therefore clearly not uncontested in the 21st century. The liberal market model comes under additional pressure from the economic shift towards East and South-East Asia, where state intervention ('managed markets') has been the dominant approach in the post-war era. As this brief discussion reveals, there are clearly limitations to the institutionalisation of global energy relations, as well as a lack of state capacity in achieving domestic and international energy policy objectives, while existing governance arrangements remain fragmented in nature.

Multilateral agreements and institutions

The bulk of international institutions are based on the principle of multilateralism, that is, 'the practice of coordinating national policies in groups of three or more states' (Keohane 1990).

Trade: WTO and ECT

One example of a multilateral international institution is GATT. GATT constituted the cornerstone of the global regime for the exchange of goods and services between states until the creation of its successor, the World Trade Organization (WTO) in 1995, which now provides for a multilateral framework for negotiating and safeguarding trade agreements. Clearly, and as discussed in Chapter 1, multilateral arrangements reflect the historical circumstances in which they were created and typically are based on specific normative principles. For instance, a key norm that guides the operation of WTO is that of free trade among its signatory parties. Thus free trade is a value that guides WTO negotiations, becomes written into its regulations, and informs international law as it arises from the trade regime. The global trade regime, however, fails to comprehensively cover energy.

As of 2013, the WTO governs trade between 159 member states. All BRICS countries have now become members of the WTO, with Russia having joined as recently as August 2012. Yet, as Selivanova (2010: 6) pointedly reminds us '[a]lthough energy is covered by general WTO rules, these rules are not well designed to address most acute energy problems'. Notably, the WTO regime generally fails to regulate energy trade and investment. Existing agreements primarily address market access, not export restrictions and investment protection. In light of an ongoing debate – whether justified or not – about the end of easy oil, resurgent 'resource nationalism', and cartels in oil (and possibly gas), the WTO's regulatory reach appears to fall short on key energy agendas. Moreover, the global trade regime does not adequately address physical transit and issues arising in cross-border trade, notably with regard to the non-discriminatory use of energy infrastructure such as pipelines. This issue gains particular importance in the context of countries such as Russia strategically using their infrastructure networks to control the energy trade of third countries, such as Central Asian gas producers seeking export markets in Europe. In addition, while GATT Article V suggests the principle of free energy transit, under existing WTO rules non-interruption is clearly not guaranteed: 'gas disputes' continue to take place and thus the institutional framework of the WTO, as it stands, must be deemed insufficient. Finally, in many states, the energy sector is characterised by monopolies, both in the upstream, downstream, and retail sectors. As such, since the WTO regime primarily addresses governments, not companies, the latter remain poorly governed by global trade regulations.

As noted above, this has in recent decades led to consistent attempts by Western powers to formally institutionalise neo-liberal (pro-market) rules in energy trade. The most ambitious example of this was ECT, which was initially a less formal agreement based on GATT trading regime rules and norms. The ECT is underpinned by a 'logic of commerce' which aims to facilitate commercial transactions and free trade through transparency, by articulating respect for property rights and contracts and by providing for a level playing field for all businesses involved. The ECT is very much the product of its time: as the Cold War came to an end, political and economic relations between the old 'East' and 'West' entered what is sometimes referred to as a 'romantic' period based much more on cooperation, and advice from the 'West' to the 'East' on how to reform their economies. This presented a clear window of opportunity to tie one of the world's leading fossil fuel exporters, Russia, into market economy rules. The ECT would have been the first legally binding multilateral agreement that included important importer, exporter and transit countries, based on a set of agreed common rules. The ECT therefore represented a triumph for the institutionalisation of neo-liberal economic practices across a wider Europe – until its eventual failure.

The ECT and the ECT Protocol on Energy Efficiency and Related Environmental Aspects was signed in 1994 and has been in force since 1998. The ECT covers five broad areas, covering the entire energy value chain: (1) the protection and promotion of foreign energy investments; (2) free trade in energy materials, products and energy-related equipment; (3) freedom of energy transit through pipelines and grids; (4) reducing the negative environmental impact of the energy cycle through improving energy efficiency; and (5) dispute resolution mechanisms (state-to-state and/or investor-to-state). This makes the ECT the only agreement dealing with inter-governmental cooperation in the energy sector with such comprehensive coverage.

From the onset, the ECT suffered from a number of political drawbacks. Key producer countries such as Norway and Russia signed the treaty but abstained from ratifying it; other such as the US and Canada retained an observer status. In 2009, Russia officially informed the Charter Secretariat that it did not intend to ratify the ECT (although some ECT provisions, that is, dispute settlement and investment protection, are still applied provisionally). Instead, Russia offered to replace the ECT by a new legal framework (Medvedev's Conceptual Approach paper of 2009). Russia's official withdrawal leaves the ECT somewhat in limbo, and significantly limits its reach as a multilateral regulatory framework in energy trade, transit and investment. The initial success and more recent struggles of the ECT provide an example of the difficulties of creating an international institution that sought to apply a certain set of values or norms across a wide range of nations.

Producer and consumer organisations: OPEC and IEA

Multilateral arrangements not only underpin the international trade regime and its energy 'spin offs' (for example the ECT), they are also crucial to the main international consumer and producer clubs – the IEA and OPEC. OPEC was created by multilateral treaty in 1960 between oil producing countries. Based on the treaty, the organisation operates as an entity of public international law, with the goal of 'safeguarding and coordinating' the policies of the oil-producing countries. The IEA, in turn, was established as an intergovernmental organisation of consumer countries within the framework of OECD, but based on the separate Agreement on an International Energy Program (IEP) of 1974. The latter constitutes a more selective multilateral agreement, and forms the legal basis for managing the IEA's strategic petroleum stocks – the organisation's main mechanism of short-term oil supply (risk) management.

OPEC is a key example of an inter-governmental organisation specific to energy. OPEC's member states include some of the world's largest reserve holders, and in total currently 12 countries (Algeria, Angola, Ecuador, Iran, Iraq, Kuwait, Libya, Nigeria, Qatar, Saudi Arabia, the United Arab Emirates and Venezuela). According to Article 2 of OPEC's Statute (2012)

A. The principal aim of the Organization shall be the coordination and unification of the petroleum policies of Member Countries and the determination of the best means for safeguarding their interests, individually and collectively.
B. The Organization shall devise ways and means of ensuring the stabilization of prices in international oil markets with a view to eliminating harmful and unnecessary fluctuations.
C. Due regard shall be given at all times to the interests of the producing nations and to the necessity of securing a steady income to the producing countries; an efficient, economic and regular supply of petroleum to consuming nations; and a fair return on their capital to those investing in the petroleum industry.

The main goal behind the formation of the organisation was to regain sovereignty over oil reserves and increase its income share from oil production at a time when the oil market was dominated by the 'Seven Sisters' (see Chapter 3). On this account, OPEC did succeed. However, despite controlling 72 percent of global crude oil reserves, OPEC controls only 43 percent of crude oil production (BP 2013). As previously discussed, OPEC possesses few tools to enforce compliance among its member states, leading to problems in maintaining the cartel. OPEC has also struggled to expand its membership to emerging producers such as Brazil, or to coordinate effectively with other major players such as Russia.

The IEA is another key example of an inter-governmental energy organisation. The IEA acted to coordinate Western consumer responses to OPEC and the effects of the two oil shocks. In response to the 1979 oil crisis in particular, the IEA contributed to growing energy efficiency, facilitated the pooling of energy supply resources, and made the storage of emergency reserves mandatory for members. Through the 1990s the IEA evolved into an organisation with multiple roles. It put considerable resources into gathering and publishing information about world-wide energy systems, fossil fuel reserves, and energy policies. These activities reflect the neo-liberal objective of 'good governance': the belief that a high degree of transparency and/or active information sharing is necessary for international markets to function properly, not least through reduced transaction costs. The IEA also advises member countries on promoting good governance in the energy sector, and undertakes regular reviews of member countries' energy policies. Consequently, the IEA has been actively promoting trade liberalisation and energy sector privatisation under the umbrella of its 'energy reform' programmes. The IEA has also begun to focus on climate change mitigation (and adaptation) and energy poverty, thereby covering the whole energy challenge Trilemma, at least in terms of energy analysis. Although the IEA has recognised the need to include emerging consumers such as China and India, it still remains an organisation sponsored by the rich world and the traditional 'consumer club' of OECD countries.

Multilateral arrangements have also gained significant importance with regards to the climate challenge. The (expiring) Kyoto Protocol and the EU 20-20-20 goals both constitute an attempt to make major carbon emitters commit to formal emission targets, with a view to fighting global warming. Climate and environment related international institutions are discussed in more detail in Chapter 5.

Limits of multilateral frameworks

As in other sectors, multilateral arrangements in energy face a number of challenges. These mainly relate to the limited regulatory scope of international frameworks and the weak enforcement capacity of some international organisations (IOs), as well as to collective action problems amongst members. In addition, global energy has more recently seen the rise of an 'energy independence' agenda that tends to undercut or weaken attempts at building multilateral frameworks.

The international trade regime is a case in point here. Besides falling short in its coverage of energy issues, the case of WTO also reveals the limited traction of the pro-market model as a principle in guiding global energy governance in more general terms. In turn, the failure of the ECT as a multilateral energy regime based on the principles of free trade is primarily due to the fact that a key participating actor – Russia – did not, as it turns out, share the main normative principles underpinning the treaty. Instead, Russia's main objective has become to de-monopolise the EU's initiatives in norm creation in cross-border energy relations. Russia feels that it was in an extraordinarily weakened position economically and politically when it signed the ECT, and now considers itself to be in a position whereby it should be able to influence how the trade in energy is organised. This vividly illustrates the fact that international energy regimes are clearly subject to political power plays and geopolitical scheming. Part of the problems that multilateral approaches face result from the constant shifts in the policy agendas of key players and the power distributions among participating actors.

Furthermore, many multilateral arrangements suffer from weak enforcement capacity. Whilst most energy challenges exceed national borders and jurisdictions, regulatory power and the enforcement of international agreements hinges on sovereign nation-states. In fact, with the exception of a few states who have explicitly transferred executive power to a supranational authority (such as the European Community for Coal and Steel or Euratom), multilateral arrangements in energy usually lack a powerful watchdog able to maintain existing arrangements and punish defectors. Even multilateral regimes such as the Non-Proliferation Treaty depend on the goodwill of the participating countries and on their willingness to stick to common rules. In this case, a powerful or hegemonic country such as the USA will typically act both as the source of the norms that underpin multilateral regimes, and the 'enforcer of last resort'. In addition, there exists an inherent 'shadow of the future': at any point in time, player will be considering the benefits and costs of leaving the commonly established framework. This may provide for some incentive to comply with existing rules and arrangements, as the long-term benefits may outweigh the short-term costs. Yet, it may also be a rational choice to leave the existing framework altogether, as Russia demonstrated when effectively turning its back on the ECT in 2009.

Related to this, multilateral regimes typically suffer from collective action problems. Probably the most obvious example is OPEC, as discussed in Chapter 3. OPEC faces a classic prisoner's dilemma: each member of the organisation has a clear incentive to cheat on individual quota targets, with the effect of the whole organisation losing its power to effectively cartelise the oil market (Colgan 2014; Goldthau and Witte 2011). OPEC's counterpart, the IEA, in fact faces a somewhat similar problem. With the aim of stabilising oil markets against supply shocks, IEA members built up strategic petroleum stocks, to be released onto the market in case of emergency. However, this system enables emerging oil consumer heavyweights, such as China or India, to free ride: reaping the benefits of having a safety net, but leaving the costs of maintaining strategic reserves to IEA member countries. In public policy terms, such reserves in fact constitute a global public good, as they create benefits that are non-rivalrous and non-excludable in consumption. Encouraging non-members to join the organisation would not only require overcoming the entailed collective action challenge; it would also mean creating a complete global agreement between oil consuming nations. This, however, would probably create too many veto players for an effective multilateral regime to operate. Moreover, countries like India and China, whose governing frameworks for energy are not pro-market, are unlikely to sign up to the IEA's good governance related transparency requirements.

Finally, multilateral international frameworks have been weakened in recent years due to the increasing traction of realist perspectives on energy affairs. After decades of the neo-liberal economic paradigm dominating the international energy order, with its promotion of deregulation, privatisation and free market exchange, the pendulum had started to swing back towards a more state-centric approach by the turn of the millennium. As noted previously, a number of major oil producers have brought their energy sectors back under state control. Examples include Venezuela nationalising PdVSA, Russia's state-owned Rosneft acquiring Yuganskneftegaz from Yukos, and more recently, Argentina squeezing Spain's Repsol out of YPF, the country's national oil company. At the same time, China started to adopt a mercantilist approach to securing oil supplies by building direct, bilateral operational and trade relationships with reserve holding countries in Africa, Central Asia and elsewhere.

In both the USA and Europe debates surrounding 'energy independence' resurfaced in response to such events – revealing a growing strategic discomfort in the West in the face of the apparent decline of the neo-liberal paradigm. Fears were fuelled by record highs in oil prices of almost US\$150 per barrel in 2008, as well as by the series of 'gas disputes' between Russia and Ukraine. Russia, a reliable supplier for decades, began to be perceived as an actor using energy as a geopolitical tool, rather than as a business partner in energy markets. As a result, OECD countries have started to rethink their approach to energy security, with a renewed emphasis on enhancing domestic production, and with national policies taking priority over multilateral frameworks. As a case in point, a surge in domestic natural gas (and oil) production in the USA has led to a debate over whether energy exports should be allowed. Washington – the traditional advocate of free trade regimes, the historical sponsor of pro-market institutions like the IEA, and a long-term critic of OPEC's export restrictions – had enacted an energy export control regime in the aftermath of the two oil shocks. Moving toward exporter status in natural gas and oil, the country may now be prioritising low domestic energy prices over the benefits of strengthening the global free energy trade, and abstain from lifting the export ban.

Regional institutions in energy governance

Energy governance challenges can also be regional in nature – not least due to historically inter-connecting energy infrastructure. It is therefore hardly surprising that various forms of regional energy regimes or organisations have emerged. Some of these arrangements (such as those within the EU) are explicitly tied into international multilateral governance regimes, whereas others (such as the ASEAN Energy Cooperation) shave yet to find their role in global energy affairs. Nevertheless, regional approaches to energy governance clearly can complement global frameworks, by strengthening their legitimacy and by 'anchoring' them in regional contexts.

The European Union

The EU is probably the principal example of a regional multilateral organisation having clear roots in energy agreements. It is also arguably the longest-lasting and the most comprehensive regional body of energy governance. The 1951 ECSC, complemented by the 1957 European Atomic Energy Community (Euratom), laid the foundations of what later became the European Union, an organisation exercising supranational authority in key areas such as competition policy, single-market regulation and trade. The main mechanisms on which the EU was built relate to market integration and to 'an ever closer Union'. It is worth briefly noting here that although the first European agreements were based around coal and nuclear, energy sectors were specifically left out of Jacques Delors' 1992 EC internal market arrangements. It has only been more recently that three 'energy packages' have been adopted, with a view to fully integrating and liberalising European energy markets, and to make the neo-liberal economic paradigm the main principle of regional energy governance in Europe. The 1998 directive aimed at market liberalisation, albeit limited and gradual. It was complemented by two additional energy packages in 2003 and 2009, which separated energy transport from trading services, ensured third party access to energy networks, and established stronger national regulators. The EU's efforts to liberalise energy markets has also given rise to a new set of national regulators, which are organised under the independent EU-level Agency for the Cooperation of Energy Regulators (ACER), and are aimed at fostering the pro-market agenda.

Although the EU is often painted as the poster child of energy multilateralism, the world's most progressive region in energy terms fails to fully live up to its own aspirations. To date, the internal market remains scattered while energy has remained primarily characterised by national markets. As a case in point, efforts to 'unbundle' energy generation and sale operations from transmission networks have been repeatedly blocked by a coalition of market-sceptical member states, led by France and Germany. Several countries such as the UK have already unbundled ownership unilaterally, but in others there has been considerable delay in transposing the 2009 'Third Energy Package' into national law. The European Commission – the EU's supranational watchdog for market affairs – has undertaken infringement proceedings against member states, with some cases reaching the courts. Prominent cases in the last few years include Ireland and Slovenia (for not fully transposing the gas directive), and Bulgaria, Romania, Poland and the UK. Furthermore, while a 1968 Directive requires all member states to maintain 90 days of strategic petroleum reserves, it was not until 2010 that the EU started to require member states to keep strategic stocks in natural gas – rather late for a region with high gas import dependency rates and related supply side risks. Finally, price distortions and uncompetitive behaviour persist among energy corporations active on the European market. The EU Commission at least seems determined to address these problems, as demonstrated by recent investigations into producer collusion and possible oil price rigging (involving BP, Royal Dutch Shell and Statoil), as well as investigations into anti-competitive behaviour by Russia's Gazprom.

Regarding its external energy policy, the EU has mainly come to rely on a liberal internationalist approach. Official policy goals refer to external energy policy to be achieved by fostering market interdependence (notably between producer states such as Russia and European consumers), positive-sum cooperative security and 'rules-based governance'. Of course, these rules are to be set by the European Union, for example through the ECT, and there are a number of issues with the EUs attempts to promote its energy agenda into 'third countries' in the developing world (see Keating 2012a). Of particular concern here is that recently EU governments themselves have begun to question the EU's market-based approach to regional energy governance. Producer states have become more assertive with regard to their short term national interests; a series of ongoing disputes between Russia and Ukraine (culminating in the 2014 Crimean crisis) have made gas supplies to the EU appear unreliable; and fierce politics surrounding transit routes such as the 'Southern Corridor' have become part of a 'great game' regarding Caspian energy supplies (see Chapter 8 for a more detailed discussion of pipeline politics and the transit dimension). So far, the Commission has responded to these challenges through its regulatory powers. Allegations of market distorting activities led to dawn raids in offices of Gazprom's subsidiaries in several European countries in 2011. The following year, the Commission launched an anti-trust case against the Russian state company. This can be seen as an attempt to address the challenge of an external monopolist supplier through a pro-market and liberal approach. The EU has also begun to sponsor agencies and frameworks to promote a pro-market regulatory approach to energy companies in EU neighbour states, for example through the ECSEE (see Box 4.2).

Nevertheless, there exists a prevalent fear among certain member states, notably in Central Eastern European states dependent on Russian energy supply, that the internal market may allow third country producers (or their agents, such as Russia's Gazprom) to gain too high an influence in domestic energy affairs and ownership of national energy infrastructure. Furthermore, there are concerns that the EU does not possess sufficient leverage to negotiate reciprocal liberalisation for their investments in producer states. It is no surprise, therefore, that the 'Third Energy Package' of 2009 gives European states leeway to decide whether big energy contracts need to be based on producer states providing reciprocal access to their markets. The initially proposed, and eventually dropped, 'reciprocity clause' – dubbed by the media the 'Gazprom clause' – in fact sought to impose on Russian suppliers a degree of liberalisation and 'market discipline' that member states are unwilling to impose on their own energy companies. Now all deals involving

Box 4.2 The Energy Community of South East Europe (ECSEE)

The Energy Community of South East Europe (ECSEE) is a perfect example of the EU's rule-based approach to energy and its aspiration to foster liberal norm diffusion beyond its borders. ECSEE, established in 2006, effectively extends the EU's internal market rules for energy to non-EU South East European countries and the Ukraine. Contracting Parties commit to adopt and implement the energy acquis (the EU's legal apparatus) and to adhere to the principles guiding the latter. This involves, among other things, the obligation to set up a market-oriented, rules-based regulatory framework, liberalisation of the energy sector, enhanced energy efficiency requirements in line with EU goals, and procedures to ensure reliable energy statistics are produced. In addition, signatory states are obliged to transpose EU directives and regulations, including the 2009 Third Energy Package.

Observers have pointed to the difficult legal and political environment in which the ECSEE operates, and have expressed doubts over the effectiveness of the rules-based approach. In addition, if the Third Energy Package was ultimately transposed into Ukrainian law, this would directly run counter to interests of Russia's Gazprom, which has in the past sought to maintain unhindered access to the crucial Ukrainian gas transit infrastructure. It therefore remains to be seen whether this attempt to extend the EU's rules-based energy regime will succeed, or whether it will fall prey to the vested interest of local elites, the larger geopolitical interests of key suppliers such as Russia, or both.

non-European companies have to be approved by national regulators, which can block them in case of security of supply risk. In other words, member states have ensured that they will not be required to abide by an approach based on market interdependence, when geopolitical trade-offs may be required.

Of course, the EU's significance in regional energy affairs goes beyond security of supply aspects. The EU has in fact adopted a series of policies creating region-wide environmental standards and requirements for environmental protection. These are covered in more detail in Chapter 5.

Non-EU regional energy governance

Although the EU represents the most elaborate and powerful regional approach to energy governance, a number of alternative frameworks and initiatives have emerged in other world regions. The most important ones among these arguably are regional free trade agreements. A key example here is the North American Free Trade Agreement (NAFTA), signed by the US, Canada and Mexico. Although NAFTA – like most other free trade agreements – does not explicitly deal with energy, it covers the sector with specific provisions relating to energy investment and to cross-border trade in energy services. Mexico, a country that seeks to retain state control over the energy sector, has in fact been exempted from the energy related provisions of NAFTA, which restricts NAFTA's energy chapter to the US and Canada. This, again, demonstrates the limitations of liberal and pro-market arrangements to energy governance in more general terms.

Petrocaribe, an agreement between several Caribbean states, represents a regional framework explicitly using energy to foster political integration. Driven by oil-rich Venezuela, Petrocaribe might be regarded as an attempt to foster this country's regional geopolitical agenda. Caracas offers energy supplies to Petrocaribe's member states at favourable payment modalities that are stretched over long periods of time. That way, it uses energy as a resource to project its political – and often openly anti-US – agenda onto its neighbouring countries. Venezuela's rising economic problems and the death of President Chavez in 2013 have however started to put in question the long-term prospects of this 'oil-for-friends' approach to regional integration.

There are also numerous examples of agreements for energy cooperation in Asia. The South Asian Association for Regional Cooperation (SAARC) has energy as one of its main areas for cooperative inter-state activities. However, the region is energy poor, and so the main emphasis is on promoting the development of renewable energy sources, particularly hydropower – which is deemed to be underdeveloped in the region. SAARC also seeks to cooperate in promoting energy efficiency and energy conservation, but more interestingly, plans to increase power interconnections and build a regional power market are under discussion, with support from the Asian Development Bank (ADB). In Central Asia, energy cooperation agreements have been signed between Kazakhstan, Kyrgyzstan, Uzbekistan and Tajikistan. Of course, these amounted to the admission that these states are part of a single energy grid system that was developed prior to the break-up of the Soviet Union, and on shared rules to ensure continuing energy security in this context. More recently, the Eurasian Economic Union (EEU) signed by Belarus, Kazakhstan and Russia has resulted in an economic region with massive energy resources in coal, oil and gas. A common electricity market is planned for 2019.

The Association of Southeast Asian Nations (ASEAN) has set very strong targets for sustainable energy supply in the region. Plans include a strong emphasis on biofuel production, as well as on the Trans-ASEAN gas pipeline (TAGP) and an ASEAN-wide power grid (APG), based on a competitive, open single market – as well as on expanding electricity access to the millions of energy poor in the region. ASEAN energy cooperation builds on the success of this institution in broad terms, but also on energy-specific agreements such as the 1975 establishments of the ASEAN Council on Petroleum (ASCOPE), the 1986 ASEAN Energy Cooperation Agreement, and the 1999, 2004, and 2010 ASEAN Plan of Action on Energy Cooperation five-year plans (see Shi and Malik 2013). Topics covered by ASEAN Energy Cooperation include conventional and renewable energy, technology transfer and traditional energy security.

However, Asian regional energy agreements can be seen as not really leading, so far at least, to substantial integration in the energy sector among participating countries. ASEAN's 1986 agreement on ASEAN energy cooperation, for example, is typical of ASEAN regional agreements: it is deliberately non-institutionalised, and constitutes a rather loose platform for regional cooperation among ASEAN countries in the energy sector, rather than providing for a robust legal framework. Of course, the history of ASEAN suggests that greater cooperation can be achieved in the region through informal frameworks than through formal agreements which states will not be drawn into signing in the first place. The Shanghai Cooperation Organization (SCO), by contrast, represents a formal framework for cooperation between Russia, China, and the Central Asian states. Whilst it was created to foster regional cooperation in areas such as security and the economy, energy investment and trade has become a focal point of attention. Despite overlapping interests between energy-exporting Russia and energy-importing China, there also exist conflicting agendas particularly in regard to the Caspian. Both China and Russia maintain a competing interest in the energy-rich region, as an oil and gas supplier (China) or competitor for vital markets (Russia). It is therefore unlikely that the SCO will emerge as a powerful regional energy organisation any time soon.

The role of corporations in governing global energy

Whilst international agencies play an important role in governing and shaping international energy relations and markets, energy companies are equally important actors. In fact, as much as 'high politics' has historically centred on organising producer versus consumer interests in global energy, developments on the corporate level often mirror the different paradigms informing these struggles.

International oil companies (IOCs)

As discussed in Chapter 3, Western oil corporations (or international oil companies – IOCs) have dominated international energy affairs since the early days of the oil industry. This changed in the 1960s with the formation of OPEC and subsequent waves of nationalisation in key producer countries, notably in Venezuela, Iran, Iraq and Saudi Arabia. More recently, IOCs have again come under pressure from state-owned national oil companies (NOCs), this time from emerging economies such as China and India. Nevertheless, IOCs are among the most profitable energy companies, indeed of all companies, in the global economy. In fact, judged on revenues, the largest oil and gas companies remain privately owned. ExxonMobil, Royal Dutch Shell and BP plc tend to all have higher revenues than state-owned companies like Saudi Aramco, the Saudi NOC, despite Aramco's vastly superior asset base. This is partly because producer NOCs such as Saudi Aramco and Norway's Statoil tends to produce their assets at a slower pace than privately owned companies. IOCs tend to operate on a value-based management system, whereby shareholders expect a return higher than the competition. By market value, the most valuable company in the world in 2013 was ExxonMobil, ahead of Apple and other 'new economy' companies.

The role of IOCs in both international energy affairs and domestic governance remains ambivalent. On the one hand they have for long been the backbone of the global oil industry and helped drive technological progress and innovation. The profit motive has fostered specialisation and the emergence of a global oil and gas service industry, represented by sector leaders Schlumberger and Halliburton. On the other hand, their activities have repeatedly led to criticism, and come with a track record in ecological damage, political upheaval, and arguably in causing conflict. A case in point is Shell's engagement in the volatile Niger Delta, which is associated with environmental degradation and rising conflict among ethnic groups. As a consequence, IOCs have been linked to human rights violations and the undermining of democratic regimes in the developing world, as well as being accused of having excessive influence over Western energy-related foreign policies.

Arguably also, IOCs have come to miss out on key trends in energy technology. A case in point is the US 'revolution' in shale gas and oil. It was small 'wildcatter' companies such as Mitchell Energy that were at the forefront of developing the novel fracking technology and making it ready for market, not the established oil majors. In order to regain momentum in the rapidly growing unconventional fossil fuel sector, IOCs had to engage in a series of expensive takeovers. ExxonMobil, for instance, in 2009 acquired XTO in a $41 billion deal, the eighth largest in the energy sector so far.

National oil companies (NOCs)

National oil companies have recently returned to international prominence. NOCs are broadly defined as companies which are owned, and sometimes run, either directly or indirectly, by a national government. Despite the use of the term 'oil', these are companies which own a wide range of energy assets including natural gas reserves, pipelines, refineries and distribution networks in the downstream sector. NOCs now control access to over 80 percent of world energy reserves, which is an almost complete about-turn from the days when the 'Seven Sisters' controlled access to the same degree. In fact, the NOCs can be seen to constitute a new 'Seven Sisters': Saudi Aramco;

JSC Gazprom (Russia); CNPC (China); NIOC (Iran); PdVSA (Venezuela); Petrobras (Brazil) and Petronas (Malaysia). To date, 55 percent of global oil production is in the hands of the NOCs, according to EIA statistics. The resurgence of NOCs in recent years stems from the rise of 'resource nationalism' in the mid-2000s, with Russia and Venezuela at the forefront of states seeking to regain national control over the oil industry. Furthermore, a new category of NOCs started to gain importance, this time companies owned by (net) energy importers. The most prominent examples are China's Sinopec, CNOOC and CNPC, which have started what might be described as a global 'shopping spree', investing in numerous energy upstream projects in Africa, Central Asia and South East Asia, and more recently also in Canada and other Western countries.

The rise of NOCs has been met with growing concern in the West, given that the NOCs may benefit from significant diplomatic and financial support from host governments ('energy diplomacy'), as indeed the Seven Sisters had. This might afford them extra leverage when bidding for international projects against Western market actors. In addition, NOCs are assumed to be guided by national policy rather than driven by profit maximisation. This can mean that they invest for strategic reasons, for example in pipeline projects to new markets, rather than for economic ones. NOCs are also alleged to invest in countries deemed hostile to US interests and democratic 'free-market values'. Moreover, NOCs tend to be less transparent than IOCs about reserves and production – undermining multilateral efforts to support global markets with information and knowledge.

It should be noted, however, that NOCs operate in a variety of different ways and bunching them together in one category can be misleading. For example, Statoil of Norway is commonly regarded as a very well-run company which operates on a global level. Statoil is very different to Gazprom, a company which remains close to Russia's political leadership, which in turn operates differently from NOCs like Saudi Aramco, a company whose actions are primarily restricted to Saudi Arabia. Chinese NOCs, in particular, tend to sell most of their equity oil on global markets rather than shipping it back to their 'home market', thus strengthening the supply side. Furthermore, whilst NOCs, and particularly Chinese state-owned companies, are often blamed for operating in their host countries with a 'no strings attached' attitude, Western IOCs have an equally problematic track record. It is therefore not the existence or dominance of NOCs per se that gives some cause for concern. Rather, it may be that despite favourable access to cheap capital, NOCs may not have the ability to invest sufficient resources in exploration and production activities going forward, so as to support growing demand for oil and gas. This entails the danger that global reserves might not be developed at the pace necessary, so that the amounts of oil and gas supplied to world markets might come at a price that is unaffordable for importing countries. As the IEA estimates, some US$1.6

trillion in annual investment is needed in supply infrastructure alone across the coming decades in order to meet burgeoning energy demand (IEA 2012). Combined with a global transparency problem in oil and gas, this may indeed constitute a real threat to international energy security. Of course, it should be noted that discussion in the West of moving to an energy future dominated by renewables will do little to encourage NOCs to invest heavily in long-term production capacity.

A changing landscape: Emerging actors and institutions

Global energy affairs are clearly characterised by significant change, and new institutions and actors continue to emerge. The BRICS, a set of populous, high-growth economies which increasingly look like new power centres in the global political economy, are having an impact in energy also. Yet, as discussion of the significance of the BRICS grows, it is important to remember that these countries should not be grouped together in terms of energy fundamentals: Brazil and Russia are large-scale energy exporters whereas India and China are large-scale net importers. Furthermore, key non-Western states in energy supply and demand, such as Saudi Arabia and Indonesia, are excluded. So while the BRICS will certainly impact on the global political agenda in coming decades, it remains to be seen to what extent the BRICS are able or willing to assume a leadership role in shaping international energy affairs. However, the G20, an extended G8 platform that reflects the changing political economy of global economic power distributions, is inclusive of the BRICS as well as key Western consumers and Saudi Arabia. The G20 was of course initially intended to address the global economic crisis of 2008, but it has since adopted an energy agenda, targeting fossil fuel subsidies and oil price volatility. Nevertheless, given the highly heterogeneous energy interests of its member states, it is also unlikely that the G20 will assume the role of a global 'steering committee' in energy.

Consequently, the creation of institutionalised fora for producer-consumer dialogue might be more productive. Triggered by spiking oil and gas prices in the 2000s, there has been a growth in such dialogues, both in bilateral and multilateral forms. Examples include initiatives between the EU and energy-rich countries or regions (such as the EU–Russia Energy Dialogue, EUROMED or EU–GCC), enhanced producer–consumer dialogue between IEA and OPEC, and most importantly the International Energy Forum (IEF) (see Box 4.3). The IEF's remit is to provide a platform for consumer and producer nations, including non-OPEC exporters, to engage in regular dialogue and information sharing on a largely informal basis – similar to the ASEAN model. The IEF sees itself as a 'neutral facilitator', and marks itself out from IEA or OPEC in that it specifically declines to set formal rules that all members need to follow. Crucially, the IEF runs an IEF Business Forum, underlining the importance of the private sector to

---

Box 4.3 The International Energy Forum (IEF)

The IEF was set up in 1991 and formally institutionalised in 2003. It brings together key energy producer and consumer nations, including non-members of OPEC or IEA such as Brazil, China, India, Mexico, Russia and South Africa. Its membership reflects over 90 percent of world supply and demand and it is supported by a secretariat based in the Diplomatic Quarter of Riyadh, Saudi Arabia. Instead of relying on binding rules and norms, the IEF's focus is on discussion, dialogue and knowledge transfer – its motto is 'energy security through dialogue'. Energy Ministers from each member country meet once every two years to conduct an open and informal global energy dialogue, and in addition the IEF supports regular symposia, workshops and training sessions. Despite the genuine attempt to promote multilateral dialogue and cooperation, the IEF is often used as an open venue for bilateral contacts between Energy Ministers, as well as with and among top-level executives from the energy industry. The primary achievement of this organisation has been the Joint Organisations Data Initiative (JODI) which has helped to improve transparency by extending monthly reporting to non-OECD countries such as China.

---

global energy affairs, and making the producer–consumer dialogue more than an inter-governmental affair.

As much as political and economic shifts have triggered the emergence of new players and institutions in global energy, new policy issues have also added to the patchwork of the existing global energy governance architecture. UN Energy, for instance, is the United Nations' response to the energy poverty challenge, aimed at enhancing energy access while simultaneously increasing energy efficiency and the use of renewables. Taking this further, the World Bank has partnered with the UN in coordinating the Sustainable Energy for All (SE4ALL) initiative, making the development agency an important player in global energy governance. Addressing the low-carbon challenge, IRENA aims at promoting a sustainable energy transition. Created in 2009, IRENA supports countries across the globe in regulatory reform, capacity building and technology and policy transfer. Another fuel-specific organisation, the Gas Exporting Countries Forum (GECF), is a product of the attempt by states to capitalise on the changing dynamics of international gas relations, particularly given high gas prices in the first decade of the 2000s. Essentially, GECF is a gas producer club in the making, uniting some 70 percent of global conventional gas reserves under one umbrella organisation. GECF aims at coordinating production and export policies among its member countries and might be compared to OPEC. So far, however, it has been unable to reproduce OPEC's success in the 1970s, as it suffers from conflicting interests between member states, and a lack of enforcement mechanisms.

Conclusion

This chapter has provided an overview of global energy governance, focusing on the international and regional levels, and on the role of non-state energy actors. In understanding the mechanisms of global energy governance, and particularly in realising the stark limitations of the contemporary global energy system, the extent of global energy challenges – and the difficulties in addressing them – becomes clearer. The following chapter builds on this by addressing a specific area of global energy governance, and one of the key elements of the global energy challenge trilemma – the relations between energy, the environment and climate change.

Chapter 5

Energy, Climate Change and the Environment

Almost all climate scientists now agree that humankind has influenced global warming, partly through the combustion of fossil fuels. This is referred to as the 'climate consensus'. As it now stands, a wide variety of elite political institutions including governments and inter-governmental organisations (IGOs) accept this consensus, and so are trying to establish ways to lower greenhouse gas emissions. One of the most common routes to climate mitigation is to seek a sustainable or low-carbon energy transition of global proportions. Climate change mitigation has therefore become a core objective of energy policy for much of the world. In addition to these more formal or traditional governance institutions, new groupings of state, civil society and corporate actors are emerging to work towards climate mitigation and sometimes also towards the promotion of specific new technologies.

The ongoing process of mitigating climate change through an energy transition has proved far more difficult and complex than many predicted. It requires a major transition of inter-connected regimes, each with their own social, economic and technological aspects. Energy transitions have happened before (see Chapter 2), but this planned low-carbon transition faces new barriers and constraints, not least because serious time limitations are involved. Furthermore, previous energy transitions all involved greater use of energy – not less – as such policy-makers, non-governmental organisations (NGOs) and others involved in this transition are learning as they proceed. Finally, it must also be recognised that there are vested interests that oppose a sustainable energy transition, and that even amongst those who do want to act, there are disagreements about how to proceed and hesitancy in the face of uncertain consequences.

This chapter focuses on understanding arguments for action on climate change, and how these have evolved into a climate consensus. Some of the governance institutions that are most actively involved in climate mitigation are also introduced, along with the policies and strategies they are pursuing and the governance instruments and agreements that have been put in place. This chapter also introduces some of the key ongoing energy-related debates within the complex global politics of climate change. Further discussion of the role of technologies within climate mitigation and important technological advances takes place in Chapter 9.

Environmentalism, climate change and global energy politics

The environmental movement gained broader political momentum in the 1970s, when it became a key issue dealt with under the auspices of the United Nations through various conferences on the Human Environment. Only recently, however, has the environmental perspective on climate change – outlined in Chapter 1 – started to have a significant impact on the political economy of energy.

Climate science and knowledge credibility

It took many decades for the scientific climate consensus on anthropogenic climate change to establish itself and to gain the support of political elites – and this battle is for many not yet over. The formation of this consensus highlights the importance of credibility (believability) and legitimacy (the extent of support) in debates over complex and controversial policy areas. It is important to recognise that ideas or arguments can become more credible and legitimate over time. Indeed, once a new set of ideas successfully challenged old perspectives and achieved credibility, they can emerge as a new paradigm or 'fact'. Similar arguments were made in Chapter 3 in relation to the neo-liberal paradigm, and the degree to which its ideas became influential over economic policy in the 1990s and early 2000s. In this way history shows us that what is credible and legitimate one day may be subsequently dismissed.

Credibility and legitimacy are highly relevant to the environmental movement and its attempts to promote climate change mitigation. As can be seen in more detail below, a range of IGOs, NGOs, governments, businesses and civil society movements are working hard to engender changes in how we produce and use energy in order to limit greenhouse gas emissions. Significant changes have begun in some countries, but a massive increase in the worldwide effort is still required – some say of revolutionary proportions. This implies that more people need to become active in promoting these changes, and become generally more supportive of climate change mitigation policies. Suffice it to say that those who produce and use energy – which covers a high percentage of the world's population – are central to enabling a successful and sustainable global energy system transformation. However, and this is what makes credibility so important, people are less likely to want to change if they do not believe in the arguments put forward to support the necessity of such change.

This is where the situation gets more complicated. Scientific knowledge about climate change continues to grow incrementally, but it is also open to contestation and challenge. As the well-known sociologist of science Thomas Kuhn famously observed, scientific knowledge, like many aspects of human life, is itself socially constructed (Kuhn 1962). At any point in time there will be a dominant paradigm within an area of science, be it physics or biology, about how things work. This paradigm, in turn, may be widely supported within society, and viewed as a credible source of knowledge or facts. The paradigm itself may be treated as 'fact'. However, it is also possible that a new body of evidence may emerge – perhaps after decades of research and analysis – that challenges the current consensus, and disproves some of its core theoretical claims. As Chapter 3 explained, a paradigm shift may then be seen to occur. This, arguably, is where we now are in relation to scientific research on anthropogenic climate change, which has recently shifted towards the 'climate consensus' position.

In other words, there has not always been an international consensus amongst scientists about anthropogenic climate change and some scientists remain climate sceptics. Paradigm shifts seem easier to understand, and to have taken the form of sudden breaks, when looking back on them historically. But when living through paradigm shifts, it becomes evident that there are myriad debates, contestations and arguments as new knowledge seeks to establish itself as credible, and become the new dominant paradigm. During such times, as we see now with the climate change consensus, those who do not support change, perhaps because they feel they might lose out from alterations in how we produce and use energy, can utilise data and analysis from climate sceptics to argue against change. Far from a clean break between paradigms, change appears to be difficult, messy and uncertain.

The recent history of climate debates clearly demonstrates how the work of climate sceptics has been used to question the credibility of emerging knowledge about climate change, as well as to argue against the necessity of measures to mitigate global warming. In 1995, when the Intergovernmental Panel on Climate Change (IPCC) produced a report concluding that the effects of humankind on our climate had become discernible, the lead scientist faced personal accusations of drawing conclusions from a lack of evidence. The US Administration, under George W. Bush, also took a more sceptical position on anthropogenic climate change – a position that was supported financially by multinational oil and gas companies and their associated industry groups. During this period climate sceptics received a greater amount of funding and media 'air time', while the USA refused to become a signatory of the Kyoto Treaty. The USA, however, is an interesting example of how political support for new ideas can emerge rapidly. Al Gore's climate change documentary, 'An Inconvenient Truth', along with his Nobel Peace Prize of 2007, did much to create legitimacy and credibility for anthropogenic climate change arguments in the USA. Although climate scepticism has by no means disappeared in US political and public circles, the Obama Administration, for example, has been pro-climate action and sought to make some, at least in US terms, unprecedented policy changes as a result.

As suggested above, however, new knowledge about anthropogenic climate change is still evolving and is therefore open to contestation – albeit from an increasingly small minority of scientists. There are also a number of institutions that are dedicated to clinging to the old consensus: that global warming is a natural phenomenon that would occur at the same pace without human action. Think tanks such as The Global Warming Policy Foundation and The Global Warming Hoax or blogs such as the 'Climate Change Sceptic' are examples of this. Whilst the debate continues, it is hard for wider populations to make up their minds about exactly how credible and legitimate the notion of anthropogenic climate change actually is, let alone to decide whether they should become an active part of a wider energy transition. As a result, polls show wide variations in the degree of support for climate action in different countries around the world. European countries in particular show relatively high levels of active popular support for a low-carbon transition; in other states populations may rather prioritise accelerated economic growth based on existing energy systems.

Science and the climate consensus

Despite the sceptics and the continuing debates, a global warming consensus emerged within the scientific community that puts human actions, and the potential to change these actions, at the centre of global warming. This is not to say that the planet would not otherwise be getting warmer, but simply that the actions of humankind have exacerbated the rate of change, and that levels of greenhouse gases (GHGs) in the atmosphere have increased markedly since the industrial revolution and continue to rise. The specific scientific argument that the atmosphere is warming partly as a result of increased concentrations of GHGs in the atmosphere was set out in Chapter 1.

Clearly, the movement to recognise anthropogenic climate change emerged not only due to environmental pressure groups, but also from environmental analysis informed by such scientific discoveries. Within the climate change consensus, scientific discussion and attention has recently encompassed the recognition that while average planetary temperatures continue to rise, actual climate changes will be variable. Different geographical areas will be affected differently, while weather phenomena such as droughts, floods and seasonal storms (hurricanes and cyclones) will become both more common and more extreme, with particular effect on areas already vulnerable to these weather events. Organisations such as the Intergovernmental Panel on Climate Change (IPCC) (see Box 5.1) are crucial to bringing together scientists from around the world and thereby advancing the scientific knowledge that underpins the climate consensus.

Climate change is expected to have a huge impact on the natural world, including the destruction of valuable ecosystems such as coral reefs and the removal of habitats for many other species. But climate change is also a major social issue. As humans live and operate within the confines of the Earth and its atmosphere, we are all in some way connected to climate change – making it the ultimate global problem. In fact the list of potential implications for humankind of warming above 2 °C (over pre-industrial levels) is long, and makes terrifying reading: melting polar ice caps, rising sea temperatures and levels, floods, famines, mass intra- and transnational migration, war and potentially deaths on a genocidal scale. The World Bank estimates that by 2025 climate change will cause 1.4 billion people across 36 countries to

Box 5.1 The Intergovernmental Panel on Climate Change (IPCC)

The IPCC was formed in 1988 by the United Nations Environment Programme (UNEP) and the World Meteorological Organization (WMO). It was set up to provide the world with the current state of scientific knowledge about climate change, as well as its potential environmental and socio-economic impacts. It does this by collating data from around the world and bringing this together in Assessment Reports on a four-year basis. It is therefore one of the main organisations through which we can trace the development of global, scientific understandings about anthropogenic climate change.

It has so far produced five assessment reports. Each report is split into four sections, covering different aspects of climate science as well as different impacts and solutions. 195 countries are currently members of the IPCC and each country sends its experts to be part of the working groups that produce the various assessment reports. The IPCC is therefore a global organisation that represents views from all countries represented when compiling data, engaging in analysis, and reaching conclusions.

The latest round of IPCC reports has brought to light new information whilst also providing a greater depth of empirical information about how and why our climate is changing. Working Group I, which focuses on the physical science basis, has argued that the warming of the climate system is now unequivocal and concentrations of CO_2 have increased to levels unprecedented in at least the last 800,000 years. One of the measured outcomes of this was considerable cumulative ice mass loss between 1992 and 2012 in Greenland, Antarctica and across the world's various glaciers. This alone has severe implications for global mean sea levels and, in particular, for (small) island countries (IPCC 2013). Furthermore, if we are to meet the target of keeping global temperature increases caused by global warming to below 2 °C, then by the year 2100, only 790 billion tonnes of carbon can be emitted. Yet, to date we have already released 535 billion tonnes. Reducing future emissions levels to within the allowable 255 billion tonnes will require a substantial and sustained reduction in current rates of emissions, far stricter carbon budgets in the future, and clearly, large changes in the nature of the world energy system.

face crop or water scarcities (Grevi et al. 2013). A related prediction is that global warming will result in 26 million 'climate displaced people' in the next 20 years (see Burnell 2012: 818). The likelihood of such events, as well as the scale of their potential impact, rises with each 1 °C increase in global temperatures (IPCC 2007). The implications for civilisation as we know it are stark.

Target setting and the energy–climate nexus

Even if the global political consensus on climate change was unchallenged, the question of *how* to mitigate for climate change would remain contested. There has been a long debate between 'radicals' and 'reformist' positions on the environment (see Chapter 1), and this has morphed into a debate on whether the climate change agreements reached between and within countries so far, which can really only be described as 'reformist', could succeed in preventing severe climate change events. Even countries like Germany and Sweden that have strong political and public support for action on climate change are reformist, in that they support the view that economic growth should not be negatively affected by climate mitigation policies. The principle of economic growth is also enshrined within UNFCCC agreements on climate change, as evidenced by clauses on differentiated responsibilities (see Box 5.3).

One particularly controversial aspect of climate change mitigation plans is determining what targets should be set, and for which states. The primary agreed target so far is to limit global warming to 2 °C above pre-industrial levels and, in order to do so, to reduce emissions of greenhouse gases. Targets have more recently extended directly to the energy sector. Energy production has long been a focus for environmentalists, not least based on the estimate that 60 percent of global emissions come from energy, but new and innovative energy policy is becoming increasingly understood as a route to change. This has been referred to as the *energy–climate nexus*.

Energy and climate policy-making are certainly becoming increasingly inter-linked and interdependent in practice. Energy policy around the world is increasingly based on setting achievable national emissions reduction targets, as well as specific renewable energy and energy efficiency targets (see Box 5.2). In fact, 144 countries now have clear renewable energy targets in place, and globally renewable energy, including hydropower, did provide for an estimated 10 percent of global energy consumption in 2012. By 2013 global investment in renewable energy technologies had reached US$249 billion, making it one of the fastest-growing sectors of the global economy (REN21 2014). Solar PV, on- and offshore wind, hydropower and biofuels are common targets for renewable energy investment (see Chapter 9).

Creating a more sustainable energy system requires changes to the way in which energy is used, as well as how it is produced. Energy efficiency can mean different things: a reduction in energy consumption, more flexible usage (in order to reduce the disparity between peak and base-load electricity demand) as well as the more efficient production of energy sources. The latest World Energy Outlook from the IEA emphasises the central role that energy efficiency policy should play in emissions reduction, suggesting that 49 percent of needed reductions could come from specific energy efficiency measures (IEA 2013: 10). Once this is recognised, energy policy becomes even more salient to achieving climate mitigation, and as a result energy efficiency targets have been set by the EU and in a number of states.

Efficiency targets, however, have tended to be both less prevalent and less stringent than emissions reduction and renewable energy targets. This is partly because reductions in energy demand may be more complicated to achieve. They imply widespread behavioural changes: from industry, across the service sector, and into households. In many countries, furthermore, energy for large

Box 5.2 Energy policies for climate change

The basic principle behind climate and sustainable energy governance has been to limit global warming to 2 °C. So far governments, NGOs, IGOs and more locally based authorities have focused on achieving this aim in the following ways:

- Setting targets for:
    - Greenhouse gas emissions reduction
    - Production of energy from renewable sources
    - Improvements in energy efficiency and/or demand reduction

- Implementing emissions and other trading schemes
- Providing support for energy production from renewable sources
- Encouraging more local and/or within-community energy production and supply (distributed energy)
- Improving the performance of cars and other appliances

One example of an energy policy framework with these objectives is the EU 20/20/20 agreement, which includes targets for emissions reductions, renewable energy and energy efficiency as well as provisions for an emissions trading scheme. Other examples include CAFE standards in the USA, feed-in-tariffs to support renewable energy investments in Germany and Denmark and energy efficiency obligations in the UK.

industries is still subsidised, whilst in others, industry may be exempted from emissions reduction schemes and enjoy lower energy tariffs. Industry can, of course, be politically important for many reasons, and particularly so in some developing states where industry is considered central to continued economic growth. Encouraging energy demand reductions therefore may be politically difficult. Most efficiency and demand reduction measures, however, do offer the potential to decouple economic growth from growth in energy demand.

Achieving energy efficiency in the household sector is equally important and just as complicated as it is for industry. It has been estimated that in the European Union home energy use is responsible for 25 percent of energy-related greenhouse gas emissions (EEA 2014). Much of the existing housing stock across Europe, and especially in Eastern Europe, is very badly insulated and this is a significant part of the problem – as is particularly evident in cold winter months. In countries where electricity usage has been or remains subsidised, attitudes towards energy usage can be quite lax, and electricity supply may well be taken for granted. There is little economic incentive for efficiency gains when costs are artificially low. Energy demand reduction measures also generate financial savings, but as these are spent elsewhere, demand for these new, additional services again increases energy demand (the 'rebound' effect). Finally, in the developing world there are plans to massively extend electricity access (see Chapter 6). This implies growing global demand, rather than reductions – a point explored in more detail below.

Energy and climate governance

As a scientific consensus on anthropogenic climate change has formed, political elites around the world have responded by beginning to shift energy policy towards achieving climate targets. Indeed, it is apparent that there have been concomitant shifts in thinking about climate change outside of scientific communities, resulting in a steady proliferation of institutions dedicated to addressing climate change in various ways. Many governments, IGOs and regional organisations are now attempting to design governance systems that will facilitate transitions to low-carbon energy systems. This section looks in more detail at the institutions involved in energy and climate governance, and what exactly they are doing to address climate change.

Global governance and the Kyoto Protocol

As explored in the previous chapter, there are various 'levels' at which governance can take place and we start here with a brief look at global or multilateral governance institutions. As political recognition of climate issues has grown, and given that it is understood by many to be the ultimate global problem, one obvious way of working towards a sustainable energy system has been via the system of IGOs already in place. Most international energy institutions, in particular the International Energy Agency (IEA), are now very active in promoting climate mitigation policies. In addition, the International Monetary Fund (IMF) and the World Bank have become increasingly involved in both energy and climate governance.

The highest-profile multilateral climate governance system is, of course, the UN itself. Within the UN system there are a number of organisations that are specifically oriented towards climate issues, sustainability, and energy policy, in particular the United Nations Environmental Programme (UNEP) and the IPCC (see Box 5.1). With regard to developing states, the United Nations Development Programme (UNDP) has been particularly active. The UNEP has been hosting environmental conferences and organising protocols and agreements for many decades now, and has made some progress. For example, in the Montreal Protocol of 1987, UN member states agreed to reduce the production and use of certain industrial chemicals (such as chlorofluorocarbons, CFCs) that were deemed by scientists to be harming the ozone layer (Haas 1992). The Rio Earth Summit of 1992 produced the UN Framework Convention, which garnered 166 signatories, and agreement to evaluate emissions and report annually.

The closest that the world has come to a global agreement on climate change remains the UN Framework Convention on Climate Change's

(UNFCCC) Kyoto Protocol. The Kyoto agreement brought countries together in an attempt to keep global warming to 2 °C above pre-industrial levels by setting greenhouse gas emissions reduction targets. It also included new measures such as the Clean Development Mechanism (CDM), through which developed/OECD countries could support climate programmes in developing states, and use the results to offset emission levels in their domestic economy (see Box 5.3). The protocol was initially adopted in 2005, and was ratified by 191 countries. The 37 full signatories to the protocol ('Annex 1' countries

Box 5.3 Historic and current polluters

UN protocols and climate agreements operate on the principle of 'common but differentiated responsibilities', as adopted at the Rio Earth Summit of 1992. What this means, in essence, is that more developed countries should shoulder the financial burden for necessary economic adjustments in poorer countries in order to reduce carbon emissions. There is an element of 'climate justice' at play here – developed countries enjoyed long periods of industrial development in their histories and therefore developing states should be allowed the same.

Consequently, rather than pointing the finger at states which are investing strongly in coal-fired power stations designed to fuel industrialisation and development (such as India and China), OECD countries (the 'Annex 1 countries') should be reducing their own emissions, developing low-carbon energy alternatives, and then facilitating technology transfer to developing states. In fact, no mandatory targets for emission reductions were set for developing states ('Non-Annex 1 countries') under the Kyoto Protocol. This structure to the treaty has obvious consequences for energy policy, as it provided little incentive for developing states to engage with a low-carbon transition, outside of participation in the CDM and carbon trading.

Some BRICS countries explicitly prioritise rapid development and industrialisation over the environment, and primarily look to oil, gas and coal to meet energy needs, which are often easier to access, cheaper, and less technologically demanding to produce than low-carbon alternatives. China, Russia and India are now amongst the world's top five emitters of greenhouse gases in absolute terms – along with the USA and Japan. It has been estimated that by the year 2035 China will have twice the emissions of the USA. Adjusted on a per capita basis, however, BRICS countries still tend to emit less than many OECD countries (CDIAC 2015). It should also be noted that China, in particular, may open a new coal-fired plant on an almost daily basis, but has also been very successful in recent years at developing new energy technologies and in boosting energy production from renewable sources.

Some low-lying Pacific island states are, by contrast, strong supporters of mandatory targets. States with limited energy resources may also see the Kyoto Protocol as an opportunity to increase development aid disbursement, albeit into specific areas of their economy such as renewable energies. There are a number of vehicles for achieving this, including through the World Bank and the United Nations Framework Convention on Climate Change (UNFCCC).

in the language of the Kyoto Protocol) committed to legally binding carbon emissions cuts of 5.2 percent over 1990 levels by 2008–2012. Other countries that ratified the protocol agreed to continue evaluating and reporting emissions annually.

The Kyoto Protocol agreement period ended in 2012, and so its reduction commitments are no longer legally binding. Unfortunately, progress on further commitments in a post-Kyoto agreement has so far been slow and difficult. At the Copenhagen Conference of Parties (COP) industrialised countries agreed to mobilise funding for climate mitigation of US$100 billion in developing states by 2020. At the Doha COP a second commitment period, January 2013 to December 2020, was agreed, but full signatories are almost exclusively EU countries: important emitters such Japan, New Zealand, Russia, USA and Canada would not make a commitment. Agreements are continually frustrated by the idea that greenhouse gas emission reductions in signatory countries will be rendered meaningless because of rapidly growing emission levels in countries like China and India. Such issues must be addressed, and so the 2015 United Nations Climate Change conference (COP21) in Paris will be crucial if the UN climate process is to be maintained.

It is worth drawing attention here to a fairly new form of actor in international climate change. Just as energy institutions such as OPEC emerged as a reflection of vested interests in fossil fuels, so new international institutions are emerging to promote new technologies and energy sources in response to recognition of the seriousness of the climate change issue. These institutions may not strictly be IGOs: while they often rely on support, and include representatives, from various nation-states, they may primarily revolve around civil society and private sector entities. They constitute more of an international PPP model, where the private sector includes for-profit businesses and their representatives, and not-for-profit third sector actors such as NGOs and social movements, and their representatives. Examples IRENA, which promotes, facilitates and supports the expansion of renewable energy, and the DESERTEC Foundation. DESERTEC is a civil society organisation but it also has industry membership and some state support, in particular from Germany. It seeks development, and job growth, through the deployment of low-carbon energy technologies in a variety of countries (see Chapter 8). It is a movement that represents in practice many of the ideas of 'Green Growth' discussed above. Other examples include policy networks such as the Renewable Energy Policy Network for the 21st Century (REN21), which includes a broad array of members across the political, corporate and social spheres, and the Renewable Energy & Energy Efficiency Partnership (REEEP). REEEP was formed in 2002 alongside the World Summit on Sustainable Development, runs an open clean energy information portal, and has to date invested around US$20 million in clean energy projects across 58 different countries.

The 'trilemma' and positive policy interactions

There is another way in which climate and energy policies come together in practice which is worth addressing, and which helps provide a broader perspective on energy and environment issues. Most IGOs involved in energy governance have three simultaneous energy policy objectives, the 'trilemma' of global energy challenges: energy security, reducing energy poverty, and climate mitigation. It appears, however, that the compatibility of these objectives is largely taken for granted. Some policies are certainly viewed as 'win-win' scenarios, such as energy efficiency measures that boost long-term energy security by reducing energy requirements. Furthermore, while strong emphasis has been placed on the need to boost renewable sources of energy for climate and environmental reasons, it has become increasingly commonplace for pro-renewable groups to also claim that renewables boost energy security by, for example, reducing the need for imports. The most recent report by REN21 makes similar claims about the usefulness of renewable energy:

> Today, renewable energy technologies are seen not only as a tool for improving energy security, but also as a way to mitigate greenhouse gas emissions and to provide direct and indirect social benefits. (REN21 2014: 5)

Some interactions between energy and climate policies may in practice be more complicated. Nevertheless, it does appear that one of the drivers behind the growth of renewable energy in many countries, including Sweden and Germany, has been a desire to reduce dependence on fossil fuel imports (Giddens 2009).

Box 5.4 The Kingdom of Tonga and the energy–climate nexus

The Kingdom of Tonga is a small Polynesian country with a population of only 103,000. Under the leadership of its first elected government, it has recently adopted a series of new energy policies that have put it on the world renewable map – and gained it membership of IRENA. It plans to achieve 50 percent renewable energy by 2020 via the Tonga Energy Roadmap 2010–2020. The roadmap is both ambitious and (necessarily) innovative, stipulating that all parts of government, as well as Tonga's development aid partners, must work together to achieve an energy transition. While Tonga is open about its vulnerability as a small island to climate change and rising sea levels, the early initiative for this boost in renewable energy production came from its exposure, as a heavy net energy importer, to rising international fossil fuel prices in 2008. Here, renewable energy can be seen to operate as a panacea for long-term energy security, affordability and climate-related problems.

Another area where energy policy objectives are understood to be concomitant is energy for development (see Box 5.5). There are currently a number of aid programmes that promote greater access to sustainable energy in developing states, for example the United Nations General Assembly's SE4ALL. SE4ALL has four core objectives to be met by 2030:

- Universal access to electricity
- Universal access to safe household fuels
- Double the rate of improvement in energy efficiency (reducing energy intensity)
- Double the share of renewable energy in the global energy mix (30 percent by 2030)

A massive expansion of energy access in the developing world implies greater global energy demand, but with an emphasis on sustainable energy projects, it is hoped that developing states can 'skip' a phase of development, and leapfrog over the carbon-intensive energy system that characterised development in OECD states (see Box 5.5). Certainly, for a global low-carbon transition to take place, both economic growth and human development need to be 'de-coupled' from energy intensity (Urban and Nordensvard 2013: 12).

Box 5.5 Sustainable development and energy poverty

The theory of sustainable development is based on a core premise: that economic growth can be compatible with environmental protection (UNCED 1987). What was once considered a zero-sum game between environmental and developmental considerations is therefore re-cast as a positive-sum game (Connelly and Smith 1999). However, sustainable development also argues that there are strong links between poverty and environment. On the one hand, global environmental problems are likely to affect the poor more severely, and on the other, the livelihoods of the poor – driven by necessity – are likely to exacerbate environmental degradation. Although the poor may live harmoniously with the ecosystem upon which they rely, this is not necessarily the case. The poor may be living in a tenuous relationship with the environment, and climate change can exacerbate drought, flood, desertification and soil erosion issues that affect the most vulnerable socio-economic groups. Furthermore, the consequences of climate change may simply be most severe in places where the poor are found – such as the Sahel region of sub-Saharan Africa. Population pressures only increase the incentive for the world's poor to increase levels of environmental exploitation. Finding a sustainable energy pathway for the world's poorest people, therefore, has become an international priority. These issues are explored more thoroughly in Chapter 6.

Regional climate and energy governance

International climate and energy governance agreements and policy formulations also take place at the regional level. Indeed, regional-level agreements with fewer veto players and positive spillovers from cooperation in other policy fields may be more effective. There has in fact been a proliferation of regionally based environmental institutions over the past decade or so – not least for the purposes of negotiating at COPs to the UNFCCC. One such regional movement has been the coming together of African Ministers of the Environment who, in conjunction with the Conference of African Heads of States on Climate Change (CAHOSCC), agreed on a unified African position for the Warsaw COP in 2014. Another established regional group is the Asia-Pacific Partnership on Clean Development and Climate, which includes Australia, Canada, China, India, Japan, Korea and the United States amongst its members. This regional body seeks to promote cooperation in the development and diffusion of cleaner technologies and practices.

However, of all regional institutions, the EU is clearly at the forefront of climate policy. The EU was an early leader in recognising climate change as an issue and in seeking policy responses, but crucially, it then made climate commitments that were simply more ambitious and far-reaching than other regions. The cornerstone of the EU approach has been to lead by example. Progress at the multilateral level, it is argued, can best be assisted by pushing ahead with emissions reductions inside the EU, and by being generous in providing climate financing to developing states. The EU was a firm supporter of the Kyoto Protocol – something that is rightly publicised as one of the most significant symbols of the EU commitment to rules-based multilateralism. It was in part at the EU's behest that Kyoto exempted developing nations from emissions reduction targets, thus facilitating an agreement with key developing states such as India and China (though at the expense of the USA's withdrawal from the treaty).

It is EU member states that have primarily committed to UN 2020 emissions reduction targets, though it is necessary to point out that most of these states had already made equivalent climate change commitments in the context of domestic environmental politics. Furthermore, the EU has set out collective regional carbon reduction targets. In March 2007, the European Council agreed a '20/20/20 by 2020' plan, committing to 20 percent reduction in greenhouse gas emissions, 20 percent of energy to come from renewable sources, and a 20 percent increase in energy efficiency. It has also proposed that the EU will increase its greenhouse gas emissions reduction target to 30 percent if non-EU countries also commit to emissions reductions. Furthermore, the EU's Emissions Trading Scheme (ETS) is the world's most advanced cap-and-trade mechanism for reducing emissions. The EU recently established two new bodies, the Directorate-General for Climate Change (DG Climate) and the Directorate-General for Energy (DG Energy), in order to establish and enact further climate and sustainable energy policies. The EU is also at the forefront of establishing and enforcing energy efficiency standards on a wide range of appliances.

The EU is on course to meet its emissions targets, if not the energy efficiency targets. However, this is in part thanks to the ongoing global economic crisis, which has slowed the rate of energy demand growth in the EU. Furthermore, by transferring heavily carbon-intensive industries to developing states, the EU can meet its 20 percent target while EU companies increase their overall emission levels, and without reductions in overall energy consumption. Critics also argue that the EU's carbon trading scheme (ETS) is poorly designed, and unlikely either to promote significant reductions in emission levels, or to provide the incentives necessary to bring breakthrough environmental technologies to the market. For example, ETS allowances are so generous that the carbon price has remained low, a problem exacerbated by the ongoing recession. Over 150 of the most heavily polluting sectors of the economy remain outside the scope of the ETS. Furthermore, the ETS does not really promote multilateral energy or environmental cooperation – it simply allows European countries to purchase 'cuts' in emissions from third countries. In practice, as long as EU member states remain divided over exactly what the climate mandate should be, the EU's ability to credibly commit to international carbon reduction emissions will be weakened. This was apparent in recent negotiations regarding 2030 targets: Germany was strongly in favour of specific renewable energy targets; the UK was against.

Climate and energy policy at state level

Despite the best efforts of IGOs and regional organisations it is looking increasingly likely that the international community will fail to take the measures necessary to avoid a 2 °C increase in global temperatures. Institutions such as the IPCC and the IEA, amongst others, have been developing forecasts of temperature rises according to various scenarios based on current or potential new climate and energy policies and trends. And even on the more optimistic 'new policies' scenario, the IEA's World Energy Outlook (2014) predicts that the 2 °C target will not be met. Instead the world currently appears to be on track for long-term warming of between 3.6 °C and 5.3 °C compared with pre-industrial levels – most of which will happen this century. As such, it is clear that further, more profound policy measures are required to avoid the potentially devastating impacts of such temperature rises.

Consequently, emphasis is moving away from multilateral and regional settings, and being placed back on nation-states. The importance of the national level reflects the observation that international targets alone have little effect on national emission levels. For emissions targets to be met, policies to enable this – and to manage the socio-economic consequences of policy changes – must be introduced at the national level (Carter 2010: 57). On the bright side, a great many countries have greenhouse gas emissions reduction targets as part of global or regional agreements, and departments or ministries for energy and/or environment are also commonplace. 144 countries currently have renewable targets, with 138 also having support strategies and policies in place to meet these targets (REN21 2014). But only a few countries have separate, national emissions targets that exceed their international commitments. The UK, for example, through the 2008 Climate Change Act, set a legally binding emissions reduction target of 80 percent by 2050, as well as a series of five-year carbon budgets.

Nevertheless, recent policy innovation has largely been taking place at the national level, particularly with regard to renewable energy. However, approaches have differed substantially between countries. For example, in the electricity sector, policies to support renewable energy include public tendering or auctions, renewable portfolio standards and/or quotas, net metering and, crucially, FITs (see Box 5.6). Other examples include heat obligation in the heating and cooling sector, and biofuel blend mandates in the transport sector (REN21 2014: 7-9).

Sweden, Denmark and the Netherlands are key examples of states with successful national-level renewable energy strategies. But perhaps the most important case study of national policy success is Germany. Phase I of this policy was the 'Energy Concept' (the 'Energiewende'), put into law through

---

Box 5.6 Feed-in-tariffs (FITs)

A number of options for promoting renewable energy are available to governments, but the most popular and effective to date has been FITs. Eighteen EU member states now use FITs, along with 50 other countries including China, India and Mongolia. FITs set a guaranteed rate for each kilowatt-hour (kWh) of renewable electricity fed in to the grid operator – the cost of which, usually higher, is passed on in electricity bills to consumers (Mitchell 2008: 181). In many countries (such as Germany) an obligation is placed on electricity grid operators to buy renewable electricity at the set price, often on long-term contracts, and to give it priority access to the grid over non-renewable fuel sources. This model appears to be more successful in promoting renewable electricity, and more cost effective, than non-FIT alternatives. In 2013, for example, FITs enabled Latin American states to build onshore wind and solar PV installations without the need for government subsidies. As the technology costs of renewable energy fall over time, FIT rates can also be reduced. Properly designed, with an initial cap, FITs can also lower the risk levels for renewable energy investors in entering well-established energy markets.

FITs can, however, prove controversial. Although they offer the best support to emerging renewable technologies to enter electricity markets and gain market share they are not 'market' based. A recent report by the EU Competition Commission, for example, recommends that countries start to reduce FITs and replace them with more market-based instruments. Clearly, FIT structures are a form of government intervention that creates distortions in market incentive structures. On the other hand, given the extent of global fossil fuel subsidies, energy markets might already be seen as severely distorted.

the Renewable Energy Act of 2000. Germany is now in Phase II of this energy system transition, designed to reach fruition by 2050. This is a real and radical energy transition in design – on top of tough low-carbon targets nuclear energy is to be phased out. The targets, measured against 2008 levels, include greenhouse gas emissions reduction of 80–95 percent and reductions in primary energy use of 50 percent. The renewable energy target is 60 percent of final consumption (Agora 2013: 1). Germany has significantly increased renewable energy supply from a very low base (mainly solar PV) using its 'risk free' FIT schemes. Renewable energy supplied over 26 percent of German electricity demand in the first half of 2012, a seven-fold increase since 1991. In addition, this energy is largely owned by local collectives or individuals. Germany has also pursued policies to improve household insulation, the national grid and localised energy distribution systems. This process has had its opponents and caused much internal debate, particularly over high energy prices, but Germany can be said to have shown a greater degree of political commitment to energy transition than any other state.

China and the USA, two of the most significant aggregate greenhouse gas emitters, are usually perceived as climate change 'laggards'. This is partly due to the Kyoto Protocol, which the USA withdrew from, and which set no binding targets for China. However, in recent times, both have made policy moves towards energy sustainability. China has enacted renewable energy and efficiency strategies, and in 2013 was the world's largest investor in renewable power – with its renewable investments exceeding its fossil fuel investments. In fact, China's investment levels in this period exceeded all of Europe's combined (REN21 2014). The USA is also a large investor in renewable energy in absolute terms. In 2014, furthermore, the Environmental Protection Agency (EPA) announced a new federal sustainable energy plan, seeking to cut carbon pollution from existing power plants by 30 percent over 2005 levels by the year 2030. This is the first ever attempt by a US President to regulate carbon pollution from power plants. However, as the plan was passed through President Obama's executive authority, it can easily be overturned by future administrations. Nevertheless, emission levels in the USA are starting to trend down, partly as a result of the switch from coal to gas for electricity production that followed from the 'shale revolution'.

Sub-national measures and movements

Important energy and climate change politics and policy measures also take place at the sub-state level. However, the local politics of climate change contains a number of tensions. For example, civil society groups have played important roles in raising the profile of climate change both amongst elite political institutions and within wider society (see Box 5.7). Furthermore, the general awareness of anthropogenic climate change amongst the general public is growing along with support for specific climate policies, including

Box 5.7 Civil society networks

Civil society groups, particularly environmental NGOs, have played a significant role in raising the profile of climate science and of anthropogenic climate change (Garner 2011: 162). However, as new knowledge about climate change and mitigation strategies is produced, and as new technology continues to emerge, even more is needed from civil society. New knowledge needs to be diffused, and civil society organisations may have the networks, expertise and resources to communicate clearly to actors at different levels of society and across national borders. One organisation which has risen to this challenge is the Climate Change Network. Representing 365 amalgamated NGOs and over 20 million concerned citizens, this network seeks to diffuse knowledge, but also to mobilise governments and apply pressure on corporations and business institutions. The European Climate Foundation, supported by both civil society groups and corporate donations, is also highly active in climate change mitigation debates in Europe.

for renewable energy. Yet people who are in principle supportive of renewable technologies can also object strongly to wind farms, solar PV farms or new transmission grids being built close to where they live. This problem may be exacerbated by the centralised grid systems that have historically predominated – as a rule the public is unaware of exactly where their energy comes from. For others, realistically, climate change is simply low on the list of political and economic priorities.

The sub-national level also includes local production and transmission systems, as well as local social movements that unite communities in collective action. A number of influential climate thinkers suggest that if a sustainable energy transition is to occur, this is just as likely to result from a local groundswell of citizen involvement as from top-down processes of governance. Such ideas touch a chord with the 'radical' version of environmentalism discussed in Chapter 1. The ambition is that the more distributed and collaborative relations necessary for the emerging green economic era will in turn drive a wider breakdown of the conventional top-down organisation of society (Rifkin 2011: 36).

A community-led energy revolution implies that the ways in which energy is produced and used will switch from a centralised to a diffused and flexible energy system (see Chapter 9 for more details). Examples of increasingly distributed energy systems can be seen in Germany, Denmark and some US states. Indeed, in Germany in 2013, 35 percent of renewable energy was owned by private citizens, and another 11 percent by farmers. However, while local communities and local interest groups have been crucial to organising and coordinating renewables-based electricity generation and distribution, support from local or municipal authorities or through national governmental programmes has also been essential. In federal systems such as the USA, some US states have made far greater strides in promoting local renewable energy production than the US federal government has achieved – particularly California. Finally, crucial new sources of support for sustainable energy and of innovative environmental practices have emerged in the form of large cities. Key examples include the C40 network, the Global Cities Covenant on Climate, the Cities for Climate Protection Programme, and the International Council for Local Environmental Initiatives.

The current politics of climate change and energy: Debates and issues

This final section turns to the complexities of the contemporary politics of climate change. The emphasis here is on broader debates concerning the role of energy policy and energy systems within processes of climate change mitigation. Other debates are much narrower in scope, so despite their importance cannot be covered here in any detail. For example, the question of how climate change efforts should balance investments in mitigation and in adaptation strategies is an important one for policy-makers (see IPCC 2007), but is secondary to the question of the role that energy policy plays in the first instance.

As already hinted at above, there remains a strong debate about the role of public and private institutions within energy and climate governance, as well as in regard to the wider process of a sustainable energy transition. Debates about the relative role of states and markets in energy governance have raged for decades (see Chapters 3 and 9), but the determination of the appropriate balance of responsibilities between governments, regional actors, corporations, IGOs and NGOs in facilitating a low-carbon transition is yet to be made. Even more complex and unclear is the question of whether it is possible, or indeed advisable, to coordinate all of these different actors, and how this might be achieved. What is apparent, as this and previous chapters have outlined, is that states are currently becoming more involved in energy systems again – not simply because of the securitisation phenomenon, but also because of the apparent limits of the market in driving a sustainable energy systems transition.

States, markets and investment

Debate over the state–market balance is particularly evident with regard to energy investment. This is the case for the research and development of new technologies, in building renewable energy generation capacity, and in related policy areas of storage, networks and interconnections. One argument, evident across environmental and transitions literatures and debates, is that only state entities can provide the scale of investment that is required for a successful energy transition. This is partly because of the growing perception that markets have thus far failed to deliver sufficient levels of investment. However, an alternative to more state investment and economic intervention might be to create clearer governance structures and energy sector investment rules and regulations, thereby encouraging more private sector investment. On the other hand, the kinds of niche inventions and technologies that will emerge during an energy transition probably require state subsidy or protection, before they can develop and diffuse more broadly (see Chapter 9). Historically, all new methods of producing energy have suffered from underinvestment at initial phases – but this could be compensated for through targeted state investment. Furthermore, it might be pointed out that it is not only the renewable energy generation part of the global energy system that needs investment. A great many energy-consuming economic sectors could facilitate more sustainable energy usage (for example the automotive and agricultural sectors), and government finance might be equally well used in this regard.

One leading thinker in this area is the economist Marianna Mazzucato, who argues that states should invest more in directly nurturing new technologies (Mazzucato 2013). In support, one can only look at the role of various US federal bodies in creating the conditions for research and development in some of the most successful contemporary technologies (the Apple iPhone for example). Certainly the idea of the state as the initiator and facilitator of new investments is accepted in many countries. States have now initiated and/or funded a number of banks with heavy roles in sustainable energy investment (see Box 5.8). Mazzucato suggests that states should go one step further, and not just invest directly in companies and other institutions seeking to develop new technologies, but also maintain those direct stakes for long enough to make a positive return on investment.

Box 5.8 Sustainability banking

There are now a number of banks that are active in 'green' or 'sustainable' investments. Well known examples include the Brazilian Development Bank Banco Nacional de Desenvolvimento Economico e Social (BNDES) which, although it focuses on development projects broadly, invests heavily in supporting sustainability projects such as the Luz Para Todos project (see Chapter 6). Other examples include the newly set up Green Bank in the UK, and the KfW Bank in Germany. The KfW Bank has a long history – it was initially set up in order to spend German development funds after World War II (as the 'Reconstruction Credit Institute') – but it now has sustainability as one of its primary business targets. Crucially, this bank is very well capitalised, better in fact than the World Bank. Consequently, it is able to lend to sustainability projects at very low interest rates, and it recycles repaid monies into new sustainability projects. It actively supports energy systems change, and encourages forward-looking ideas in Germany, Europe and throughout the world.

Managed transitions and distribution of benefits

One of the principal questions within academia, think tanks, and more recently political circles is whether there should be a greater role for government strategic 'planning' in a low-carbon energy transition. This is because processes of transition need to be managed: any energy system change will create an uneven distribution of costs and benefits across various social coalitions and demographic groups. Carlotta Perez, in her historical analysis of previous technological revolutions, has identified that the state has in every instance been called upon to manage new technologies so as to ensure that it is not only those that can afford expensive new technologies that benefit (Perez 2002). A common example is the central role of most OECD governments in the last century in rolling out electricity generation and transmission systems so as to provide universal access to electricity. Given that the near-term economic costs associated with climate programmes, such as efficiency mandates or renewable schemes, are in many countries passed directly on to consumers, this appears to be a valid point. In some cases it appears that multinational fossil fuel companies and heavy industry have been protected by governments, while household consumers pay disproportionally for the costs of energy transition. This, as will be seen below, can exacerbate energy poverty. States with strongly supportive welfare systems or governments that explicitly seek to equitably distribute the costs of energy transition can, by contrast, mitigate such outcomes.

One argument, supported by Transitions Management groups, is that energy and climate governance needs to become a great deal more reflexive, interactive, coordinated and visionary. This is based on the understanding that any sustainable energy transition would be unprecedented, both in terms of the time frame envisaged, and because of the centrality of new scientific knowledge about humankind's relationship with the environment, rather than of new technologies and their uses.

Social practices across society as well as entire infrastructure systems need to change, and this will only happen by taking a 'learning-by-doing' approach. Both established and new government institutions will be required to provide clear leadership, to help disseminate new climate knowledge within society, and to coordinate and foster new networks and partnerships between evolving research and development institutions. However, the role envisaged for government is overall less of a 'hierarchical' or top-down one, and more as facilitator, coordinator and visionary. Indeed, arguments have recently emerged in favour of an 'entrepreneurial' state, able to actively create new markets and encourage technological revolution.

However, in the contemporary political economic climate, fiscal austerity has become the accepted wisdom in many OECD countries. This is part of the ongoing consequences of the global financial crisis that began in 2007. As such, governments that are cutting back on public spending are required to choose between a range of very worthy and necessary causes. This has made it very difficult to justify increased spending on climate change and energy transition.

Technology debates

Energy and climate policy decisions are often mediated by different states' pre-existing energy system. For example, states with highly developed fossil fuel systems, in particular exporters, have tended to show greater resistance to any sustainable transition – not least because existing elites face large potential losses, and may have the ability to resist change. There have been debates about whether governments should be specifying what the future energy mix should look like, or making binding decisions about centralised versus distributed electricity systems. However, the technology debates discussed here focus on the future of two key fuel sources for electricity: gas and nuclear.

Supporters of the gas industry have proposed for a decade or so now that gas should act as the 'bridge fuel' between today's high-carbon, fossil fuel dominated energy systems and future low-carbon systems. This is largely because it is understood that this transition will not happen quickly, and gas, which is increasingly widely available, is relatively low-carbon compared to coal or oil. Furthermore, carbon capture and storage (CCS) technologies, should they ever become commercially viable, would allow gas to complement renewables in power generation. This is because gas generation can quickly be turned on or off, and can therefore be used to balance the variable output of wind and solar. Certainly switches from coal to gas for power generation in the UK in the 1990s, and in the USA in the 2010s, has resulted in lower overall emissions. Critics, however, argue that investing money in long-term gas projects will, in overall terms, further exacerbate global fossil fuel system 'lock-in', and make the switch to renewables both slower and more complex.

The second major technology debate is whether to include nuclear as a long-term electricity supply source (see Box 5.9). Proponents of nuclear power heavily emphasise its low-carbon status, as well as the fact that it can be produced domestically – thereby allowing countries to reduce imports of other raw materials needed for electricity production (especially gas). Furthermore, once nuclear power plants are established (and before decommissioning starts) they run at very low costs in comparison to other forms of electricity supply. Electricité de France (EDF), one of the largest nuclear power companies in the world, has been quick to both emphasise and capitalise on the low-carbon and security credentials of nuclear energy. Their annual report of 2009 heralded a 'global nuclear revival', pointing to the IPCC and the Council of the European Union's adoption of positive stances on nuclear in 2007.

However, counter-arguments to nuclear have grown in influence since the Fukushima disaster of 2011 (see Chapter 2). Many environmental groups have of course long opposed nuclear power on the grounds that, despite being low-carbon, it poses a great many other rather serious environmental and social risks. The narrowing down of environmental debates to focus on climate change has therefore been to the benefit of the nuclear industry. Nevertheless, there are also questions about the full economic costs of nuclear

Box 5.9 Renewables versus nuclear

For many the energy debate is really a debate over whether to support renewables or nuclear power. Nuclear has the opposite problem to intermittent renewables – it cannot be turned off. Nuclear power and renewables therefore do not combine well within energy grid systems, implying the need to make a choice between these two sources of power. At a spatial level there is also a clear contrast – nuclear power would require the continuation of the centralised generation model. Large nuclear power stations would feed in to a large-scale transmission system, whereas renewables can sit much closer to centres of energy demand and operate on a diffused basis. From an environmental perspective, nuclear energy also carries with it a problematic history of toxic leaks, unresolved issues surrounding how to decommission toxic waste, and catastrophic safety failures. Waste from nuclear plants needs to be stored for tens of thousands of years, and establishing safe storage facilities has proven very difficult for many countries.

There have of course also been criticisms of almost all proposed renewable energy sources: wind, biomass, solar, wave, CCS and hydro-electric. Critics point to high variability (especially wind), high associated costs, high energy levels involved in producing certain renewable systems (such as wind), and for biofuels they point to competition with traditional agriculture exacerbating food security issues. However, the production of renewable energy is still in an early phase, and significant learning (and further cost and risk reduction) can still take place.

Indeed, it increasingly looks like a combination of innovation and building economies of scale is rapidly reducing the cost of producing energy from a range of renewable sources. Wind turbine costs are estimated to have dropped by one-fifth since 2007, while solar costs have fallen even more dramatically. For example, in spring 2009, a standard crystalline-silicon photovoltaic (PV) module cost US$4.20 per peak watt. By the end of 2012 it was only US$0.62 per peak watt (Clean Technica 2013). Such evidence is used by anti-nuclear protagonists to argue a cost-based case for renewable energy over nuclear.

power: up-and-running costs may be low, but building and especially decommissioning costs can be enormous. When these are factored in, nuclear power starts to look more expensive than almost all other sources of electricity, including renewables (Schneider et al. 2011).

Many countries, however, still have nuclear power plans in place – including the UK, Finland and India – not least because of its low-carbon and military credentials. In fact the IEA, together with the Nuclear Energy Agency (NEA), predicts that nuclear power will grow from 14 percent to 24 percent of world electricity production by 2050. By contrast, however, some countries like Germany have since Fukushima overtly rejected the nuclear power option. In seeking to move to a nuclear-free low-carbon future, the Germans can start to design energy infrastructure that moves further away from centralised power than would otherwise be the case. Energy infrastructures that allow for greater distributed energy, as well as flexibility, may result.

Conclusion

This chapter sought to assesses the energy–climate nexus and the politics of low-carbon transition. In examining the governance institutions involved in the energy–climate nexus at the global, regional, national, and sub-national levels, as well as the roles of different types of actors in climate governance, we can gather some insight into the first aspect of the 'trilemma' of global energy challenges – environment and climate change. While this first global energy challenge contains its own debates and difficulties, such as the renewables vs. nuclear debates, it is also clear that one of the main tensions is between energy policies for climate change mitigation and the two other aspects of the trilemma – achieving energy security, and promoting energy access in the developing world. It is this latter global energy challenge that the following chapter addresses in more detail.

Chapter 8

Transit and Infrastructure

Infrastructure is the physical plant necessary to support technology for transport, communications, and governmental and industrial processes. It facilitates the production of goods and services and the provision of public goods for example in education, health care, and of course energy services. Energy infrastructure is essential for the functioning of energy systems and modern societies, and for maintaining welfare. It connects producers and consumers of energy across geographical distances, it brings oil, gas and electricity to people and companies, and it provides for essential services such as heating. Because energy infrastructure is inextricably linked to economic development, it represents a significant part of a state's stock of physical capital. A McKinsey study estimates that infrastructure, including energy infrastructure, typically amounts to around 70 percent of national GDP (Dobbs et al. 2013). Much of this infrastructure is dedicated to transit: the problem of moving energy sources from where they are in abundant supply to where demand is found. The geographic disparity between supply and demand in energy makes transit, and transit infrastructure, a key aspect of the global energy challenge.

Energy infrastructure and energy transit is therefore important to states both in political and economic terms. More to the point, it emerges as crucial on two fronts. First, as the geography of oil and gas production and demand has shifted, energy trade has become increasingly internationalised. This is particularly the case for oil; but gas, which has historically been more regional in nature, is rapidly following – partly due to the growing trade in LNG. Energy trade, therefore, is increasingly dependent on international shipping and waterways, as well as on pipelines that cross national jurisdictions. This, in turn, subjects energy infrastructure and transit issues to international relations, geopolitics, and the changing distribution of global economic power.

Second, energy infrastructure has an important role to play in promoting a global low-carbon transition, and in fighting energy poverty (see Chapters 5 and 6). Providing the world's poor with electricity, whether in rural Africa or developing Asia, is an immense challenge in itself. Yet expanding access to modern energy services for development should not come at the expense of climate change mitigation. Energy infrastructure building in the developing world therefore not only needs to overcome enormous problems with accessing finance, but also needs to answer tough questions about exactly what kinds of infrastructure investments are to be made.

This chapter investigates these two sets of problems in order to better understand the global energy challenge. The chapter first discusses sea-borne and network-based transit issues, and explains why energy infrastructure presents a multi-scale governance challenge. The chapter then sheds light on the security dimension of energy transit and infrastructure. It looks at two case studies, the Caspian Basin and the Persian Gulf, both of which exemplify the difficulties in securing pipeline routes and sea-lanes. The chapter then moves on to examining energy infrastructure beyond the scale of the nation-state. Discussion focuses on the oil industry, addressing the oil refining segment of the global oil industry, and on the benefits of, and prospects for, joint exploration and development projects. Attention then turns to the regionalisation and/or internationalisation of electricity networks, looking at the costs and benefits of prospective 'supergrids'. Finally, the problem of electricity storage capacity, which runs concomitant with the shift to a low-carbon economy heavily reliant on intermittent renewable sources, is addressed.

Transit and infrastructure as a global energy challenge

Given that global oil and gas transit proceeds in largely unseen ways it is often simply taken for granted until some crisis emerges. At such times, we come to realise how vulnerable global energy systems are, the range of different issues that affect transit and infrastructure, and how many different parts of the world – including producer and importer states as well as transit states – experience difficulties when problems do arise. It cannot be overstated: transit is fundamental to international trade in oil and gas, and so to world energy security.

Sea-borne energy transit: Straits and choke points

Open sea-lanes are crucial to the international trade of crude oil. Today, about half of the total world oil supply was shipped by tankers on maritime routes. Sea-borne energy trade is in fact becoming increasingly important as trade in LNG continues to grow. Consequently, 'choke points' (see Box 8.1) can become issues of security concern. The Strait of Hormuz, for example, is home to 35 percent of seaborne global oil trade but could potentially be blocked by a number of adjacent countries. The impact of this on global energy security was made evident in 1984, during the 'Tanker War' between Iran and Iraq, where each country tried to curb the other's ability to finance their war effort by stopping oil exports. Concerns resurfaced in the 2000s in the context of the dispute surrounding Iran's nuclear programme. Since 9/11, furthermore, shipping lanes are seen as vulnerable to terrorist threats and pirate attacks – the most common contemporary example being the pirate attacks on international shipping off the coast of Somalia.

Transit problems do not necessarily constitute a threat to oil supply. As discussed in Chapter 2, oil is a fungible commodity and as such global markets normally ensure that reductions in supply from one part of the world are compensated for by increases elsewhere. However, interrupted supplies have in the past led to significant price hikes and this entails potentially serious economic risks. Indeed, most post-World War II recessions in the United States correlate with sudden increases in the price of oil (Balke et al. 1999). Oil price shocks also threaten the growth paths of transitional and emerging economies, including the BRICS. Their high oil intensity (the amount of oil needed to produce a unit of GDP) equates to a greater exposure to price fluctuations than most OECD countries face. Sea-lanes, therefore, are strategically important for the smooth functioning of both oil markets and the global economy as a whole.

Box 8.1 Bottlenecks: Choke points in global oil trade

The US Energy Information Administration (EIA) lists seven 'choke points'; that is, narrow straits on global sea-lanes through which large volumes of oil are shipped:

1. *Strait of Hormuz*: The world's most important oil choke point is located between Oman and Iran and plays host to some 17 mbd (million barrels per day). It connects the Persian Gulf, the world's most important oil producer region, with the Arabian Sea.
2. *Strait of Malacca*: the Singaporean strait represents the shortest sea route between the Persian Gulf and emerging Asian economies. It links up the Indian and Pacific Oceans with around 15 mbd.
3. *Bab-el-Mandab*: Located at the Horn of Africa between Yemen and Eritrea, this 3.4 mbd strait represents a key entry point to the Red Sea and the Suez Canal.
4. *Suez Canal*: The canal is crucial for some 3 mbd of oil trade, particularly from the Persian Gulf to European markets.
5. *Bosporus*: The Turkish strait is an important export route for around 3 mbd of oil from Russia and Caspian region countries.
6. *Danish Straits*: Connecting the Baltic Sea and the North Sea, the Danish Straits (Kattegat and Skagerrak) transit around 3 mbd of Russian and Norwegian oil exports.
7. *Panama Canal*: While no longer the centre of the US oil trade, the Panama Canal transits around 0.75 mbd of oil. Plans to double the Canal's capacity may increase its strategic significance.

Source: EIA 2012

Ship-based oil and gas transit primarily takes place in 'international' rather than sovereign waters. Sea-borne trade and maritime security is therefore often subject to the Law of the Seas, a specific field of public international law that governs how states interact in maritime matters. This gave rise to a regime in the shape of the United Nations Convention on the Law of the Sea (UNCLOS), which was established in 1982 and came into effect in 1994. UNCLOS now serves as the main framework for international maritime security cooperation, and is linked to a range of international bodies with a similar focus, the most important being the International Maritime Organization of the United Nations.

Of course, the capacity of international regimes to enforce decisions, governance standards or rules is an ongoing problem in international relations. Policing the oceans, fighting piracy attacks and keeping choke points open requires a sizeable naval fleet capable of credibly enforcing rights of free transit. Few countries in the world have such capacity. Since 1945, the United States of America, a sponsor but not a signatory to the UNCLOS convention, has been primarily responsible for securing smooth global oil transit. This, however, is a public goods problem: free shipping routes are a global public good, but if one actor voluntarily takes on the task of securing maritime transport routes, then other states can benefit from this in effect as free riders. In constantly patrolling the Persian Gulf and the Strait of Malacca, the USA might be seen to have for decades provided both oil producers and consumers with a 'good' that none of them paid for. We will return to this issue later in the chapter.

Network-based energy transit: Pipelines

Pipelines, arguably the least overtly visible form of transit, have served as the main form of infrastructure through which oil and gas move from well to market. They are in some ways more complicated than shipping, as physical infrastructure must be both built and operated. This requires agreements signed between the pipeline owner/operator and multiple other parties: the producer state, the consumer state, and all the states through which the pipeline will run (the transit states). Each state, in turn, has its own political and economic objectives, legal and regulatory system, particular internal interests and social coalitions to manage, as well as historical and perhaps even problematic relations with the other states involved (see Box 8.2).

It is also possible that one party in an infrastructure building agreement holds more bargaining power than the others. This can result in uneven transit terms, and further down the road to disputes and renegotiations as circumstances, prices, and/or governments change. For example, once the physical infrastructure is built, the domestic or foreign companies involved will have sunk costs – making it hard for them to 'exit' the project and inherently transforming bargaining power. Transit states, by contrast, gain something of a 'geographical monopoly' over energy trade between producer and consumer

Box 8.2 Friendly disagreements: The Keystone XL pipeline

The planned Keystone XL oil pipeline illustrates the complex political dynamics of cross-border energy infrastructure. Keystone XL is intended to link Alberta, Canada to Nebraska, USA where it would join the existing pipeline systems to Illinois and Oklahoma, and further on to refineries on the Gulf of Mexico in Texas. The pipeline would provide an important export route for oil produced from Alberta tar sands as well as oil produced in the US Bakken field (which is currently primarily transported by rail). Actors directly involved in the authorisation process are the US State Department, the US President, the Canadian government, and Trans Canada, which is the company that would build and operate the proposed pipeline.

For their part, the Canadian government fully endorses the project as it opens up much-needed export routes for Albertan oil. However, US authorities have been more hesitant, largely because of domestic political opposition. Environmental groups in the USA oppose the use of Canadian tar-sands oil, which is massively carbon intensive. By contrast, proponents of the project in the US Congress argue that the job creation benefits and the gains in energy security for the USA, and for North America as a whole, outweigh any costs. The result is something of a stalemate, with the pipeline construction permit pending since 2008. This demonstrates that even in the context of friendly international relations between states, pipeline politics can be difficult.

states. Consequently, they may try to leverage increased political or economic benefits from their strategic position. Energy pipeline projects, therefore, entail considerable political, economic and regulatory risks.

Transit agreements will usually feature a number of clauses aimed at hedging risk for the various involved parties, and set out 'transit terms', in effect the payments that are made to transit countries in return for allowing the pipeline to operate. In most cases this takes the form of a transit fee, but it could also include set terms under which gas or oil pipeline 'off-take' can substitute for payment. Other standard features include dispute settlement mechanisms, which in the case of conflict between the parties will stipulate a range of measures from establishing external councils to arbitration procedures. The dependence on physical infrastructure for natural gas trading, along with the fact that natural gas is less fungible a commodity than oil, has resulted in gas market politics being largely regional in nature (see Chapter 1). In stark contrast to oil, natural gas transit disputes create immediate supply risks for consumer states for whom switching to alternative sources may be expensive and difficult, if not impossible, in the short term. Producers, in turn, may find it hard to export gas to other consumer states if relations with transit countries become strained.

In gas, in particular, pipeline agreements tend to be based on LTCs that tie both producers and consumers to clearly defined volumes that the supplier must deliver, and which the consumer must take, at fixed or indexed prices. The North American market's emphasis on spot prices is a notable exception to this. For the rest of the world, however, LTCs reflect the long business time horizon for gas that pipelines give rise to. As a consequence, international relations in natural gas have generally been quite stable. As a case in point, West German–Soviet gas contracts of the 1970s were consistently honoured by both parties despite the ongoing Cold War. Since gas relations signal long-term commitment, pipeline projects have sometimes been proposed in order to foster better bilateral relations. The planned Iran–Pakistan gas pipeline, also known as the 'Peace Pipeline', is an example of this form of gas diplomacy.

Nevertheless, there have been cases of transit disputes or contractual disagreements over natural gas. In 2012, despite decades of stability, and massive sunk costs in gas transit infrastructure, Egypt sought to cancel a 20-year natural gas contract with Israel, putting into question the 1979 peace treaty between the two nations. Here, domestic political change in Egypt is seen to affect international energy relations, which in turn could have serious consequences for international relations more broadly. The recent 'gas wars' between Russia and Ukraine also demonstrate how fragile the network-based international energy infrastructure that drives natural gas markets can be (see Box 8.3).

These ongoing gas disputes serve as a reminder that energy is as much a political as an economic subject. Energy infrastructure and transit is for many analysts inextricably linked to a realist/mercantilist perspective, and to what in the field of international relations is sometimes termed *Realpolitik*. Indeed, for such analysts, Russia's actions in particular highlighted the possibility of oil and gas producers emerging as 'energy superpowers'. Russia has in fact pursued an active strategy of gaining control or influence over regional energy infrastructure more broadly, with a particular focus on pipeline transit routes. Russia has sought to exchange subsidised Russian gas for a share in the ownership of national energy infrastructure, or for rights to invest in national energy infrastructure, both within former Soviet space and beyond.

Russia has also responded to the Ukrainian transit problem with two offshore pipeline projects designed to circumvent Ukraine. Nord Stream, a 55 bcm pipeline, crosses the Baltic Sea and connects Russia's Vyborg with Germany's Greifswald. South Stream, a 63 bcm pipeline, was planned to run through the Black Sea, connecting Russia's Russkaya compressor station with Bulgaria's Varna. Plans for South Stream have in 2014 been replaced by a new 63 bcm project titled Turkish Stream, which takes a similar route as South Stream but lands in Greece. Taken together, the pipelines will have the capacity to replace the volumes currently transiting through Ukraine. Nord Stream has been operational since 2012, but the pipelines

Box 8.3 Unfriendly disagreements: Gas transit between Russia and Ukraine

Russia inherited from the Soviet era a pipeline grid system that supplies gas to Ukraine but which also transports the bulk of Russia's gas exports to Europe, Gazprom's main market. However, continuing poor relations between Russia and Ukraine in the post-Soviet era have resulted in conflict over gas transit, in 2005–2006, in 2008–2009 and again in 2013–2014. In January 2009, in the middle of a cold winter, gas consumers in Central-Eastern and South-Eastern Europe (particularly Bulgaria, Serbia, Bosnia-Herzegovina, Moldova, Slovakia, Greece, Austria and the Czech Republic) were cut off from supplies from 7–20 January, bringing these states' industry and public life to a standstill. The causes of these crises were both economic and political in nature.

In regard to economics, it is a question of Russian energy subsidies to Ukraine, and of Ukrainian debt to Russia. Until 2005, Russia delivered gas to Ukraine at US$50/trillion cubic metres (tcm), which according to Gazprom was less than the cost of production. This subsidy is explicable both as an historical anachronism – a hangover from the Soviet era – and as a reflection of Ukraine's ability to extract rents from its geographical transit monopoly over Russian gas exports to Europe. However, there were also accusations that Ukraine was siphoning gas off from the pipeline system, and Ukraine's Russian debt – in part a reflection of Russia's claims of Ukrainian gas extraction – rapidly mounted.

In political terms, energy relations began to deteriorate with the election of the pro-Western Yushchenko regime that rose to power in the wake of the 2005 'Orange Revolution'. As a consequence, and against a backdrop of sharply rising international gas prices, Russia began to reduce its gas subsidy to Ukraine. By December 2008, gas prices reached US$230/tcm, while Ukraine's Russian debt reached US$1.5 billion. Russia warned that if the debts were not paid, then the price of gas would rise to the netback market rate, and supplies might be suspended. Russia and Ukraine failed to reach agreement on gas prices and volumes for 2009, triggering a cut-off of Ukrainian gas supplies. On the 19th of January 2009, a new ten-year supply and transit contract was signed between Russia and Ukraine, and the following day gas supply was reinstated. However, it was clear that as Russian gas bound for Europe had continued to flow through the pipeline, Ukrainian transit companies had been able to respond by diverting this gas to their domestic market. In passing the gas shortage on to European gas consumers, Ukraine demonstrated that it was willing to use its critical transit state status as political leverage (see Pirani et al. 2009).

planned to circumvent Ukraine in the south remain in the planning phase. It is therefore unclear whether these projects can fulfil the second of Russia's geopolitical objectives: to cement exclusive access to Central Eastern European markets.

This gas dispute certainly had wide geopolitical ramifications in Europe, where a strategic response to both the potential consequences of overreliance on Russian gas and the potential for Ukraine to act as a 'rogue' transit state became necessary. The EU response was threefold: to try and present a more unified front in terms of energy foreign policy; to actively seek alternative sources of supply, particularly from the Caspian Basin; and to establish alternative routes for gas supply to the Ukraine transit corridor. It is telling that even in the absence of a clear economic case, pipelines are planned and built specifically to bypass transit countries perceived as 'difficult'.

However, some observers argue that globalising gas markets might change the geopolitics of gas, and reduce the importance of network-bound gas trade. Liquefied natural gas (LNG), which already accounts for some 30 percent of internationally traded gas, is crucial to this process. Inter-regional gas trade is projected to expand by more than three-quarters within the next 20 years. If gas markets became more liquid, and gas trading less dominated by LTC models and pipeline infrastructure, then consumers would have more options over supply channels, gas market prices would become more comparable to oil, and transit issues would become less significant. Producers, on the other hand, would increasingly compete in global spot markets, and would be less able to use preferential or embedded access to national or regional markets for political purposes. On the other hand, gas markets would also take on the security problems facing oil markets, in particular the security of sea-borne trade. Furthermore, given that 40 percent of current LNG production capacity is in the hands of OPEC countries, a growing LNG market might also open up the possibility of a gas cartel.

In contrast to sea-borne oil trade, there is no international regime governing (gas) transit through pipelines. The Energy Charter Treaty, discussed in Chapter 4, included a Transit Protocol aimed at regulating precisely these issues. It also envisaged a dispute settlement mechanism for issues pertaining to energy transit among signatories. In fact, the EU sought to apply the Energy Charter Treaty dispute settlement mechanisms to bring agreement between the Ukraine and Russia during the 2009 crisis, but this attempt failed. Russia's withdrawal from the ECT in August 2009 leaves pipelines and network-based energy transit subject to tailored agreements between participating parties. These agreements will outline the specific 'dispute settlement regime' that governs each specific piece of transnational pipeline infrastructure.

Energy infrastructure as a multi-scale governance challenge

State involvement in the building of network-based energy infrastructure is a reflection both of perceived national interests, for example in ensuring energy security, and the fact that the energy infrastructure in question has public goods characteristics. Once in place, multiple parties benefit from energy infrastructure whether they have paid to provide it or not. Consequently, private actors may undersupply energy infrastructure, or fail to provide it altogether. Furthermore, cross-border public goods problems are particularly difficult to solve, necessitating both state action and inter-state cooperation, on a dynamic or continuing basis. Energy infrastructure needs are a global energy challenge that states must address, despite the problems of scale, time horizons and cost.

According to estimates by the International Energy Agency (2012), to meet demand increase alone, energy infrastructure investment up until 2035 needs to amount to a total of US$1.6 trillion, or 1.5 percent of global GDP. Tackling the energy poverty challenge adds another US$1 trillion to the bill (IEA 2013). In addition, to stabilise greenhouse gas emissions at the 450 ppm atmospheric concentration benchmark would require an additional US$16 trillion overall, with infrastructure a significant share of this cost (IEA 2012). Energy infrastructure is long lived, designed to last decades – hence choices, once made, have long-term significance. This reflects the magnitude of both the physical infrastructure required in the sector, and the capital investment needed to build it. Energy infrastructure choices taken today create path dependency, affecting the pattern of future energy supply and use – a problem addressed in more detail below.

Pipelines are designed to stretch across countries, as are power transmission lines that connect national energy markets. While national regulatory systems are crucial, clearly the governance capacity of supranational bodies, such as the EU, may also be significant. However, energy infrastructure requires governance capacity also at the local level (as discussed in Chapter 6). Local storage infrastructure, for instance, is crucial to maintaining national or regional grid stability, and in buffering variations in gas supply and demand across jurisdictions. Local solar power systems feed into municipal distribution networks, which themselves are embedded in national-level electricity infrastructure and regulation. Energy infrastructure therefore presents complex governance challenges, involving multi-level institutions, regulations and policies (see Box 8.4).

The security dimension of energy transit and infrastructure

This section explores in further detail the security dimension of energy transit and infrastructure. It does so by examining two regions with strong geopolitical characteristics to their energy production and trade: the Caspian Basin and the Persian Gulf. The Caspian has in recent years been the site of intense 'pipeline diplomacy' between Europe, Russia and China. The Gulf, as a key region for world oil supplies, has continuously hosted a strong military presence, primarily in the form of the US Fifth Fleet.

Box 8.4 Infrastructure challenges in 'going green': The German *Energiewende*

Germany's electricity infrastructure was designed to operate at the sub-federal government (*Laender*) level, while to ensure full national coverage electricity was mainly produced by coal-fired or nuclear power plants. The German energy system as a whole therefore is characterised by both centralisation and the significantly decentralised regulatory responsibility given to the Laender. Established utility companies also operate (and may enjoy a dominant position in power generation and distribution) at the Laender level, for example RWE in North Rhine-Westphalia and EnBW in Baden-Württemberg. The German *Energiewende*, initially strongly anti-nuclear in focus, has moved towards the promotion of renewable energy – thereby creating new infrastructure challenges. As electricity generation becomes increasingly decentralised, transmission infrastructure needs to be expanded between German states so as to manage peak-load problems and ensure grid stability. This necessitates a fundamental change in the governance of power networks within Germany, as well as an overhaul of the incumbent energy system and its underlying infrastructure.

But infrastructure that has evolved over decades can prove resilient to change. The rise of decentralised photovoltaic energy production through a feed-in-tariff model has been financially damaging to incumbent energy utilities in that they failed to invest in renewable energy. They now demand reform to what is otherwise seen as one of the most successful aspects of the German low-carbon transition so far. Furthermore, efforts to enhance federal-level infrastructure through a proposed *Suedlink* transmission line across Germany have been hampered by *Laender*-level opposition. The case of the *Energiewende* clearly demonstrates the possibilities for inertia in established centralised systems of energy infrastructure. This is in fact one of the main obstacles to Germany's ambitious decarbonisation goals. However, as Germany comes to terms with these challenges of multi-scalar governance, key lessons may emerge for other states seeking a low-carbon transition.

Eye on the Caspian Basin: Grand games and pipeline races

Since 2000, gas supply from the Caspian Basin has figured prominently in international energy politics. This former Soviet region is the focus of an ongoing 'pipeline race' because major consumers such as the EU and China believe they can 'lock-in' gas reserves this way. Caspian Basin countries are landlocked between Europe and Asia, their prospective consumer markets, and this geographical fact means that a large number of new pipeline projects are being planned and built. These countries also border on their competitor oil and gas producers, particularly Iran and Russia.

The region's known energy reserves are significant, at around 11 percent of global gas and 2.5 percent of global oil reserves (BP 2013). However, it is the future potential of the region which arouses the most interest, with the IEA expecting oil and gas exports from the Caspian Basin to more than double over the next two decades. Kazakhstan's Kashagan field was the largest oil find in over 30 years, such that Kazakhstan is likely to become one of the world's largest oil exporters. There is large gas potential also, with the Kazakh government committed to tripling output by 2015, and most earmarked for export (given modest domestic demand growth). Turkmenistan is ranked as the sixth largest natural gas reserve holder in the world, and could become a key supplier for both Eastern and Western consumer markets in the future. Finally, Azerbaijan, arguably the world's oldest oil producer, and currently a top-20 oil exporter, has following the collapse of the Soviet Union once again become a prime target for European oil companies. Azerbaijan has also become a natural gas exporter thanks to the Shah Deniz field, which since its discovery in 1999 has proven to be one of the world's largest natural gas finds.

In light of these facts, and as a reflection of their own search for energy diversification, the EU and China have both invested heavily in the region. However, the geopolitical dimensions of energy are made clear by the intricacies of 'pipeline diplomacy' in the region. For Europe, Central Asian energy supply must currently transit through Russian pipelines, enabling the latter to both exert political influence and derive economic rents. Europe, with support from the USA, has therefore sought to foster alternative pipeline routes linking the Caspian Basin to European consumer markets. These efforts are primarily directed at circumventing Russia, not least because of ongoing problems in Ukraine. The proposed infrastructure projects for the 'Southern Corridor' are the key to these plans (see Box 8.5), not least because more low-key EU initiatives in Central Asia (Traceca and Inogate) are seen to have failed. The European Commission has also sought to enhance its diplomatic presence in the region. A proposed coordination of EU member states with regard to Caspian region gas purchasing would signal long-term security of demand to Kazakhstan, Uzbekistan and Turkmenistan, and perhaps constitute a better deal than they can get from alternative consumers.

'Alternative transit routes' that avoid Russia have also been promoted with regard to oil. The Baku–Tbilisi–Ceyhan (BTC) pipeline, for example, received strong support from the Clinton administration. However, this attempt at a concerted assault on Russia's strategic energy position with regard to Europe has also met limited success. The EU's difficulties in establishing a Southern Corridor again points to the public goods characteristics of energy infrastructure: without state support it is unlikely to be built, particularly in a politically volatile environment such as that in countries adjacent to the Caspian and Black seas. The EU needs to provide determined political and financial support to make the Southern Corridor a reality, which involves solving its own internal public goods problems. Furthermore, even a united Europe on energy issues would need to find strategies to deal with the new veto players that these alternative pipeline routes would create. Turkey, for example, might in future become a key transit state – but it might also be willing to use this

Box 8.5 Fostering diversification: The EU's Southern Gas Corridor

Europe's drive to diversify gas supply sources and transit routes away from Russia and Ukraine has led to a search for alternative natural gas import routes from Central Asia and possibly the Middle East. The 'Southern Gas Corridor' proposed by the European Commission in 2008 included four potential pipelines: Nabucco; the Interconnector Turkey–Greece–Italy (ITGI); White Stream; and the Trans Adriatic Pipeline (TAP). The Southern Corridor is slowly taking shape but it has been hampered by divisions between European leaders over the different competing pipeline projects. As a further problem, the political ambition for pipeline diversification has not always been backed by economic fundamentals. This is ironic, given the EU's liberal market emphasis in its energy diplomacy.

The Nabucco pipeline was the most ambitious of the proposed projects, intended to bring 23 bcm of Azeri gas through Turkey and South Eastern Europe to Austria's Baumgarten. Nabucco was widely seen as a rival to the Russia-sponsored South Stream project, which was backed by Hungary, Italy, Bulgaria and Greece. (In December 2014 Russia announced that it would cancel South Stream and tabled a new pipeline project called Turkish Stream.) Nabucco eventually lost the pipeline race to the much smaller TAP pipeline, led by BP and the Azerbaijan NOC, SOCAR. TAP links up with the Trans-Anatolian Natural Gas Pipeline (TANAP) and will bring 10 bcm of Azerbaijani gas to Europe by 2019. Nabucco was certainly undermined by political quarrels among EU member states, but the economic problems of this project were also significant. Pipeline projects typically include the upstream producers who are seeking to get their gas to export markets. Nabucco, by contrast, was a consortium of consumer-state companies that never managed to get firm guarantees of supply: in effect, there was never any gas to fill this pipeline.

Finally, White Stream was a proposed pipeline from Georgia to Romania through the Black Sea, possibly crossing Crimea. Clearly, the chances of this pipeline going ahead may have been severely diminished by the ongoing Russia–Ukraine conflict that began in 2014, by the likely future instability of this region, and by the annexation of Crimea by Russia. The latest Ukrainian crisis has increased pressure within the EU for a single EU-wide energy market, and for greater diversity of energy import routes to avoid strategic bottlenecks. As Russia is increasingly perceived as an assertive energy power, and therefore not reliable, and as the Ukrainian situation continues to deteriorate, the Southern Corridor model is becoming increasingly central to a burgeoning 'European geo-strategy'.

strategic position for political advantage against the EU (or to advance its case for entry to the EU).

China also actively courts Caspian region oil and gas companies, and is busy building pipelines designed to move energy eastward. Various agreements between China and Central Asian countries have been signed since the early 2000s, and one 55 bcm per year pipeline (the Central Asia–

China Gas Pipeline) was recently completed. Turkmenistan already exports more than half of its gas output to China, and agreements have been reached with Uzbekistan and Kazakhstan worth another 65 bcm of gas exports to China. The now completed Kazakhstan–China oil pipeline is China's direct link to Central Asian oil reserves. Beijing has flanked these pipeline projects with diplomatic moves, including regional investment strategies and fiscal incentives such as the multi-billion dollar loans given to Turkmenistan and Kazakhstan in 2009 in exchange for access to oil and gas. China also maintains energy relations with Russia, hoping that Russia's Eastern Siberian gas fields will exclusively serve the Chinese market, rather than being forced to compete with Europe on existing Russian fields. The Power of Siberia pipeline project, to bring 38 bcm of Russian gas to China, is key to Beijing's strategy.

Russia, for its part, wishes to both secure export markets in Europe and expand into potential Asian gas demand – particularly in China. Consequently, Russia has been attempting to 'lock-up' key Caspian Basin gas supply, either by using its pipeline grid to limit Central Asian gas exports to Europe, or by directly investing in Caspian gas supply sources. For example, a 2007 deal saw gas from Turkmenistan reach Europe through Russian pipelines. However, after an explosion in the Central Asian export pipeline in 2009, Russia was able to permanently reduce throughput of gas from Turkmenistan, pushing Turkmenistan to seek new export routes towards Iran and China. In 2010, Russia offered to buy up all future gas output from Azerbaijan, which would otherwise have fed planned pipelines in the Southern Corridor. However, while Russia may have had some success as a spoiler of Europe's alternative Caspian supply route plans, Moscow has long failed to reach a significant gas supply deal with Beijing. This is due to both to Chinese refusal to pay European prices, and Russian refusal to cover the costs of the multi-billion dollar pipeline needed to transport Siberian gas to China. While a 30-year/ US$400 billion deal on Russian gas exports to China signed in 2014 provides some impetus to Moscow's 'Eastern Strategy', Russia is increasingly drawn into competition with China over Caspian regional reserves, even as it is able to limit Europe's access to them.

Eye on the Persian Gulf: US securing sea-lanes

The Strait of Hormuz is key for oil market stability, with some 17 million barrels (35 percent of sea-borne global oil trade) passing through every day. Blocking the strait would undoubtedly send shockwaves through energy markets across the globe and cause the price of oil to skyrocket. The United States has therefore maintained a strong military presence in the Persian Gulf at least since 1943, when President Roosevelt declared the defence of Saudi Arabia (and its oil) as vital to US interests. That the US Fifth Fleet has continued to ensure that this sea-lane remains open is at least in part explained by the fact that the USA is the world's largest consumer of oil, and has for decades been the biggest importer of oil from this region. The Carter doctrine of 1980 and Operation Desert Storm in 1990 both need to be seen in the context of the US trying to prevent an external or regional power from controlling Gulf hydrocarbon reserves. This also reflected the strategic nature of oil supplies for the USA and its allies during the Cold War.

The USA has also projected military power into other choke points, including the crucial Strait of Malacca (see Box 8.1). However, beyond purely strategic considerations, there was also an ideational driver for the US presence in the Gulf: the historical conviction that it was in the US national interest to promote free trade. The USA was ready to invest in providing the physical preconditions (secure free shipping routes) necessary to achieve this objective. From this perspective, free sea-lanes for energy trade are part-and-parcel of the larger US effort to promote the liberal market model, and to ensure cost-effective trade can take place by both land and sea. Oil markets, in other words, have globalised on the back of the US model of general economic globalisation – free trade underpinned by military power. From a public policy lens, the USA might also be seen as being in the position of a 'natural monopoly' supplier of the good of 'sea-lane security' simply because of the size of its economy and its consequential military might. It is therefore unsurprising that the USA takes on the role of single-handedly policing international sea-lanes – this is simply the most cost-effective solution. Nevertheless, if the USA produces a global public good, then that suggests that a classic free rider problem may be at work (see Box 8.6).

Box 8.6 US policing of sea-lanes and the free rider problem

In public policy terms, protecting sea-lanes represents a classic free rider problem: whilst the task is taken on by only one market participant (in this case the USA), the benefits can be enjoyed by everyone, even when choosing not to pay for it. This is what Europe, China and other oil importing nations have done in past decades: none of these countries maintains a significant naval presence in major choke points. Exporting nations have also profited from the US policing of sea-lanes – none of the Gulf countries has built up a brown water or blue water fleet sizeable enough to secure crucial export routes, whether individually or collectively. The costs of providing the global public good of free sea-lanes clearly falls on US taxpayers, who have essentially paid for a smooth world oil trade and for functioning global oil markets since the end of World War II. Because the USA maintains a global naval presence for a variety of reasons, it is difficult to establish an unambiguous estimate for the actual costs associated with securing sea-lanes for oil. One 2009 RAND study estimated that the costs amounted to US$83 billion per year (Crane et al. 2009). For the direct costs associated with keeping the Strait of Hormuz open, however, the annual operating costs of the US Fifth Fleet may serve as a reasonably good proxy for a price tag.

More recently, however, observers have argued that the USA might rethink its global leadership in securing sea-lanes. The main driver of this possible rethink is soaring US unconventional oil production, which has led to a jump in domestic crude oil output. Oil production in the USA increased from 6.7 mbd in 2008 to 9 mbd in 2012 (BP 2013). The IEA projects that production will stand at 11.6 mbd in 2020 (IEA 2013), which will make the US the world's top oil producer, ahead of Russia and Saudi Arabia. The IEA expects the country to be close to energy self-sufficiency by 2035, and US oil imports will decrease along with dependence on foreign oil. As a result, Washington might no longer be inclined to invest massive amounts of money in keeping far away sea-lanes open. An increasingly inward-looking American society, coupled with strained public budgets, may lead the US leadership to reconsider the scale and focus of its global engagement. The USA might, for example, call on its European allies to increase their (military) presence in crucial trade routes, or leave some of their traditional fields of operation to China – a country eager to resume a more visible role in world energy affairs. In this case, much will depend on these countries' willingness to step in and fill the void that the US would leave behind. If this does not happen, or does not happen quickly enough, then oil price stability may be at significant risk, with severe repercussions for oil markets and the global economy as a whole.

To be sure, there are important reasons to believe that the USA will stay engaged in securing global sea-lanes. As the world's largest economy, it has a vital interest in facilitating international trade of goods and services in more general terms. The USA has also historically considered its allies' national security in its geopolitical strategy, and energy has certainly been part of these considerations. Furthermore, soaring domestic oil production will not shield the country against price fluctuations. As the oil market is global and integrated, disruptions in one part of the world translate into price increases everywhere, regardless of whether a country is a net importer or exporter of oil. It is therefore in US interests to remain engaged in securing sea-lanes, including the crucial Strait of Hormuz. However, in the future, the USA may push more aggressively for burden sharing, particularly with its own allies.

International energy infrastructure

Meeting global energy challenges also requires the building and maintaining of infrastructure that is international in nature. This can include the building of pipelines or electricity cabling that crosses national boundaries, exploration and extraction in disputed marine territories, and resolving bottlenecks (for example in the processing of energy) in a global energy market where key suppliers may lack technological capacity.

Oil refining

Beyond the well, building oil refineries is one of the major infrastructure investments required for the global oil industry. However, global oil refining currently faces two seemingly contradictory structural problems. First, global refineries have averaged only 80–90 percent capacity utilisation over the last two decades. Clearly, system-wide overcapacity problems exist. Whether these can be addressed, however, depends on the balance between growing oil demand, particularly from China and India, and the extent to which these two states, along with a range of Middle Eastern countries, build their own oil refineries. It is altogether possible that a shift in the geographic location of global oil refining will occur to some extent. Western states, if they end up on the sharp end of mounting global overcapacity problems, may be forced to rationalise refining capacity.

Second, refining has long been identified as a serious bottleneck to the global oil industry. This contradiction is explained by the fact that there is a mismatch between the kinds of petroleum products most refineries are designed to produce, and the kinds of petroleum products the global marketplace requires. Refineries were historically designed to work with light, sweet crude oil that is now increasingly rare and expensive. Consequently, these refineries may lack the 'deep conversion capacity' necessary to sufficiently refine the now more common heavy crude into 'middle distillates'. Yet, it is in these middle distillates that the most significant global demand growth is taking place: in 2010, for example, diesel-fuelled cars constituted over 50 percent of the European passenger car market. This refinery capacity mismatch is a global problem, though it is particularly apparent in the USA.

Underinvestment in refineries can be explained by looking at the economics involved. For example, refinery profits depend on the price of refined oil relative to the price of crude oil. The cost of refinery operations is also a factor, but this has become a particular problem for refinery investors given the widespread underutilisation of refining capacity. Refineries are, in effect, missing out on economies of scale, and not delivering full returns on investment. Furthermore, as Chapter 3 detailed, the oil industry often features oligopolistic pricing practices, one of the historical consequences of which has been high crude oil prices, leaving very small margins in the refining phase. With growing climate change concerns refinery operations face further rising costs in meeting emissions regulations, while new competition from alternative energy sources, even in transportation systems, is also leaving its mark. However, there are some incentives for investment in new refining capability. As with any mineral exploitation, downstream processing can serve a number of economic functions. Reduced dependency on foreign refined imports can be an important step towards energy independence, and the benefits of economic diversification from the primary into the secondary sector can be enormous, including the creation of new high-skilled jobs, and support industries and services.

Oil refining remains an international process in large part due to the number of developing states which, while rich in oil reserves, lack the finance, political stability and/or technical skills to build, maintain and operate their own oil refineries, or which struggle to attract international investment into domestic refining capacity. The key example of this is Nigeria, which, as detailed in Chapter 6, has to import refined oil for its domestic economy despite being one of the world's foremost producers of crude. Oil refineries are expensive to build, and obviously there are economies of scale, such that it may not make financial sense for small states, on Africa's eastern seaboard for example, to invest in national refinery capacity in any case. Finally, it must be noted that the security concerns which surround energy infrastructure as a whole also apply to refining. Both state and non-state actors can pose a threat to refineries, and there is clear vulnerability of the world refining system to 'Acts of God': 21 percent of US refinery operations were shut down due to Hurricane Katrina (Yergin 2006).

Joint exploration and development

Disputes between states over mineral rights have historically presented serious problems for the oil industry, but here infrastructure building (in this case in the form of joint exploration and development projects) can provide a solution to these problems. According to Valencia (1986: 661):

> the success of joint development agreements is dependent on the given knowledge of actual deposits, good political relations, practical mindedness, and cooperative private companies.

Joint exploration can be a good strategy for states that dispute borders or maritime boundaries where oil and gas reserves may be present. By agreeing to jointly extract resources, mutual profits can be gained, inter-state relations stabilised, and perhaps most importantly, the risks (and costs) of such ventures can be shared. There are myriad such arrangements, and a range of different mechanisms for dealing with issues that occur with joint exploration and development agreements have been established as part of these arrangements. These mechanisms can be intricate, and processes of legal harmonisation between states can be very difficult: particularly if national legal systems are themselves insufficient either in their coverage of energy, corporate law, or contract law related issues, or in their ability to enforce legal decisions on key actors (Becker-Weinberg 2014: 139).

The Malaysia–Thailand Joint Development Area (JDA), managed since 1991 by the Malaysia–Thailand Joint Authority (MTJA), is one of the best examples of such strategies. Both states have made territorial claims over the Gulf of Thailand, and this may in other circumstances have been a cause for conflict between states. Yet, the route of cooperation was chosen – while

neither state has withdrawn its claims, they have engaged in mutual development and administration of the project, and since 2005 they have shared the
benefits of significant gas production. According to the MTJA website, this
authority assumes:

> all rights and responsibilities on behalf of the two Governments to explore
> and exploit the non-living natural resources, particularly petroleum, in this
> overlapping area.

Part of the area disputed between these two states is also claimed by Vietnam,
and a similar joint development strategy has been set out to also manage this
disagreement peaceably. Energy infrastructure, in this instance, both builds
upon and contributes to the regional peace that has existed since the formation
of ASEAN in the 1960s.

A more problematic example relates to the exploration of Lake Albert
between the Democratic Republic of Congo (DRC) and Uganda (see Litvinoff
2012). Lake Albert is Africa's seventh largest lake, and is important to local
agriculture and livelihoods, both in terms of its biodiversity and with regard
to the tourism industry. Oil extraction might threaten all three of these economic activities. Furthermore, although relations have in overall terms been
improving, the DRC–Uganda border has been a significant historical zone of
conflict, from Rwanda in the South to South Sudan in the North. Nevertheless,
oil exploration has been taking place since the 1990s, but with major finds
confirmed in 2006 and 2007 the question of whether, and how, to exploit Lake
Albert's oil resources has become more serious. Lack of transparency from
both sides, and political instability (particularly in DRC) have delayed oil
production significantly, while questions still remain about how any extracted
oil could reach coastal areas on a stable basis (Uganda being landlocked), so
as to enable export revenue to be derived from extraction. While political and
technical cooperation, similar to that of Malaysia and Thailand, is necessary
for full oil extraction processes to take place, mutual distrust between states,
lack of faith in agreements already reached, and fear on both sides of anti-
government forces operating in the Lake Albert region make this a difficult
prospect. There is also a concern that private companies are in Lake Albert to
reap super-profits without necessarily contributing to local community development, or taking appropriate care for sustainable practices. Lack of agreement and the possibility of escalating accusations of 'theft' of each other's
natural resources means that in this case the inability to reach joint agreements
on energy infrastructure could in fact drive conflict.

Regionalising/internationalising electricity

At the domestic level, energy infrastructure creates economic and political
questions that policy-makers must address. The electrification of the world is
increasing and the number of end-uses for electricity proliferating, not least due

to changing technologies in other sectors of the economy. Growing demand can cause energy costs to rise, but the costs of energy infrastructure increase also. The question of *how* to pay for new infrastructure requirements very quickly morphs into the question of *who* is going to foot the bill. However, in democracies with short-term election cycles, simply passing costs on to consumers can trigger considerable political backlashes, as Chapter 6 noted with regard to Indonesia. Furthermore, not all Western consumer markets are as tolerant of high prices as the Germans, as various fuel crises and protests in the UK, Australia and the USA demonstrate. Politicians in these countries have attempted to use climate change as a policy narrative to explain the necessity for rising energy bills, but this has been unpopular, and in Australia, disastrously so for the 2007–2013 Labor government. In the UK in 2011, it was widely reported in the media that nearly a quarter of households were 'fuel poor' (calculated as spending over 10 percent of their monthly income on heating and electricity). The difficulties for governments (and private companies) in managing price rises to cover necessary infrastructure investments in this context are clear. Impacts are felt particularly in cold winters, when deaths can escalate (often, but not always, in elderly segments of the population) if heating is unaffordable.

Change often takes place at a cost – financial, social and political. However, given the difficulties of meeting these costs, particularly in the post–2007 global crisis financial climate, the incentives to lower costs through more efficient energy systems are very strong. Electricity transmission has historically been seen as particularly sensitive to distance, with the increasing losses that have come with distance explaining the lack of international cooperation and coordination in the electricity sector. While it may be technically feasible to produce electricity in one continent and consume it another, it has never been economically justified. Now, however, building economies of scale in the electricity sector appears as a potential strategy for cost reduction, at least for small or middle-sized states. Electricity – which has tended not to feature strongly as a subject in international relations, in foreign policy strategies, or for international organisations (IGOs and NGOs) – is consequently becoming increasingly regionalised or internationalised in order to mitigate some of the risks involved in meeting energy system infrastructure needs.

Exporting electricity, as opposed to the fossil fuels from which energy is generated, is therefore a strategy used by states for several reasons. Small states in particular may find the gap between peak- and base-load energy too severe. They are forced to build extensive energy production capacity, at great expense, but are only able to use the electricity generated during peak demand times (morning and evening). The rest of the time, expensive energy infrastructure is redundant. However, as the European case shows, if small states can build cross-border energy infrastructure, and link grids with states that peak at slightly different times, then costs might be offset to some degree. This is partly why the EU drives towards EU-wide electricity grid structures, the economic benefits of which are derived from reductions in peak-load only electricity production.

A further reason for electricity exports is where states are struggling, perhaps due to relative economic weakness, to meet growing energy demand that neighbouring states can provide. Indeed, Russia, China and South Africa, surrounded by states that are struggling to build their own energy supply capacity, number among the world's top 15 electricity exporters. In the case of Mozambique, energy exports to Southern and East African countries in fact provide a significant share of overall GDP revenue, notwithstanding Mozambique's extremely low internal levels of electrification. The Southern African Power Pool (SAPP) to which both South Africa and Mozambique belong can be considered something of a success. However, SAPP has struggled with the move away from cooperation in power production to a regional competitive power market: short-term trading has increased, but most energy trade remains based on long-term bilateral contracts (ESMAP 2010: 4).

Managing electricity generation through export strategies can also become increasingly important as states move towards decarbonisation. As the percentage of energy produced from renewable sources grows, so production increasingly reflects variations in wind and sunlight, rather than variations in demand for electricity. This can create problems with meeting peak demand, but also problems with excess electricity or 'surplus production' at times when demand is low. As decarbonisation proceeds, states, particularly in Europe, increasingly seek to solve the logistical problems of their changing energy sectors through export strategies (see Lund and Muenster 2003). Denmark, which on average produced around 33 percent of its electricity through wind power in 2013, both imports and exports large quantities of electricity depending on demand variations and intermittent renewable energy supply.

Building energy supergrids

The economic feasibility of different modes of addressing energy needs can alter very rapidly in response to both technological change and political circumstance. Advancements in high-voltage direct current (HVDC) electric power transmission in the 2000s allowed for connections between European countries such as Northern Ireland and Scotland, France and the UK, Finland and Estonia, and Italy and Greece. There are plans to extend these interconnections to facilitate renewable electricity production, though difficulties associated with authorisation processes must be addressed. Indeed, given recent efficiency gains in renewable technologies, growing opportunity to bring renewables into the energy mix, and the ability of renewables to adapt to local contexts, supergrids may serve as a necessary infrastructure investment to facilitate a transition to low-carbon energy production. But despite this, it must be recognised that today only 3 percent of Europe's electricity travels across national borders.

The European Commission predicts that in the near future this will rise to 10 percent, but political efforts may be needed to make this prediction a reality. One key advocate of cross-border electricity infrastructure building in Europe is 'Friends of the Supergrid'. This conglomerate of companies and other organisations, with either an economic or political interest in enabling a low-carbon transition in Europe, seeks to link up offshore wind farms with onshore demand, as well as to increase electricity network connections between European countries. Whereas there are numerous examples of coordinated company lobbying and political influence in the energy industry, particularly in the oil, gas and nuclear sectors, this group seeks to present a renewable-based, large-scale alternative. However, in promoting a European supergrid, 'Friends' understand that it is necessary to move beyond national energy infrastructure investment planning, towards a European-wide strategy. This is, of course, in itself a difficult task.

Perhaps the most ambitious concept for generating cross-border electricity infrastructure is the Desertec Industrial Initiative (DII). Formed in 2009 as a private consortium of companies, Desertec proposes investing around €400 billion in concentrated solar power (CSP) plants in the Sahara Desert – producing cheap electricity across North African states as a result of leveraging the enormous solar generation capacity of this region. Electricity would then be delivered to the Middle East, North Africa and the European Union through HVDC power lines. Coming out of Germany, Desertec has received support from states and civil society, particular with regard to job creation prospects for North Africa and the potential for reduction in carbon emissions. This project is long-term in nature, and includes initiatives to promote new technologies and increase R&D investments through the Desertec University Network. Advances that have already occurred include the new hybrid solar and natural gas plant in Kuraymat, Egypt.

However, critics have identified numerous political problems, including (given the instability of the region) the vulnerability of the infrastructure to terrorism, sabotage or conflicts within or between North African states. There are also questions about whether these states would see any benefit from Desertec investments in terms of their own development, as despite their current electricity shortfalls, the proposed Desertec system would be controlled by private interests. Alternatively, state involvement by North African governments could create a potential 'energy weapon' against the EU, particularly if the latter becomes strongly dependent on electricity imports from the Maghreb and Mashrek regions. In economic terms, the danger is that such investments would quickly become obsolete, or surplus to requirements given Europe's domestic renewable energy supply growth. The project also rests on the creation of multi-continent supergrids at a time when decentralised energy solutions are gaining ground (Irving 2010).

Previous chapters also raised the problem of carbon 'lock-in' and the role of grid systems in facilitating this process. Obviously, this is one of the most serious problems that energy system infrastructure faces: enormous sunk costs in existing infrastructure that creates path dependency for further energy sector investments. It makes little financial sense to provide subsidies, say, to decentralised, renewable energy sources, when billions have already been invested in creating national (or international) grid systems. Yet, as costs fall for such generation technologies, and as climate change pressures mount, it is precisely the decentralisation of energy system infrastructure which may be required. Isolated or dispersed rural communities in developing states, furthermore, are more likely to achieve energy access through such strategies in any case. Continuing governmental focus on grid systems may mean electricity in key urban centres, but beyond this the costs may well be prohibitive. However, decentralised approaches also require decentralised systems of governance. While this may be a problem, given poor governance capacity in many parts of the world, it is also an opportunity, as the spill-overs of electricity access (see Chapter 6) may be supplemented from governance spill-overs also.

Electricity storage capacity

The shift to renewable energy also creates other problems that need to be addressed through energy infrastructure. Storage is a serious issue, both because of the growing disparity between peak demand and the results of increasingly variable generation capacity, and because energy storage has historically been a weak point in the energy system: it has always been more efficient to not produce unneeded energy than to store it for use later on. However, as wind and solar PV power generation in particular become increasingly prevalent in the energy mix, the issue becomes far more complex. Power storage becomes necessary for stabilising the energy system, but investment in this area has fallen behind in relation to investments in increasing the efficiency, or expanding the scope, of wind and solar power generation. Nevertheless, different storage technologies currently used include capacitors, flywheels, electrochemical batteries (including lead-acid, nickel-cadmium and lithium-ion), compressed air energy storage (CAES), superconducting magnetic energy storage (SMES), pumped hydro-electric, and thermal storage, which is commonly used in 'green buildings'.

The basic economic strategy used for energy storage is 'electric energy time-shift', which involves purchasing electricity when prices are low, storing electricity, and then selling on or using this electricity when prices are high. Obviously, storage efficiency is a key issue in determining the cost-effectiveness of any storage strategy (Eyer and Corey 2010). Some research suggests that for investments in power storage facilities to be commercially successful, they need to operate as adjuncts to and in cooperation with generation systems, rather than in competition with them (Roberts and McDowall 2005). However, in the case of the EU, this may go against the grain of competition policy, and perhaps reinforce the sense that strategic intervention by government in the energy sector may be necessary to supplement market activities. Of course, the more accelerated the renewable energy strategy, the greater problems there are with energy storage – particularly for Germany. Germany has recently responded to the storage crisis that solar and particularly wind investments have created by seeking to lower the costs of energy storage. Using a decentralised model, €50 million over two years was allocated to home energy storage capacity, beginning in May 2013. Storage also takes a prominent place in the country's national energy research programme. In any case, sufficient investment in electricity storage capacity may be required to support decarbonisation and/or supergrids that significantly rely on intermittent renewable technologies.

Conclusion

This chapter sought to explain the crucial role that transit and infrastructure play in the global energy challenge. It discussed sea-borne and network-based transit issues, notably with regard to choke points such as the Strait of Hormuz, and large-scale pipelines such as Keystone XL, Nord Stream and South Stream. It also assessed the security dimension of energy transit and infrastructure looking specifically at the Caspian Basin and the Persian Gulf. Finally, cross-border and cooperative infrastructure issues were addressed, notably with regard to the role of electricity networks and regional grids in the context of low-carbon energy transitions. The following chapter addresses the final missing piece of the puzzle for the trilemma of global energy challenges, particularly with regard to this low-carbon transition – the role of technology and innovation.

Chapter 9

Technology and Innovation

Energy technology innovation is widely regarded as a key element in addressing the global energy challenge. Novel technologies such as low-carbon appliances, demand-side response mechanisms, energy storage devices and renewable energy sources are expected to place the planet on a more sustainable pathway whilst providing the energy poor with access to crucial energy services. However, such a technological shift would be both shocking and transformative, both within energy systems and beyond (Rosenau 1990). As we saw in Chapter 2, the Industrial Revolution led to the spread of energy technologies which had an enormous impact on economic activity throughout the world – the steam engine being a clear example. Radical changes to human social organisation will also have unintended consequences. The environmental consequences of the global fossil fuel economy which resulted from the Industrial Revolution, for example, are only now becoming apparent. However, as scientific knowledge catches up with changing energy systems, we are far more informed about how different energy systems interact with ecosystems, and so how we can produce and use energy in more sustainable ways.

The purpose of this chapter is to focus on questions of technological innovation, and how processes of innovation relate to other societal structures. Following the socio-technical transitions literature, energy systems are understood in technical as well as social terms, in that they deliver economically important goods and interact with a range of important political concerns (see Markard et al. 2012). Indeed, it is crucial to view technology as the product of dynamic interactions with society. As Robert Cox puts it, technology is 'being shaped by social forces at least as much as it shapes these forces' (Cox 1987: 21). Consequently, we cannot sit around and wait for energy technology innovations to occur. It is necessary to actively generate structures for change, and for change of a more sustainable variety than that of previous transformations of energy systems. Understanding technological change, by extension, requires us to analyse the political and economic incentive structures that guide and structure innovation, as well as energy systems themselves. Indeed, energy is a crucial subject area for the study of innovation, as promoting technological change in this field has clearly generated problems that the dominant neo-liberal paradigm, with its preference for letting the market drive change, has struggled to provide answers to. Furthermore, energy technology is complicated – not simply in a technical sense, but also because of the interaction between different development, environmental and security-based drivers of change.

This chapter begins with an overview of different ways in which innovation is understood and conceptualised, and discusses the different ways innovation might build upon or disrupt existing energy systems. We then look at the role of the state in energy innovation in some detail, looking at different strategies states use to promote new technologies, and the benefits of these both for specific objectives, such as facilitating a low-carbon transition, and broader objectives such as improving international competiveness. Such strategies include public funding, leveraging research and development (R&D) investments, and capacity building in terms of regulation, governance and promoting network collaboration for innovation – in effect, enhancing national innovation systems. The chapter then turns to the global level, looking at the impact of the rise of knowledge economies, the significance of global financial and commodity markets (and the competition that takes place within them), and the impact of the global division of labour on how different states can integrate into the emerging global structures of energy technology innovation. Finally, the chapter looks in detail at energy technology in the context of developing states, and finishes up with a discussion of the role of technology transfer in solving energy-related problems pertaining to developing states.

Innovation and technology

Innovation can broadly be described as the introduction of a new process, device or method that somehow improves on previous ways of doing things. Following Schumpeter (1912), innovation can be divided into two basic forms: product innovation and process innovation. Taken together, products and processes can constitute entire systems. Both product and process are important in energy terms, not least with a view to fostering sustainable energy innovations (see Box 9.1). New energy management tools such as smart meters are matched by the increased efficiency of products such as household heating systems and small-scale electricity generators. Process innovations can completely change the carbon footprint of a product before it even reaches end-users. Consequently, while government policy and regulatory regimes have an important role to play in fostering innovation in energy technologies, private companies are also key players.

Energy innovation: Exogenous or endogenous?

Debates over innovation can be simplified into two basic approaches: neo-classical and neo-Schumpeterian. Neo-classical economics typically views technological change and innovation as *exogenous*; that is, as external to the economic system. In other words, it is usually assumed that there is a given rate of technological change. This assumption can lead to a *deterministic* view of technology as simply a function of the historical evolution of markets, and the incentives markets create for innovation (see Box 9.2). Furthermore,

Box 9.1 Examples of sustainable energy innovations

Sometimes it is hard to picture what is meant by an 'innovation'. Some countries (e.g. Denmark) and states (e.g. California) have a particularly strong record of energy-related product and process innovation. Here are some contemporary examples of potential innovative changes to energy systems, as compared to traditional (fossil) systems:

Traditional energy products	*Innovative energy products*
Gas central heating	Ground source heat pumps
Cars run on diesel/petrol	Cars run on electricity (with storage)
Electricity produced by coal/gas	Electricity produced by wind; solar; water/wave
Estimated meters for electricity	Meters that deliver regular data/smart meters

Traditional energy processes	*Innovative energy processes*
Companies that supply energy	Companies that provide demand reduction services
Centralised electricity production	Decentralised electricity production
Unresponsive transmission	Flexible transmission systems

energy and environmental regulations are deemed *transaction costs*. As the government imposes more and more such costs, this distorts the allocation of economic resources. The result is lower levels of economic wealth. Consequently, the greater the degree of regulation (or 'red tape'), the worse the economy will perform overall.

However, given the breadth and depth of energy challenges facing the world today, there may be good reasons to move away from the neo-classical approach. Attention might also be paid to the role of institutions, systems of governance and government policies upon the rate of innovation. In fact, these turn out to be critical, such that technological change and innovation can more accurately be seen as Schumpeter saw them: *endogenous*. This leads to very different policy measures in relation to technological change, particularly with regard to energy systems and environmental concerns. Energy innovation is now understood to reflect policy measures such as promoting energy R&D investment, social preferences for sustainable products, and regulatory measures that promote or discourage certain industrial processes. Indeed, historical evidence suggests that state policies played a crucial role in diffusing the benefits of energy technology innovations to

Box 9.2 Cornucopians and neo-Malthusians on innovation

Cornucopians (derived from the legendary ancient Greek 'Horn of Plenty') do not believe that resources will run out, and tend to put their faith in technological fixes. This is similar to the Prometheans discussed in Chapter 1, and is particularly evident with regard to environmental problems (see Friedrichs 2011). From the Cornucopian perspective, as long as science and technology continue to advance, so too economic growth can continue unabated. This is because new advances will, put simply, create new resources, and reduce the need for resources that are becoming scarce, expensive or environmentally problematic. This results in a 'reformist' agenda for addressing problems of energy and environment through technological change (Garner 2011). Mainstream conceptions of sustainable development, such as ecological modernisation, reflect this approach, which is also shared by a range of international organisations that lean more towards neo-classical or neo-liberal economic perspectives. Technology and innovation enable sustainable development, therefore, because they both reduce problems with environmental depletion, and promote economic growth.

Neo-Malthusians, by contrast, argue that there are insurmountable planetary environmental limits, and that logically this limits prospects for economic growth and our ability to exploit natural resources. Radical ecologists and environmentalists usually take such a position (Friedrichs 2011). This approach picks up on the work of famous liberal economists Thomas Malthus, who in *An Essay on the Principles of Population* (1798) argued that population growth would always outpace any increase in resource limitations. Neo-Malthusians tend to view technology as being a leading cause of environmental problems, and view the never-ending accumulation of 'technological fixes' promoted by Cornucopians as likely to make environmental problems worse. While such a perspective was common amongst environmentalists at the early UN Earth Summits in the 1970s, the rise of the sustainable development paradigm in the late 1980s has led many environmentalists to adopt the more reformist position of the Cornucopians that is currently dominant in international organisations (Bernstein 2001).

wider society, for example in the building of national electricity systems in many Western countries in the 20th century (see Perez 2002).

Furthermore, because neo-Schumpeterian economics recognises that innovation occurs in complex systems as a result of feedback loops, it is able to explain how endogenous factors such as regulations can promote innovation and entrepreneurship. Strong environmental regulations might drive heavily polluting businesses and industries out, and create incentives for greener industries and energy producers to emerge. However, heavy polluters can also adapt: through accelerated innovation, they can develop new technologies to meet stricter regulatory requirements. These new technologies then drive economic growth and profit making in the global economy. This, for neo-Schumpeterian economics, is harnessing 'creative destruction' so as to maximise the innovative drive which is at the heart of the economic system. In practical terms, the innovators have generated 'first mover advantage' for themselves, getting the jump on the competition in new technology markets, or creating new markets altogether.

The classic example of the innovative potential entailed in a confluence of social, political and economic incentives is Germany in the 1980s. While recognition of the problem of acid rain in Europe began in Scandinavia, it was the acid rain falling on the Black Forest (*Schwarzwald*) that created widespread political dissatisfaction in Germany after 1980. Emotive mass media campaigns against acid rain may well have overstated both the extent of the damage and potential future impacts: one programme in 1982 held that over half the forest had been destroyed, while in 1983 the damage from acid rain in Germany alone was estimated at US$250 million. Nevertheless, these claims had a significant impact on German politics, and part of the explanation for the entry of the German Green Party into the Bundestag in 1983 can be found here. Crucially, Germany introduced mandatory gas desulphurisation technology requirements for heavy industry as a result of the acid rain problem. German heavy industry protested fiercely about the requirements on the grounds that this would affect international competitiveness, but the political solution was to make these requirements mandatory across the European Community – as was achieved in December 1983. Indeed, a string of international sulphur conventions followed (see Newberry 1990; Menz and Seip 2004). Germany also became a key supporter of the 1979 international Convention on Long-Range Transboundary Air Pollution (LRTAP), a regime initially designed to lower sulphur dioxide (SO_2) and nitrous oxide (NO) emissions, which also came into effect in 1983.

While neo-classical economics predicts that increasing environmental regulations on heavy industry would be detrimental to economic activity, in practice German companies were able to adapt quickly with new technologies and innovations, reinforced by the existence of local entrepreneurs ready to test out new production patterns. Companies in other European countries followed, and further waves of environmental regulation on the EU level followed in the 1990s and 2000s. This has kick-started what is now the global environmental technologies market. Taken together, the global low-carbon technologies and environmental goods and services sector is already worth US$5 trillion annually, making it larger than the aerospace industry (UK Department for Business Innovation and Skills 2012).

It is obviously difficult to empirically demonstrate the link between government incentives and innovations in the absence of a counterfactual (Gagelmann and Frondel 2005). However, it has been argued that in the US the stringency of government regulation of sulphur emissions was also a key factor in driving innovation, as well as subsequent processes of knowledge diffusion (Rubin et al. 2004). More generally, the example of sulphur

---

Box 9.3 The role of crises in energy innovation: The 1970s oil shocks

It is quite common in both politics and economics to assume links between crisis and change. The oil crises of the 1970s, discussed at length in Chapter 3, led some states to employ radical strategies to change their energy system and reduce their dependency on oil. In the case of Japan, the UK and Germany a switch towards nuclear power took place. The success of this strategy in Germany and Japan in particular – both states with historically high levels of intervention in the economy – in part underpins the confidence of these states in once again restructuring their fuel mix in response to both the decarbonisation imperative and the 2011 Fukushima disaster.

Brazil, by contrast, shifted towards domestic ethanol manufacturing for car fuel, arguably both a product and process innovation. This domestic energy strategy was useful not only in terms of lowering pollution levels (and reducing greenhouse gas emissions) but also because it created work in the agricultural sector. In the 1980s as many as 80 percent of Brazilian cars were ethanol-based, although by the 1990s any price advantage had disappeared. Since 2003 Brazil has been pursuing a flexi-fuel strategy. Although the level of fuel efficiency is low, the flexi-fuel system allows consumers to adapt by switching to whatever fuel is market competitive at any point in time. Consequently, this is an energy technology adaptation well suited to the level of economic development in Brazil, which like many developing states struggles to insulate itself against global price fluctuations that affect different fuel sources (Juma and Yee-Cheong 2005: 81–2).

---

emissions impacting heavily on the environment and habitat points to the important role that crises can play in fostering innovation with regard to energy products and processes. Crises are seen to create new conditions within which profound market, policy, institutional and/or ideational change might occur (see Box 9.3).

Energy innovation: Disruptive or sequential?

It is important to distinguish between different types of innovation. From the viewpoint of path dependency (a concept usually used by historical institutionalists) innovation is likely to occur in a *sequential* manner. Also termed co-evolution, path dependency holds that the prospects for innovation are a reflection of existing values, patterns, rules, laws and institutional arrangements, and that resulting innovations tend to work by changing or adapting the existing system. Energy innovation, therefore, must be understood in relation to the larger socio-technical system that energy serves – economic sectors (e.g. transport), regulatory regimes (e.g. energy laws) and specific industries (e.g. coal mining or photovoltaic production). In terms of specific products, sequential innovation takes the form of a series of incremental enhancements, which leave the underlying technological framework unchanged (see Box 9.4). Regulations do their share in this context, as they can work to the benefit of existing economic interests, particularly if they increase entry costs into the market.

However, energy technology can also become 'locked-in' or embedded, proving resistant to change. This is not a problem per se, as sequential innovation can maintain economies of scale, reducing costs for both businesses and consumers. Overall production systems also become more resilient to external shocks. However, lock-in of obsolete technologies can in some instances cause serious difficulties. This is particularly evident with energy systems, where both fossil fuel energy sources and centralised grid system technologies for energy distribution demonstrate some characteristics of lock-in (see Unruh 2000). The core issue is that where radical change is needed, sequential innovation or path-dependent evolutionary change is insufficient. As previous chapters have discussed, this appears to be the case with regard to the global energy challenges posed by the imperatives of security, environment and development.

Box 9.4 Sequential innovation: Deep-sea drilling and shale oil

Since the first oil well was drilled in 1859, exploration and production of oil has tended to occur in 'easy access' locations such as Pennsylvania, USA or the south-western part of the former Persia. However, more recently we have seen a shift towards deep-water offshore projects such as Brazil's Libra fields, or in Arctic waters. The exploitation of conventional oil reserves has also expanded into unconventional sources such as Alberta's tar sands, or shale oil in North Dakota, and the IEA (2013) estimates that by 2035 nearly half of global oil production will be from unconventional sources. In meeting the technological challenges entailed in extracting unconventionals, the oil industry has without doubt been a major source of energy sector innovation. Nevertheless, these innovations were clearly sequential in nature, focusing on improving existing technologies and industry-wide efficiency levels, while maintaining the value chain as a whole. Clearly, the objective was not to change the underlying product itself (oil) or how it is used (in carbon-intensive energy production). The IEA (2013) estimates that to match demand growth, around US$10 trillion of energy investment will be made in the oil supply chain within the next 20 years. This will increase both sunk costs and the vested interests in existing (environmentally unsustainable) technological patterns, as well as perpetuating the tendency for sequential product innovation in the sector.

The example of acid rain, however, demonstrates an alternative possibility: that of *disruptive* innovation (Bower and Christensen 1995). Here, the concept of *punctuated equilibrium* is useful, as it points to the radical disjunctures and discontinuities that can go hand-in-hand with technological innovation and change (see Box 9.5). Non-linear/non-sequential shifts in industrial organisation are akin to Schumpeter's theory of 'creative destruction' (1942), in which existing technologies and methods of production give way to novel ones. Clearly, such a non-sequential shift creates heavy transaction costs, and the greater the sunken investment in now-dated products and processes, the greater the economic costs of innovation are going to be for particular companies, industries and states.

Radical change is particularly problematic given the strong incentives for states to ensure reliable energy supplies, and how this reliability hinges on the

Box 9.5 Disruptive innovation: Electric cars

Individual mobility has become a major driver of energy consumption, and is responsible for more than 50 percent of global oil consumption. The car industry is in fact one of the largest and fastest-growing sectors of the global economy. In China alone, the number of cars is expected to rise from around 60 million today to more than 400 million by 2035. The car industry's response to climate change concerns has been to focus on increasing fuel efficiency, often in response to regulatory measures enacted in Europe and the USA. This is a classic case of sequential innovation: even if a car runs 100 kilometres on a litre of (oil-based) fuel, it would still rely on a (then very efficient) combustion engine that produces carbon emissions. Electric cars (e-cars) by contrast would constitute a disruptive innovation, in that they are detached from the fossil-fuel based socio-technical regime that surrounds the traditional car industry. The technological challenges facing e-cars are significant, particularly in regard to the battery life (and hence the range of the vehicle), refuelling systems (there is a lack of necessary infrastructure), and the source of electricity (which could still be derived from fossil fuels). Nevertheless, the production of affordable, mass market e-cars is seen as an important step in fighting climate change.

Clearly, the company able to create the mass market first will be able to derive significant economies of scale from their first-mover advantage, and are likely to emerge as 'winners' in the race for innovation. Tesla, the California based e-car producing company, is moving from high-performance sports models towards production for the mass market. Mass-market e-cars may potentially supplant combustion engine technology, but they might also have a more far-reaching consequence: putting into question the existence of the entire oil industry. The existing car industry, however, may be able to survive and adapt, if it is also able to engage in radical innovation. The Toyota Prius might be a case in point here (see Nonaka and Peltokorpi 2006), as is BMW's recent move into the production of i-series e-cars.

existing energy structures and systems. The energy sector is almost unique amongst public policy areas in terms of its enormous cost base. Given the risk of leaving behind vast stranded assets, radical shifts in energy technology (for example away from carbon-intensive energy sources) must overcome the economic and political power of public and private vested interests. It is often argued that rapid technological advancement in low-carbon technologies creates widespread business opportunities, offsetting losses elsewhere. Yet, the possibility that a 'cleantech' explosion might completely sweep away established (fossil fuel–based) companies will lead vested interests to hold clear preferences for incremental technological change, which can be controlled more easily. Clearly, any shift away from a fossil-fuel dependent economic structure will fundamentally affect economic vested interests and normalised social practices, impacting upon social and political coalitions and the prospects for consensus building (Fouquet 2010). Consequently, in a field where the need for radical technological development is most pressing, a strategy of incremental and path-dependent change appears to be followed. Such a strategy limits the possibility of significant economic discontinuities and energy supply disruptions, but also limits the creation of radical products that could enable a low-carbon transition.

Business and energy innovation

For Schumpeter (1912), the concentration of economic power leads to increased levels of innovation. The energy sector certainly features large established companies, which are both highly profitable and face strong demand growth. However, they do not appear to be a good source of energy technology innovation (see Metcalfe 2006). Contemporary studies of innovation in fact point to a range of mitigating factors between large energy companies and the development of new technologies (see Damanpour and Aravind 2006: 44–50). The extremely high levels of capital intensity may severely limit the willingness of the energy sector's large players to take risks on innovation. Furthermore, energy is a high-tech industry featuring extensive degrees of automation. This creates a rigidity that makes process innovation problematic. The energy sector is therefore characterised by a range of strong vested interests and sunken costs, such that private energy companies, NOCs and state energy utilities can all effectively be cast as different species of immovable 'dinosaurs'. Nevertheless, significant energy transitions have taken places in the past, and both the oil shocks and the acid rain example demonstrate the crucial role that crises can play in determining whether radical technological change can break through the technological inertia of sequential innovation. The Fukushima disaster may prove to have similar effects.

To understand innovation we need to look beyond particular technological inventions. For innovation to take place, the new must prove to be workable: in effect, it must be widely diffused such that old technologies and processes are actually replaced. This requires that new technologies be proved efficient or profitable in competitive markets, or that they can otherwise receive strong state support while economies of scale or further technological advances are achieved (this is discussed further below). Product and process innovation therefore is largely determined after the fact (Metcalfe 1995). Once again, the setting wherein innovation occurs is critical. As suggested above, the large, dominant energy companies appear to be a poor setting for radical innovation (Junne 1997). However, it may be the case that small and medium-sized enterprises (SMEs) in the energy sector are engaged in radical innovation, and the crucial role that non-established energy companies have played in fostering low-carbon energy technologies is a case in point here. Radical technology disjunctures in energy may therefore emerge in the near future despite the sequential strategies used within the existing regime of international energy business and states.

Of course, SMEs in the energy sector have their own challenges to overcome. The high level of capital intensity in the energy sector favours incumbents, and serves as a barrier to entry for small players. Smaller companies may also face difficulties in raising capital, and the regulatory incentive structure that states have created in energy may not be suited for small entrepreneurial activity. New technologies may need to build economies of scale to reach their economic potential, and global market demand may simply be insufficient to allow this. This may further mitigate access to capital, and in fact discourage R&D investments. Technological development in the field of energy may also be particularly difficult, though there is no way to determine this without the power of hindsight. Alternatively, take-up of new technologies may be particularly low. Finally, radical technologies may be disadvantaged by subsidy regimes, such that even if they are more cost-effective than traditional fossil fuels, these continue to receive the lion's share of state financial support (IEA 2013). As a consequence, SMEs in the energy sector are likely to be far more dependent on the provision of infrastructure by the state, on the state's role in human capital formation, and on other aspects of state intervention.

The role of the state in energy innovation

Private companies play an important role in energy sector innovation, but realising the full potential of both product and process innovation, as well as ensuring the diffusion of resulting technological systems, may require state intervention (see Perez 2002). Public intervention and support for innovation is justified by two crucial observations. First, basic research will typically not be carried out by private companies because of the low chances of developing marketable products and recuperating costs. Second, new technologies run the risk of falling short of full commercialisation, either because of a lack of financial support or high entry barriers to the market. They may not make it through what has been termed the 'Valley of Death': the gap between the pre-commercial stage of a product and full commercialisation.

The Valley of Death problem

In order to foster energy innovation, it appears that the state must take on a number of functions. It is necessary to ensure that essential funding for basic research and development is available. Financial support for applied R&D and during the demonstration phase is also required – at least up until the point where the product develops a niche market. In fact, the pre-commercialisation phase can prove to be the trickiest part: public funding and support ('push') typically focuses on earlier stages, but private investors and market forces ('pull') may not yet be ready to risk investing in full commercialisation of the product. As with other high-skill, high-tech production areas, energy innovation is likely to be of high return – but it is also high risk. Indeed, non-technical barriers may be the most difficult to overcome. As the 'Valley of Death' problem in Figure 9.1 illustrates, the state needs to promote increased risk taking across the stages of innovation, ensuring that novel technologies successfully travel the distance from the research laboratory to large-scale industrial manufacturing for the global marketplace. Extensive cross-industry and cross-value chain collaboration can be useful in encouraging risk taking, but states also need to provide regulatory and financial incentives to encourage risk taking beyond the normal logic of the private sector.

The state, in essence, can share some of these risks with the private sector, which otherwise might seriously detract from investment. The state is also crucial for providing regulatory and governance functions that support energy technology innovation, and enable business start-ups to overcome the likely high costs of entry to the sector. The state therefore faces the complex task of coordinating research and development investment, and providing 'catalysts' for energy innovation, typically in the form of tax breaks and subsidies (see Box 9.6). Furthermore, the state needs to reduce transaction costs for collaboration and networking between energy companies and the

Figure 9.1   *The innovation process: From invention to market*

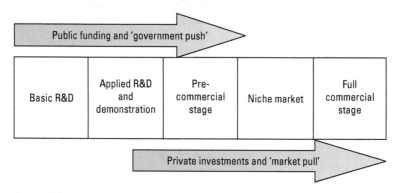

Source: Adapted from Grubb 2004; Bürer and Wüstenhagen 2009.

Box 9.6 Public policy and solar PV electricity generation in Germany

A clear example where state support has resulted in a technological break-through in energy markets is the German solar photovoltaic (PV) sector. Generous, guaranteed feed-in-tariffs over a period of several years attracted private investment into the nascent sector and helped reduce unit costs as companies 'learnt by doing'. According to Bloomberg New Energy Finance, average PV module prices dropped by 75 percent between 2009 and 2012 alone, and in many countries reached grid parity price levels (BNEF 2012). As a result, solar PVs reached full commercialisation quickly, and a sizeable industry developed, with the technology widely deployed in the German national electricity market. Smaller communities showed strong uptake of the technology, creating new supporters for renewables, and weakening the grip of the 'big four' energy companies in Germany. Today, Germany has more than 35 gigawatts (GW) of installed PV capacity, equivalent to six medium-sized nuclear power plants. Government regulation was used to ensure that PV-generated electricity had priority market access, while established coal and nuclear generators were prevented from leveraging the competitive advantage that followed from their market power and extensive capitalisation.

This example also illustrates the inter-connectedness of the global energy technology innovation and production process. While state support in Germany created the growing PV market, most production is now located in China, which has built an increasingly competitive industry on both state support and Western Europe's strong demand. Consequently, it is not necessarily national industry which is the beneficiary of state support. Of course, it can be argued that the German system of feed-in-tariffs – a policy now emulated in a number of other countries – in fact created a global public good in the form of rapidly falling costs for solar PV units. Consequently, this clean energy technology is now more affordable for everyone, including rural communities in developing states.

tertiary sector, which can serve as a hub for technology development. Finally, whether through direct investment or other means, the state must support human capital growth and technical skills development, as these underpin national prospects for energy innovation.

Energy innovation and national competitiveness

National economies are dynamic in nature, but this capacity to adapt to changing global market conditions is becoming increasingly critical to economic success. In turn, the nature of global economic change is towards 'knowledge economies', high-tech, computerised, scientific and network-based activities relating to the management of information (see Meeus and Hage 2006; Keating 2012b). The growth of these knowledge economies necessitates 'transitions management', wherein the state performs crucial coordination and networking functions, linking innovators, business and industries to researchers, universities and agents of scientific and technological development. This is the case in the energy sector as it is across the board for technology development. However, while energy innovations necessitate new forms of state intervention, they also contribute to the state capacity. In other words, the benefits of energy innovation go beyond the economic and environmental gains of particular technologies: energy innovation can, given widespread adoption, support international competitiveness, contribute to strengthening the national innovation system as a whole, and generate positive spill-overs towards other aspects of national knowledge economies.

Climate change is a strong driver of energy innovation and technology development. Though this has at times been perceived in terms of cost (for example in the USA's explanation for its refusal to sign the Kyoto Protocol), from a neo-Schumpeterian perspective, restructuring economies to foster a low-carbon transition can also be a strong driver of future competitiveness. State regulatory functions and strategies to facilitate this transition are therefore justified on both environmental and economic grounds. As noted above, states, companies and entire industries might be able to generate 'first-mover advantage' in new fields of technological development, setting standards for future sequential innovation, and thereby cementing a competitive edge in the market. For this, something of an energy technology ecosystem needs to be developed. This 'industrial ecology' would be characterised by more demonstrators, more collaboration, greater uptake of new technologies and practices, and smoother transitions from the R&D phase to the commercial exploitation of eco-products and process technologies. For example, industrial synergies offer greatly underutilised energy efficiency gains. Industrial centres tend to operate as an agglomeration of individual factories or plants, not just in economic terms, but in energy, water and transport terms also. Integrated transport systems, waste heat and other waste product recovery systems, energy flows and cross-plant energy storage facilities can all be critical to the low-carbon restructuring of geographical industrial areas. The state can play a crucial role in identifying, enabling and financing such processes.

The role of national energy innovation systems

The economic pressures resulting from the rise of knowledge economies and the environmental incentives to create industrial ecologies result in an integrated solution, in which states are required to strengthen and build upon existing 'national innovation systems' (NIS). NIS already underpin national economic competitiveness (Zysman 1996), and are clearly evident in the energy sector. Energy innovation in fact seems to be even more country-specific than other specialised high-tech areas. According to Vie (2012) this is because of the particular 'mode of knowledge production' used in energy innovation: transdisciplinary, application-based, institution-ally heterogeneous, reflexive, and likely to result from collaboration between multiple parties. The importance of national institutions, systems and regimes that promote innovation with regard to energy is partially explained by the high costs and high risks in this sector, which necessitates significant levels of social accountability. 'Competence building' with regard to research capac-ity, systems of governance and regulation, and opportunities for networking and collaboration is therefore a key issue for the state to manage in conjunc-tion with businesses and other actors.

The problem is that links between basic research and research organisa-tions and industry do not emerge spontaneously: networks and innovation clusters need to be developed and fostered, and incubation activities need to be supported. One common strategy used by state is to creation 'science parks' linked to universities, which then become central elements of 'idea-innovation chains' (Kline and Rosenberg 1986). A division of research labour can then result, in which private energy companies devolve primary research to the tertiary sector, so they can then focus on applied research based on the outputs from these research centres. In Germany, such a model has been followed in the energy sector (Mazzucato 2013). Bridging the public–private divide is crucial, however, and the state will need to both facilitate and enhance the market 'pull' of private finance into energy sector investment, as well as continuing to make public investment into scientific infrastructure and energy research organisations. Global investors, business 'Angels', and venture capital are of course more likely to be attracted to 'global' cities, which feature high levels of human and physical capital, and already existing strong international trade and financial linkages. Enabling local entrepreneurs, businesses and networks to emerge is also critical, and may also be easier in the context of large urban centres that can serve as regional or global 'hubs'.

More collaborative institutional structures *within* the tertiary educa-tion sector may also be critical for promoting radical energy innovation. In effect, the distinction between 'pure' research, 'applied' research and 'product-oriented' research may need to be dissolved completely, merging education and training with both research and research application. This requires the basic organisational structure of tertiary education to shift away from hard disciplinary boundaries and abstract knowledge, towards problem-driven interdisciplinarity. The US-based (and publicly funded) laboratories provide a working example of how successful interdisciplinary research can be organised. It may also be necessary for the state to create and support institutions tasked with the dissemination of energy research and new technologies, as well as with fostering the commercialisation of energy research (see Perez 2002). Strategies to increase the number of demonstrators, or to increase new technology uptake rates, may be more of a challenge than generating new technology and research in the first place (see Box 9.7).

Box 9.7 Accelerators: The US military industrial complex

One line of thought for promoting energy innovation is to link it to the military and defence sector. For example, the US Department of Defense (DoD) already spends US$10 billion a year on liquid fuels, and has been held responsible for 28 percent of all US greenhouse gas emissions (Alic et al. 2010). Simply transforming its own carbon footprint would be significant in terms of the global effort at decarbonisation. Furthermore, the DoD spends over US$100 billion per year on R&D. Given a remit to be a key customer for renewable energy technologies and a key investor for energy sector R&D, as well as strong targets for greenhouse gas emission reductions, the DoD could exercise a critical impact, as it did with the development and dissemination of information and communication technologies (see Mazzucato 2013).

The logic here is that it takes large players with both political and market impact to really accelerate innovation and change in the energy sector – a function that other forms of private finance, such as venture capital, are not keen on providing. Of course, innovation only begins with the new technologies resulting from R&D investment: as argued above, it is assisting these technologies towards full commercialisation that is the problem. Public procurement, although not an ideal replacement for market success, can serve to buy more time for energy innovations, and help the energy sector to create economies of scale for new technologies. Public sector procurement has in fact always been a key tool of statecraft, as the history of mercantilism demonstrates. However, with regard to energy innovation and defence spending, OECD countries have yet to catch on.

Energy innovation at the global level

As our discussion has shown, national innovation systems are essential in bringing forward novel technologies. The state has a key role to play in eliminating barriers to such technologies, and in ensuring funding for basic energy R&D. However, in a globalised economy, a global outlook on energy technology innovation is required. It is crucial that the products of energy innovation have access to the global marketplace, which provides a crucial testing ground. Export-oriented production strategies for innovative new energy technologies may be crucial, as protected national markets may not provide the competition, economies of scale or incentive structures necessary for technologies that can facilitate a global low-carbon transition. States need to come up with infant industry policies for the energy sector, enabling new energy industries, companies and technologies to participate in the booming global greentech/cleantech market.

The global marketplace also offers a potential avenue for capital investment, with globally integrated capital markets and other financial services potentially available to the energy sector. However, there is a lack of an internationally agreed upon set of rules, standards or governance arrangements for high-tech energy efficiency projects. There are also limitations to capital markets with regard to financing the SMEs that may prove crucial to energy innovation. The state may therefore need to act as a facilitator of private finance, or compensate through direct financing of energy sector R&D, or indeed do both. In any case, it is imperative that mechanisms enabling longer-term investment in energy product/process innovation are created, as private technology investment currently operates on a much shorter time horizon than is required. Building enhanced national innovation systems may break the technology barrier, but this may be the weakest of the factors preventing innovation. States need to address the incentive structures for innovation built into their own taxation regimes, for example. They must also look at the barriers to energy innovation that prevent the dissemination of new technologies beyond national borders. This means addressing the regulatory barriers and transaction costs created by different policy regimes, such as import/export controls, and promoting the international harmonisation of standards.

The support of pilot schemes for energy innovation may particularly benefit from thinking in global terms. For the state to assist in the development of radical, breakthrough technologies, it needs to take a role in building demonstrators for new technologies that might otherwise never leave the laboratory. Besides facilitating the international promotion of energy technologies, demonstration projects may also serve the dissemination of related novel secondary products and processes. Dissemination is not simply a question of state capacity either. If the state is to be in a position politically to provide this kind of function it will need electoral support over time to do so, or other forms of legitimacy to compensate in non-democratic states. Effectively new technologies need to be socially acceptable, and benefits need to accrue to broad sections of society or at least to key social coalitions, so that change is supported. Technology innovation is not a primarily technical problem. For new technologies to scale up and succeed populations need to directly benefit from them, or come to see the necessity of radical change in response to a social, environmental or economic crisis (Perez 2002).

However, the ability to generate energy-related research and disseminate cutting-edge technologies, and to compensate for the limitations of global financial service providers, is not simply a matter of state capacities and social interests or of transforming social norms. As the following section details, it is also evident that the nature of a state's integration into the pre-existing *global division of labour* (GDL) creates path dependency for their likely participation in the global energy economy and its specific research and development systems. In general terms, we can distinguish three phases in the process of production: research, design, engineering (phase 1); production, manufacturing (phase 2); and marketing, services and standard-generation (phase 3). Phases 1 and 3 primarily take place in advanced industrial economies: OECD countries. Phase 1 is both skill- and wage-intensive, which is a good enough reason in itself for OECD countries to want to focus on this aspect of the GDL. However, the early investment/R&D in phase 1 is also high-risk, such that the previous section outlined the range of different forms of state support that are apparently necessary. Nevertheless, the ownership of patents or other rights over technologies that reach the 'full commercial stage', and so diffuse widely and rapidly, are highly profitable.

As OECD countries continue to adapt to the rise of global knowledge economies, they increasingly specialise in phase 1 (and 3). Historical advantages gained from early industrialisation now enable de-industrialisation, and 'post-industrial' economies emerge. For example, the existence of large urban centres in OECD countries, with their advanced infrastructure and concentration of high-skill, high-wage citizens enables them to provide regional or global economic hubs that attract more such employees seeking work in phases 1 and 3 of the GDL. This further reinforces the advantages that OECD countries have in fostering energy technology innovation. Indeed, although patent counts are a limited way of measuring energy innovation, they reveal that between 2000 and 2005, only four countries accounted for 67 percent of all energy innovation: Japan, the USA, Germany and China. Renewable energy innovation is even more focused, with OECD countries accounting for 96 percent of all world patents in the same period. Of these, 65 percent were produced in Germany, Japan, the USA and France (Garrone et al. 2010).

Other measures of energy technology investment reveal similar results (IEA 2009), though the emerging BRICS economies are in several cases exceptions to this rule. Brazil comes in second in global biofuels investment, and Russia appears in or just out of the top ten on most indicators. China and India come in ninth and tenth on solar energy investment, and sixth and tenth on wind energy investment respectively. China has also made massive investments in electric vehicles, and both China and India have large carbon capture and storage technology R&D expenditures. Global public spending on energy technology innovation in 2009 was well over US$5 billion, with private sector investment massively exceeding public spending in some technology areas. Nevertheless, the IEA calculated that this amount was between US$30 and US$70 billion short of requirements.

In Europe in particular the concentration of economies on phases 1 and 3 of the GDL sees regional patterns of innovation emerge. Indeed, economies of scale in energy technology innovation may only be achievable for small European states on a regional (or global) scale. Cross-border research networks can therefore be critical (see Box 9.8). Where such energy innovation systems emerge, they are usually based on pre-existing scientific and technological exchange systems, and other forms of cross-country institutional linkages and structures of innovation collaboration (Garrone et al. 2010: 14). Of course, these primarily exist between OECD countries and their universities, research organisations and companies. It is the same case with other energy-innovation promoting measures that transcend state boundaries, including energy-related patent applications, international co-authorship

Box 9.8 Regional innovation strategies: The European Union

The EU sponsors regional networks such as the European Energy Research Alliance (EERA), which promotes collaboration between national energy research facilities. The EU also explicitly promotes public–private partnerships (PPP) as the centrepiece of its innovation strategy. Indeed, it aims to create synergies between PPPs and international, regional and national programmes for research and innovation (European Parliament and Council 2013: 108), not least with a view to environmental problems. The EU believes that PPPs will link energy innovation to broader industry policy and, through enhanced energy efficiency, accelerate a low-carbon transition. In effect, it is hoped that this innovation strategy will assist in decoupling Europe's industrial economies from carbon dependency. The EU therefore committed €1.6 billion between 2009 and 2012 alone – a figure matched by private sector investments, and characterised by the strong participation of SMEs (European Commission 2013). Again, this is justified on both environmental and economic grounds, as the EU believes that accelerated energy innovation and decarbonisation will strongly contribute to maintaining the EU's international competitiveness in a post-carbon era.

of energy-based research, energy-based R&D expenditures by domestic or foreign companies, and third party financing for energy technology research.

Intertwining national strategies for energy innovation with regional solutions may in fact be critical, as successfully pushing renewables into the energy mix by promoting decentralised energy systems may only trigger truly lasting innovation if it is embedded in a regional strategy. Furthermore, although greater demand-side flexibility will help address the disjunctures between peak- and base-load demand in national economies, ultimately this problem may be unsolvable on a local or national level. This problem is in fact currently exacerbated by new renewable energy sources, due to shortfalls in associated energy storage technologies. Integrating national strategies for overhauling the energy system therefore requires thinking in terms of regional coordination, for energy storage and beyond. Energy efficiency, for example, not only is the equivalent of 'low hanging fruit' in climate change mitigation, but also entails business opportunities and clear potential for energy innovation. The state can create secondary markets where clear opportunities for energy savings exist (e.g. in product and process waste streams), but again, economies of scale may only emerge on a regional level. Other regional measures include the standardisation of recycling practices and product life-cycle energy ratings, and the establishment of standard certification schemes (for example in building energy efficiency). Regional strategies to lower transaction costs that hamper innovation can also be more successful than international efforts, which can suffer from too many veto players.

Energy innovation and technology in developing states

Energy innovation also plays a crucial role in the context of developing states. On the one hand, energy technology innovation is a crucial factor for integrating these countries in the global division of labour. On the other, technology transfer is seen as a solution to a number of energy-related problems pertaining to developing states.

Energy technology and the global division of labour

To begin with, East and South East Asian states are integrated into the GDL primarily as sites for the industrial manufacturing (phase 2 of the GDL) of cheap products, which are then sold in global markets. These states offer a combination of political stability, a relatively highly skilled workforce, and structures of state support for foreign investors, as well as lower wages than in the EU or USA. They also benefit from regional processes of technology transfer (see below), as well as from regional hubs of expertise in finance, ICT and other key services. Consequently, this region also increasingly serves as a key centre of manufacturing for new energy technologies and energy-related industrial process innovations. The massive relocation of solar PV production to China is of course a case in point here. However, the fact that the Chinese government may be subsidising solar PV exports has led to debates in the EU over an appropriate response – in effect, the EU needs to decide whether its priority is cheap solar panels or the promotion of an indigenous European solar panel production industry. Meanwhile, the USA has already elected to protect its domestic solar industry by banning Chinese imports.

However, other developing states, particularly poor states in sub-Saharan Africa, find themselves excluded from the three phases of the global process of production altogether. Such states are of course still integrated into the global division of labour – but as producers of primary commodities, such as agricultural produce, or indeed the export of energy resources. Such states can be extremely vulnerable to fluctuations in global commodity markets and reliant on imports of secondary manufactures (industrial goods), and often lack the financial capital, physical capital and human capital that might underpin energy research and development. Nevertheless, sub-Saharan Africa's economic weaknesses (such as a lack of national electricity grids) and particular demographics (such as widely dispersed rural populations) can also create opportunities for energy technology development. This region could prove a crucial testing ground for a range of promising decentralised energy technologies, such as low-cost and small-scale solar power torches, distributed electricity generation using agricultural waste as feedstock, or solar-powered cook stoves that, as Chapter 6 detailed, can drastically improve the livelihoods of the rural poor.

States that are integrated into the GDL as producers of primary agricultural commodities also have the prospect of participating in one mass-scale energy phenomenon: the rise of biofuels. Strong demand growth for biomass-derived liquid fuels is evident in the West, in part as a response to climate change concerns. In the USA, biofuels constituted over 7 percent of total transport fuel consumption in 2012, while the EU set a 10 percent target for road and rail renewable energy sources by 2020, which strongly features biofuel use. As a corollary, global production rose from 9 million tonnes of oil equivalent (Mtoe) in 2000, to 60 Mtoe in 2012 (BP 2013). Biofuel production offers poor farmers a valuable cash-crop alternative, and developing states a strategy whereby they can directly benefit from climate change mitigation measures.

However, biofuel production in developing states entails obvious risks. Until second-generation biofuels emerge, replacing food production with biofuels could increase food insecurity – and there is some evidence from the USA and the EU that biofuel production has driven up food prices and increased commodity price volatility. There are obvious environmental risks that result from mono-cropping. In Indonesia, furthermore, the practice of clearing tropical rainforest to increase biofuel (palm oil) production actually increases carbon emissions, and there is little evidence that biofuel production is supporting sustainable rural livelihoods here. For poor developing states to benefit from biofuel production proper management and policies that target the needs of the poor are clearly needed (Bailey 2013). Once again, however, this simply shifts the problem to that of building necessary infrastructure, governance and regulatory conditions in the developing world. A similar problem arises with the use of animal waste biomass (dung) for electricity generation, whether through direct combustion, gasification or co-firing with traditional fossil fuels.

A shift towards decentralised energy systems in developing states might have other positive impacts, particularly in promoting sustainable rural livelihoods. As scholars have argued, small, environmentally benign power plants offer good prospects for reducing GHG emissions. Promising technologies in this respect include hydrogen fuel cells and gas-fuelled microturbines (Juma and Yee-Cheong 2005: 22), as well as technologies relying on locally available renewable energy sources. New economic opportunities for small-scale local energy providers would be created, who could tailor provision to specific local endowments of wind, solar, hydro or geothermal energy. Consequently, decentralised approaches, as well as being more financially affordable and leading to reductions in technical losses, could also increase the share of renewables in the local energy mix (Sims et al. 2007). This can also contribute to addressing problems of indoor and outdoor air pollution that increasingly threaten human development (see Chapter 6).

Energy technology transfer

Technology transfer is widely seen as a solution to a number of energy-related problems in developing states. However, adoption rates for new technologies in the developing world are low, and the dissemination and commercialisation of new energy technologies has also proven problematic. Indeed, it has been argued from the human development perspective that these low levels of technology transfer are causing 'capability deprivation' for households and businesses throughout the developing world (Cozzens and Kaplinsky 2009). Given that poor developing states in particular seem to benefit from new technologies only at a very late stage, they might do better to focus less on energy innovation per se, and more on solving the governmental and market failures that prevent the absorption, adaptation and diffusion of existing advanced energy technologies. If technology transfer could be accelerated, then even if national innovation systems in the developing world remained weak, such states could still see economic and environmental benefit from recent technological innovations. This, in turn, would increase the competitiveness of these states, contribute to sustainable economic diversification, and perhaps also strengthen domestic innovation capacity.

Various donor initiatives to facilitate energy technology transfer across all energy technologies can be identified. The IEA's Multilateral Technology Initiatives target both states and businesses in promoting both the development and dissemination of novel energy technologies. Bilateral donors such as GIZ or DfID directly support the COP-sponsored nationally appropriate mitigation actions (NAMAs), which seeks to shift both technologies and entire economic sectors onto a low-carbon trajectory. The USA's Unconventional Gas Technical Engagement Program (UGTEP) promotes the deployment of the fracking technology outside of the USA. However, technology transfer is an ongoing area of dispute between the developing world and OECD countries. Developing states want new technologies to be disseminated immediately, in order to help them 'tunnel through' the Environmental Kuznets curve (see Chapter 6, Figure 6.2). Yet the global economy operates through a system of patents and intellectual property rights. This ensures that the profits of new technologies go to inventers, patent holders, and holders of capital that can afford patents, thereby incentivising further innovation. Furthermore, it is not entirely clear whether states can indeed 'tunnel through', such that a strategy for the simultaneous promotion of rapid economic growth and a low-carbon transition is feasible in practice.

Certainly, capital-rich Chinese state-owned energy corporations have taken the opportunity to invest heavily in Western energy technology companies such as Nexen Inc., Chesapeake Energy and Devon Energy. The Chinese SOEs not only acquire these companies' assets, but also crucial skills and emerging technologies, increasing their own knowledge base and enhancing their international competitiveness. By contrast, poor developing states in particular lack both capital and technical capacity. The broad adoption and implementation of new technologies or international benchmarks and standards can be severely hamstrung in such states by extensive human and physical capital shortfalls. Indeed, the engineering, computing and technological know-how needed to manage new low-carbon energy technologies is arguably only just emerging in OECD countries. Developing states with the highest levels of absolute poverty also tend to have the lowest levels of tertiary graduates, innovation, and technology uptake. And while applications of nanotechnology in solar cells, hydrogen fuel cells, photovoltaic devices and semi-conductors, as well as other technological advances, could massively reduce the costs of alternative energy sources, particularly current solar possibilities (Juma and Yee-Cheong 2005: 73–4), this will clearly require significant technical capacity on the ground.

Consequently, increasing the levels of human capital in developing state economies is necessary to foster energy-related research, development, learning and technology adaptation, and may have the added advantage of increasing opportunities for poverty reduction. From a neo-liberal perspective, transparent, accountable, competent and effective states are most likely to be able to promote technology transfer and uptake. However, as Chapter 6 detailed, 'good governance' style solutions may be difficult to achieve in practice in developing states. Nevertheless, NGOs and local community developmental organisations in particular might be able to compensate for poor governance to some extent, if they themselves remain transparent and accountable. Furthermore, some lessons for weak states might be garnered from the national innovation systems (NIS) approach (see Keating 2012b). For example, it seems clear that where networks of cooperation between firms, researchers, NGOs, donors and practitioners can be fostered, active learning systems – a precondition for technology innovation and adaptation – can emerge. To promote technology transfer as a form of poverty reduction, however, it is necessary to ensure that innovations and practices are facilitating sustainable livelihoods for local communities. Crucially, localised and decentralised approaches to technology transfer, based on bottom-up design and adaptation, also create opportunities for mutual learning (learning-by-doing) as existing technologies and advanced knowledge and practices are integrated into local livelihoods and production structures. Forms of energy innovation can therefore follow from technology transfer.

However, the spectacular failure of several solar cookstove projects in the developing world drives the point home that energy technologies need to fit the socio-economic context within which they operate. Donor failure to grasp the conditions in which these stoves were used led to their rejection by the very people the technology was intended to serve. Furthermore, as the emphasis shifts away from the adoption of new technologies towards the 'appropriateness' of technologies and to intermediate technology solutions in the promotion of sustainable development, new questions emerge. For example, new-generation nuclear power plants such as 300 MW small modular reactors (SMRs) provide a cost-effective technological solution for energy access, but raise clear security concerns. These include both the possibility that nuclear weapons, dirty bombs, or nuclear facilities could fall into the hands of terrorists, and the technological problems that even advanced industrial countries struggle to manage (as demonstrated by Chernobyl and Fukushima).

Technology transfer is clearly not a silver bullet for energy and development concerns: it is a complex and difficult issue.

Conclusion

This final chapter sought to account for the role that technology and innovation play in driving change in the energy sector. As the discussion demonstrated, this is particularly significant for all three aspects of the trilemma of global energy challenges: environment, development and security. In detailing the risks and potential benefits of energy innovation, it becomes clearer why strategies to address one aspect of the trilemma can create problems for another aspect – and this is particularly the case with the prospects for disruptive technologies in the energy sector. Nevertheless, as national innovation systems (NIS) are closely linked to the manner in which states integrate into the global division of labour, state involvement in energy technology R&D is likely to be a strong feature of strategies to address global energy challenges in the future. Indeed, this is a part of the 'return of the state' in the energy sector, given critical reflections on the ability of the market to deliver social, economic and environmental imperatives in this field. In conclusion, we now reflect further on the future of global energy, and on the tensions and possible synergies between strategies to address the different aspects of the energy trilemma going forward.

Conclusion: Synergies, Conflicts and Energy Futures

Each chapter of this book has revealed a range of inter-connections, debates and unresolved puzzles within global energy production, trade and politics. From the study of global energy challenges, we have learnt a lot – not simply about energy, but also about broader global social, political and economic systems. Part of the explanation for all the complexity is the tendency for scholars and policy analysts to adhere to one or other energy *perspective*. There is a tendency to defend one's own view on energy issues, whether this is political, economic, environmental or technological in character (the four broad perspectives set out in Chapter 1). Yet, in practice, actors and institutions understand energy in multiple and conflicting ways. Indeed, analysis at the local, national, regional and global levels has revealed clear differences between actors in how energy objectives are determined and prioritised, and which methods are understood as most effective in meeting these objectives. Furthermore, with the realisation that the entire world energy system is in flux – in response to changing technologies, economic needs, environmental pressures and political priorities – arguments and debates in the field of global energy have become even more contested.

As this book has shown, recent decades have seen energy actors become increasingly interdependent. Energy agendas that were once disparate and only tangentially related have become increasingly intertwined and interconnected. For example, oil is now truly a global market, and while gas markets will not be globally integrated any time soon they are heading in that direction. Strong pushes for internationalisation have exposed all gas market participants to risks and externalities stemming from events such as political turmoil or natural disasters that previously seemed very remote. Furthermore, energy markets have themselves become subject to global financial markets. Oil and gas, and increasingly biofuels, are now subject to financial trading schemes of growing complexity – and even to outright market speculation. As a result, spillovers from developments in financial or commodity markets now represent an additional challenge to energy system stability. Other emerging challenges threaten to completely restructure these systems. Plans to significantly increase energy access in the developing world implies that a massive increase in energy generation is needed, while climate change mitigation implies massive decreases – or at least, massive decarbonisation. The magnitude of the funding required to fight these challenges has put them in rivalry with the more traditional supply security agenda, but it is not clear to what extent these multiple energy policy objectives are harmonious and self-reinforcing, or contradictory and likely to undermine one another's achievements.

Thinking about global energy challenges in terms of the inter-connectedness of issues raises new questions regarding how to govern global energy trade and investment, and how to generate effective and sustainable energy policies beyond the jurisdiction of the nation-state. However, some existing organisations have started to adapt to the changing global environment. The IEA, for instance, has expanded its scope of activities and now spends considerable resources on information gathering and dissemination. The IEA seeks to provide intellectual leadership in global energy analysis and advocates 'best practices' in areas that are clearly outside of its initial mandate, such as promoting sustainability and energy efficiency. OPEC, meanwhile, has lavishly re-launched its 40-year-old Fund for International Development, and now positions OFID as a vehicle to foster South–South partnerships and promote sustainable development. Other more specialised agencies, such as the state-sponsored IRENA, complements institutionalised IPPP arrangements such as REEEP and REN21 in encouraging renewable energy on a global scale.

Global energy systems certainly appear to be trending against both Western dominance and fossil fuel regimes. New interests, norms and regimes must increasingly be conceded to – but the overall effect is the dissolution and fragmentation of interests rather than the replacement of one constellation of power with a clear alternative. As this book has outlined, despite the increased political salience of global energy challenges, it is striking how fragmented and under-institutionalised the global energy governance architecture has remained. Few organisations are able to exert effective regulatory power beyond the level of the nation-state.

Energy governance, taken as a whole, seeks to address a *trilemma* of environment, development and security objectives: how to effect a low-carbon energy transition whilst maintaining security of supply (and demand); how to keep energy costs affordable; and how to provide greater energy access in developing states. Measures to address this energy trilemma, furthermore, face serious constraints. All necessary reforms and restructurings need to be achieved whilst maintaining levels of economic growth, and with as little disruption as possible to the rest of the economy. This concluding chapter, therefore, offers a final chance to reflect not simply on how energy sector inter-connections and complexities can be explained, but also on the synergies and conflicts between these different energy governance objectives.

Many governments and international organisations accept that this energy trilemma must be addressed, yet there are still debates over the relative importance of each of the objectives, and how policy measures should then be prioritised. In the past, government energy policies have certainly tended to emphasise one policy objective more or less to the exclusion of others. For example, during World War I and II, energy security trumped other energy concerns given the degree to which modern armed forces relied on oil, in particular, for their military technologies. In the post-war era, affordable, universal access to energy became the priority objective for many governments around the world. Even more saliently, there are debates concerning the relative significance of meeting specific energy trilemma objectives against achieving other social, political or economic objectives on the national agenda. Maintaining (or at least aiming for) high levels of economic growth is non-negotiable for most world governments. The fact is that strategies to meet energy trilemma objectives may, in practice, conflict with one another. If actions taken to ensure a more sustainable energy system jeopardise attempts at energy security and affordability, and vice versa, then even well-designed reforms may trigger political backlashes in broader context. This renders energy system reform strategies subject to difficult political choices, the problems of which can only be exacerbated in states with limited financial and administrative capacity.

However, a number of IGOs, regional institutions and national governments can now be seen to seriously consider how they might meet all the objectives of this energy trilemma simultaneously. Synergies between energy policy objectives demonstrably exist: energy security and climate change mitigation policies have been seen to go hand-in-hand in a number of cases. For example, energy efficiency improvements both reduce demand (including for energy imports which might increase energy security) and lower energy costs for households (thereby contributing to reductions in energy poverty). In the following section, therefore, synergies that can be achieved in addressing all three energy trilemma goals simultaneously are outlined, as well as circumstances under which trilemma goals come into conflict with one another.

Synergies and conflicts in addressing energy problems

Holistic thinking about the global energy challenge requires the recognition of both synergies and potential conflicts between different energy policy goals. Three particular issue areas appear to be key testing grounds for the balance of synergies and conflicts: a renewed focus on 'energy independence'; the emergence of 'climate security' on policy agendas; and issues of equity and energy poverty both in the developed and the developing world. Each is here dealt with in turn.

'Energy independence' and its consequences

One increasingly popular method of encouraging energy security is to focus on national (and sometimes regional) energy independence. While this approach largely reflects realist or mercantilist perspectives, it can also constitute a response to the unreliability of certain energy partners in a global market setting. Indeed, for several states that embraced the neo-liberal economic perspective (including the US, the UK and New Zealand), this did not preclude increased efforts to promote domestic energy production to counter concerns about imports from unreliable producers. Interest in energy independence is likely to become more prevalent at times of heightened international tensions or crises in international energy markets. The Russia–Ukraine gas transit disputes of 2006 and 2009 are a good example of both of these – causing energy market instability while directly affecting European Union gas imports. The currently ongoing Russia–Ukraine crisis will likely have similar effects. The promotion of energy independence (or 'home grown' energy) has also served as a useful rhetorical device for interests groups keen to promote particular forms of energy production. Both nuclear and renewable energy, for example, can be portrayed as low-carbon as well as domestic in character.

Alternatively, energy independence can be seen as a threat to energy security. Experts in energy systems security analysis, for example, are quick to point out that energy system failures occur just as often in domestic energy systems as they do in regionalised or internationalised ones. Severe weather conditions, human error, lack of capacity, or problems in economic areas related to energy production (such as transport) are problems that could occur anywhere. Independence, therefore, will not solve security problems – while increased inter-connectivity makes energy system failures in particular states less catastrophic in impact. In other words, energy independence can increase energy sector insecurity.

Furthermore, overemphasising domestic production often leads to continuing national support (including forms of economic support) for *all* forms of domestic energy production. In other words, concerns with energy independence can lead to the promotion of fossil fuels. Indeed, energy supply security arguments have been used in a number of cases to justify fast-tracking shale gas exploration and production, as well as tax breaks and subsidies for new oil and gas production in countries that have indigenous supplies. The global costs of fossil fuel subsidies in fact rose dramatically, from US$311 billion in 2009 to US$544 billion in 2012. As noted before, fossil fuel subsidies continue to massively outstrip state economic support for renewable energy (IEA 2013: 3). This is an enormously significant pot of government investment money that could be used to support new low-carbon and high-efficiency energy technologies. Instead, they fuel the resistance of existing energy systems to a transition towards sustainability. Energy security, therefore, in some contexts at least, is in direct conflict with climate change mitigation objectives.

Climate change and energy security

Despite growing concern with energy security, governments have thus far failed strikingly to address the security consequences of either climate change or any low-carbon transition. Debates over 'security and climate change' have focused instead on two issues. The first is the view that climate change, by driving resource scarcity, will cause conflict. Some analysts argue that some conflicts, like that in Darfur, are already in essence resource conflicts. The second is the prospect that climate change will lead to growing numbers of environmental refugees. Questions are asked about whether climate refugees should have, for example, the same legal rights as political refugees. But the security problems caused by climate change may well be much broader than these envisaged (and rather traditional) external security threats. The growth of disease vectors is already a problem many states are facing; and in recent years a numbers of states have been required to turn their armed forces inwards, to deal with the consequences of domestic weather events such as floods and storms.

Comprehensive energy security cannot now be conceived in terms of an illusory independence from imports. Climate change re-opens the whole issue of how 'security' can be defined and understood, in a context where a number of European ministries now openly talk of 'climate security'. The UK Foreign Office, for example, has created a new post to assess the implications of climate change for national security policy. A 2008 EU paper on security and climate change, furthermore, recognised that climate change could act as a 'threat multiplier' (Council of the European Union 2008a). Yet, this paper also acknowledged that EU had not, either at the national or regional level, addressed the security or foreign policy implications of climate change as a magnifier of conflict, migration, border disputes and/or radicalisation.

The December 2008 five-year update of the European Security Strategy certainly emphasises the links between climate change and security more than the original 2003 strategy did, and calls for EU security and climate change policies to 'talk to each other' on a far more integrated basis (Council of the European Union 2003; 2008b). However, diplomats within the EU express frustration that so little has been done in practice since 2008 to give substance to this demand. Little scenario planning has been incorporated into strategic decision-making regarding exactly what types of conflicts climate change is likely to produce, and just how severe they will be. European foreign policy, in effect, carries on as normal: no tangible adaptation or preparation can be discerned to what the EU itself has recognised as a geopolitical time-bomb in climate change. Furthermore, outside of the EU, governments, regional bodies and international institutions have in general done even less to help conceptualise climate security, or to produce concrete measures to address it.

While there are certainly synergies between energy security and a low-carbon transition, it would be naive to believe that the complicated entanglements of international energy security will simply dissipate in the face of such a transition – so they do not need to be addressed. To take the view that 'loft insulation is foreign policy', in other words, could be a serious mistake. The politics of climate change will in practice usher in a whole new structure of global interdependencies and difficult strategic balancing acts. Moreover, energy security and low-carbon transition conflicts are just as evident as any synergies. A number of European governments, for example, have enthusiastically embraced emerging energy sources such as tar sands and oil shales.

These are attractive on strategic grounds by virtue of the fact that they can be sourced from suppliers friendly to the West, but they are in carbon terms clearly 'dirty' energy sources. Climate change mitigation strategies for energy security and traditional security of supply concerns therefore still evince considerable tensions – and which side of this quandary of competing security threats states will fall on remains unclear.

Development, energy poverty, and equity issues

Most developing states maintain that they have a right to promote development, even if this means replicating the carbon-intensive energy use patterns that Western countries relied on during their own development processes. Western states are in no position to tell large developing states like China and India that their over 2.6 billion citizens do not have the right to drive the same cars and purchase the same consumer goods that underpin Western lifestyles. Yet the climate change implications of this, were it to happen, would be catastrophic. The principal hope, therefore, is that developing states can 'skip' the carbon-intensive phase of development that characterised previous historical examples (see for example Chapter 6, Figure 6.2).

For this to happen, knowledge, innovation and learning with regard to the production of sustainable energy must rapidly emerge – quickly enough to meet the projected energy demand growth of these and other emerging economies. It is imperative therefore that Western countries, in their own self-interest, develop energy systems that are socially, economically and environmentally sustainable in the first instance to serve as models for developing states. Given that such energy systems would almost certainly rest on new technologies, 'technology transfer' could be facilitated so that it might be possible to achieve, for the first time in history, state strategies that can simultaneously promote both rapid development and a low-carbon transition. However, for this to occur, the current pace of investment in renewable technology and research and development in the West will have to rise significantly.

There are some grounds for encouragement regarding climate change mitigation strategies in the developing world: of the 118 countries that currently have renewable energy targets in place, more than half are developing states. However, whether there are synergies between a low-carbon transition in developing states and the policy goal of massively increasing access to energy for the world's poorest people remains to be established. Certainly, as things stand it appears that for many developing states the dominant strategy for addressing energy poverty is through expanding traditional energy sources – for example through massive roll-outs of low-tech coal-fired power stations for which energy resources are cheap and readily available.

In developed countries where domestic energy policy is an acknowledged political issue, there is growing concern about how the costs and benefits of a sustainable energy transition are to be distributed. This is partly because the costs of supporting new technologies, and of transmission and distribution system redesign, are directly passed on to consumers. Such a strategy does not always ensure socio-economic equity. Indeed, in both the UK and Germany large industrial consumers pay the least for electricity – while less well-off households pay substantially more per kilowatt-hour (KwH) (Which 2013). Furthermore, strategies to increase car engine efficiency by financially penalising older model cars will tend to disproportionately impact on lower socio-economic groups. Promoting a low-carbon transition can also put pressure on energy prices. But given that reducing energy poverty is also an objective of energy policy, a conflict between competing energy objectives clearly exists, and must be resolved. Indeed, facing the threat of a political backlash against escalating electricity prices, the UK government has recently scaled back its energy efficiency policies.

Energy futures and scenarios

In part due to the recognition of synergies and conflicts in facing the energy trilemma, new strategies of conceptualisation and planning for energy systems transition are emerging in both private and public sector settings. They involve attempts to predict likely pathways of change over set time periods. The significance of this approach reflects the widespread assumption that the extent to which our production, transportation and energy consumption patterns need to be transformed may be quite radical. Such strategies infer a common perception that energy systems will be very different in the future. However, they also infer a common perception that the rapid and profound – read disruptive – nature of these changes will create great uncertainty. And uncertainty is not something that governments, companies, markets or indeed ordinary people are particularly fond of. As in the ancient Chinese curse, we live in 'interesting times'. Nevertheless, this uncertainty has cast doubt on the veracity of forecasting using traditional models, as a result of which many organisations are moving to what might be termed *scenario planning* in order to outline the main pathways to the most likely energy futures.

Energy analysts and scholars have also been prepared to make predictions about the future despite the high levels of uncertainty. They are, however, less interested in setting out different scenarios than in being forthright about a particular vision of the energy future. These can range from positive analyses, suggesting that the changes required will be possible by altering existing institutions and practices, to far more apocalyptic visions – such as those put forward by climate change *catastrophists* (see Monbiot 2007).

One such vision, sitting somewhere in the middle of this spectrum, is put forward by Michael Klare in *Rising Powers, Shrinking Planet* (2008). Klare's analysis is informed by geopolitics with a focus on power, international relations and conflict – interestingly, however, his rather conflict-ridden vision of the future is presented as a call for action today. The picture he paints is one in which nation-states, particularly the large-scale consumers of fossil fuel energy, become locked in conflict over access to dwindling resources. As with realist political perspectives, the production and consumption of natural resources is viewed by Klare as a zero-sum game. In this 'new international energy order', if one company or state gains, it is at the direct expense of its rivals.

When we see global energy challenges through Klare's eyes, the threat of climate change combines with the changing geopolitics of fossil fuel production to create rather dystopian future prospects. In this future, the establishment or maintenance of accepted world rules and norms for energy trade is highly unlikely, as are structures of multilateral cooperation between states. Rather, world governments will increasingly come into conflict over access to energy resources. In effect, climate change and heightened geopolitical pressures are undermining the post-war achievements (however limited these might be) of the liberal political and economic perspectives. One hopes, of course, that readers do not jump from scepticism about the seriousness of global energy challenges straight to fatalism – the view that it is too late to prevent Klare's new international energy order from unfolding.

Government and private sector scenarios tend to be more open. For government, developing a range of different futures that depend on key policy choices enables the recognition of the continuing central impact of government decision-making in terms of energy policy. It also allows them to highlight the advantages of their own particular policy choices against alternative policy pathways. These might blend different mixes of mechanisms to achieve a low-carbon transition; for example, certain levels of investment in renewable energy, against the promotion of demand reduction measures (such as energy efficiency targets). In each pathway, decisions need to be made not just at the 'big picture' level, but also within specific sub-sectors of energy systems: generation, transmission and distribution; transportation; and the regulation of end-use efficiency for cars, houses and a range of different consumer goods. A user-friendly example of this 'pathways' approach to scenario planning is the UK Department for Energy and Climate Change 2050 Pathway Calculator (DECC 2013).

Some of the most interesting scenario planning exercises are being conducted by the private sector. One of the most intensive of these projects is Shell's (2008) *Shell Energy Scenarios to 2050*, designed specifically to help both government and businesses think about the future of energy. Shell found that the various different scenarios that they worked on tended to converge into one or other of two very different models of energy futures. Consequently, this document compares and contrasts this pair of visions of the future, which were given the rather telling titles of 'Scramble' and 'Blueprints'. We are here offered clear visions of an energy future, and invited to choose between them. Scramble refers to the scramble for resources. Under the Scramble scenario, national policy-makers and corporate actors pay too little attention to energy efficiency and to reducing carbon intensity. Eventually, a string of crises caused by a combination of supply shocks and climate shocks force action to be taken – by which point energy system and climate stabilisation comes with severe long-term costs.

Blueprints, by contrast is more optimistic, a scenario through which the trilemma of energy challenges is addressed far sooner, and where the worst consequences of the Scramble scenario are avoided. Yet, at the same time, Blueprints is very different from 'pathways' type scenarios in which governments play a key role in promoting energy systems change. Blueprints is characterised by localised, decentralised climate action – NGOs, social movements, innovative companies and technology entrepreneurs are the key actors. Organised politics at the global, regional and national level can only be galvanised into action once broad social support for significant policy change already exists. In essence, political systems follow social and economic systems, rather than leading on them. Blueprints, therefore, is a more optimistic scenario that still remains deeply pessimistic about the prospects for political leadership on environmental issues. Yet, this scenario predicts a very strong role for cities as political units. This implies that strong political leadership will in fact be crucial, but that the location of this leadership will be changed; in fact, it will be localised and decentralised. In essence, small-scale localised responses accumulate until something of a 'qualitative leap' takes place. The obvious inference of this document is that with clear, positive action, even simply at the localised level, citizens and businesses can contribute to a more healthy future – and not just for those people directly involved in energy industries. It is, after all, possible to end this dissection of the global energy challenges that we all face on something of an optimistic note.

References

Agora (2013). '12 Insights on Germany's Energiewende', an Agora Insights Discussion Paper', February 2013. Available at: http://www.agora-energiewende .org/fileadmin/downloads/publikationen/Impulse/12_Thesen/Agora_12_Insights_ on_Germanys_Energiewende_web.pdf (Last Accessed 29 April 2015).

Alic, J., Sarewitz, D., Weiss, C. and Binvillian, W. (2010). 'A New Strategy for Energy Innovation', *Nature* 466: 316–7.

An Inconvenient Truth (2006). Directed by Davis Guggenheim, Performed by Al Gore. USA: Paramount Classics.

Anderson, T.L. and Leal, D.R. (1991). *Free Market Environmentalism*. Colorado and Oxford: Westview Press.

ARUP Foresight (2014). Drivers of Change: Energy. Available at: http://www .driversofchange.com/energy/ (Last Accessed 29 April 2015).

Auty, R. (1993). *Sustaining Development in Mineral Economies: The Resource Curse Thesis*. New York: Oxford University Press.

Bahgat, G. (2013). *Alternative Energy in the Middle East*. Basingstoke and New York: Palgrave Macmillan.

Bailey, R. (2013). 'The "Food versus Fuel" Nexus', in Goldthau, A. (ed.), *Handbook of Global Energy Policy*. London: Wiley Blackwell.

Balke, N.S., Brown, S.P.A. and Yücel, M.K. (1999). 'Oil Price Shocks and the U.S. Economy: Where Does the Asymmetry Originate?', Dallas, TX: Federal Reserve Bank of Dallas.

Bayart, J.F. (1993). *The State in Africa: The Politics of the Belly*. London: Longman Publishing Group.

Bazilian, M. *et al.* (2010). 'More Heat and Light', *Energy Policy* 38: 5409–12.

Becker-Weinberg, V. (2014). *Joint Development of Hydrocarbon Deposits in the Law of the Sea*. Heidelberg: Springer.

Behn, D. and Pogoretskyy, V. (2012). 'Tensions between the Liberalist and Statist Approaches to Energy Trade: the Case of Gas Dual Pricing', in Kuzemko, C. *et al.* (eds.), *Dynamics of Energy Governance in Europe and Russia*. London: Palgrave Macmillan.

Bernstein, E. (1899). *The Preconditions of Socialism*. 2002 edition. Cambridge: Cambridge University Press.

Bernstein, S. (2001). *The Compromise of Liberal Environmentalism*. New York: Columbia University Press.

BNEF (2012). *Global Trends in Renewable Energy Investment 2012*. Frankfurt am Main: UNEP Collaborating Centre, Frankfurt School of Finance & Management.

Bower, J.L. and Christensen, C.M. (1995). 'Disruptive Technologies: Catching the Wave', *Harvard Business Review* 73: 45–53.

BP (2013). *Statistical Review of World Energy*. London: British Petroleum.

Bürer, M.J. and Wüstenhagen, R. (2009). 'Which Renewable Energy Policy Is a Venture Capitalist's Best Friend? Empirical Evidence from a Survey of International Cleantech Investors', *Energy Policy* 37: 4997–5006.

Burnell, P. (2012). 'Democracy, Democratization and Climate Change: Complex Relationships', *Democratization* 19(5): 813–42.

Buzan, B., Waever, O. and de Wilde, J. (1998). *Security: A New Framework for Analysis*. Boulder, CO: Lynne Rienner Publishers.

Carmody, P. (2011). *The New Scramble for Africa*. Cambridge: Polity.

Carson, R. (1962). *Silent Spring*. Boston: Houghton Mifflin.

Carter, N. (2010). 'Climate Change and the Politics of the Global Environment', in Beeson, M. and Bisley, N. (eds.), *Issues in 21st Century World Politics*. Basingstoke and New York: Palgrave Macmillan.

CDIAC (2015). 'Fossil Fuel CO_2 Emissions: 2010 estimates'. Carbon Dioxide Information Analysis Centre (CDIAC), US Department of Energy (DOE). Available at: http://cdiac.ornl.gov/trends/emis/top2010.cap (Last Accessed 29 April 2015).

Cecelski, E. *et al.* (2005). *Rural Electrification in Tunisia: National Commitment, Efficient Implementation, and Sound Finances*. Washington, DC: ESMAP.

Cherp, A., Adeola, A., Goldthau, A., Hughes, L., Jansen, J., Jewell, J., Olshanskaya, M., Soares de Oliveira, R., Sovacool, B. and Vakulenko, S. (2012). 'Energy and Security', in Gomez-Echeverri, L. *et al.* (eds.), *Global Energy Assessment: Toward a More Sustainable Future*. Cambridge and New York: Cambridge University Press.

Cherp, A. and Jewell, J. (2011). 'Measuring Energy Security: From Universal Indicators to Contextualised Frameworks', in Sovacool, B. (ed.), *The Routledge Handbook of Energy Security*. London and New York: Routledge.

Cipolla, C.M. (1964). *The Economic History of World Population*. Middlesex: Penguin Books.

Ciuta, F. (2010). 'Conceptual Notes on Energy Security: Total or Banal Security?', *Security Dialogue* 41(2): 123–44.

Claes, D.H. (2001). *The Politics of Oil-Producer Cooperation*. Boulder, CO: Westview Press.

Clean Technica (2013). 'Plunging Cost of Solar PV (Graphs)'. Available at: http://cleantechnica.com/2013/03/07/plunging-cost-of-solar-pv-graphs/ (Last Accessed 29 April 2015).

Cohen, B.J. (2008). *International Political Economy: An Intellectual History*. Princeton: Princeton University Press.

Colgan, J. (2014). 'The Emperor Has No Clothes: The Limits of OPEC in the Global Oil Market', *International Organization* 68(3): 599–632.

Collier, P. and Hoeffler, A. (2005). 'Resource Rents, Governance, and Conflict', *Journal of Conflict Resolution* 49(4): 625–33.

Connelly, J. and Smith, G. (1999). *Politics and the Environment: From Theory to Practice*. Abingdon, Oxford: Psychology Press.

Council of the European Union (2003). *A Secure Europe in a Better World: European Security Strategy*. Brussels, 12 December.

Council of the European Union (2008a). *Climate Change and International Security: Paper from the High Representative and the European Commission to the European Council*. S113/08. Brussels, 14 March.

Council of the European Union (2008b). *Report on the Implementation of the European Security Strategy: Providing Security in a Changing World*. S407/08. Brussels, 11 December.

Cox, R. (1987). *Production, Power and World Order: Social Forces in the Making of History*. New York: Columbia University Press.

Cozzens, S.E. and Kaplinsky, R. (2009). 'Innovation, Poverty and Inequality: Cause, Coincidence, or Co-Evolution?', in Lundvall, B-A. *et al.* (eds.), *Handbook of Innovation Systems and Development Countries: Building Domestic Capabilities in a Global Setting*. Gloucestershire: Edward Elgar.

Crane, K. *et al.* (2009). *Imported Oil and U.S. National Security*. Washington, DC: RAND Corporation.

Daly, H. (1973). *Towards a Steady State Economy*. San Francisco: W.H. Freeman & Co.

Damanpour, F. and Aravind, D. (2006). 'Product and Process Innovations: A Review of Organisational and Environmental Determinants', in Hage, J. and Meeus, M. (eds.), *Innovation, Science and Institutional Change*. Oxford: Oxford University Press.

DECC (2013). https://www.gov.uk/2050-pathways-analysis (Last Accessed 29 April 2015).

Dobbs, R., Pohl, H., Lin, D-Y., Mischke, J., Garemo, N., Hexter, J., Matzinger, S., Palter, R. and Nanavatty, R. (2013). *Infrastructure Productivity: How to Save $1 Trillion a Year*. McKinsey Global Institute.

Dolowitz, D. and Marsh, D. (2000). 'Learning from Abroad: The Role of Policy Transfer in Contemporary Policy-Making', *Governance* 13(1): 5–24.

Downs, A. (1972). 'Up and Down with Ecology: The Issue Attention Cycle', *Public Interest* 28(1): 38–50.

European Commission (EC) (2013). *Communication: Energy Technologies and Innovation*. [COM(21013) 253 final]. Brussels.

EEA (2014) 'Homes Responsible for One Quarter of European Greenhouse Gas Emissions from Energy'. Available at: http://www.eea.europa.eu/highlights/homes-responsible-for-one-quarter (Last Accessed 29 April 2015).

EIA (2012). *World Oil Transit Chokepoints*. Washington, DC: EIA.

El-Khattam, W. *et al.* (2013). 'Establishing a Regional Mediterranean Electricity Market: Assessment and Strategy', *European Energy Journal* 3(1): 58–74.

ESMAP (2010). *The Potential of Regional Power Integration: South African Power Pool (SAPP) Transmission and Trading Case Study*. London: Economic Consulting Associates (ECA), submitted to ESMAP October 2009. ESMAP Briefing Note 004/10.

European Commission (EC) (2010). 'Consolidated Version of the Treaty on the Functioning of the European Union', *Official Journal of the European Union, 30.3.2010/C 82/49*.

European Commission (EC) (2014). 'Energy Security: Commission Puts Forward Comprehensive Strategy to Strengthen Security of Supply. *Press Release: IP/14/606*, 28 May.

European Commission (EC) (2015). http://ec.europa.eu/clima/change/causes/index_en.htm (Last Accessed 7 March 2015).

European Parliament and Council of the European Union (2013). 'Regulation (EU) No 1291/2013 of the European Parliament and of the Council of 11 December 2013 Establishing Horizon 2020 – the Framework Programme for Research and Innovation (2014–2020) and Repealing Decision No 1982/2006/EC (Text with EEA relevance).' *Official Journal of the European Union* 347 (20 December 2013): 104–73.

Eyer, J. and Corey, G., 2010. 'Energy Storage for the Electricity Grid: Benefits and Market Potential Assessment Guide: A Study for the DOE Energy Storage Systems Program', *Sandia Report SAND2010-0815*. California: Sandia National Laboratories.

Fouquet, R. (2010). 'The Slow Search for Solutions: Lessons from Historical Energy Transitions by Sector and Service', *Energy Policy* 38: 6586–96.

Frankel, J.A. (2012). 'The Natural Resource Curse: A Survey of Diagnoses and Some Prescriptions', in Arezki, R. *et al.* (eds.), *Commodity Price Volatility and Inclusive Growth in Low-Income Counties*. Washington, DC: International Monetary Fund.

Friedman, M. (1962). *Capitalism and Freedom*. Chicago: University of Chicago Press.

Friedrichs, J. (2011). 'Peak Energy and Climate Change: The Double Bind of Post-Normal Science', *Futures* 43: 469–77.

Fukuyama, F. (1989) 'The End of History?', *National Affairs* 16: 3–18.

G8 (Global Eight) (2006) 'Definition of Global Energy Security', for the G8 Summit 2006, St Petersburg. Available at: http://www.g8.utoronto.ca/summit/2006stpetersburg/energy.html (Last Accessed 29 April 2015).

Gagelmann, F. and Frondel, M. (2005). 'The Impact of Emission Trading on Innovation: Science Fiction or Reality?', *European Environment* 15: 203–11.

Garner, R. (2011). *Environmental Politics: The Age of Climate Change*. Basingstoke and New York: Palgrave Macmillan.

Garrone, P., Piscitello, L. and Wang, Y. (2010). 'Innovation Dynamics in the Renewable Energy Sector: The Role of Cross-Country Spillovers'. *USAEE Working Paper No. 12-136*. Cleveland: United States Associate for Energy Economics (USAEE).

Gazprom (2015). 'Gazprom Song'. Available at: https://www.youtube.com/watch?v=xGbI87tyr_4&feature=kp (Last Accessed 29 April 2015).

Ghazvinian, J. (2007). *Untapped: The Scramble for Africa's Oil*. Orlando: Harcourt.

Giddens, A. (2009). *The Politics of Climate Change*. Cambridge: Polity Press.

Gilpin, R. (1987). *The Political Economy of International Relations*. Princeton: Princeton University Press.

Goldemberg, J. and Lucon, O. (2010). *Energy, Environment and Development*. 2nd ed. Oxford and New York: Earthscan from Routledge.

Goldthau, A. (2010). 'Energy Diplomacy in Trade and Investment of Oil and Gas', in Goldthau, A. and Witte, J.M. (eds.), *Global Energy Governance: the New Rules of the Game*. Washington, DC: Brookings Press.

Goldthau, A. (2012). 'Emerging Governance Challenges for Eurasian Gas Markets after the Shale Gas Revolution', in Kuzemko, C. *et al.* (eds.), *Dynamics of Energy Governance in Europe and Russia*. London: Palgrave Macmillan.

Goldthau, A. and Witte, J.M. (2009). 'Back to the Future or Forward to the Past? Strengthening Markets and Rules for Effective Global Energy Governance', *International Affairs* 85(2): 373–90.

Goldthau, A. and Witte, J.M. (eds.) (2010). *Global Energy Governance: the New Rules of the Game*. Washington, DC: Brookings Press.

Goldthau, A. and Witte, J.M. (2011). 'Assessing OPEC's Performance in Global Energy', *Global Policy* 2 (Special Issue): 31–39.

Gonzalez, P.R. (2006). *Running Out: How Global Shortages Change the Economic Paradigm*. New York: Algora Publishing.

Greenpeace (2012). *Energy [R]evolution: A Sustainable World Energy Outlook*. 4th ed. Amsterdam: Greenpeace/EREC/GWEC.

Grevi, G., Keohane, D., Lee, B. and Lewis, P. (2013). *Empowering Europe's Future: Governance, Power and Options for the EU in a Changing World*. London: Chatham House. Available at: http://europa.eu/espas/pdf/espas-report-governance-power.pdf (Last Accessed 29 April 2015).

Grubb, M. (2004). 'Technology Innovation and Climate Policy: An Overview of Issues and Options', *KEIO Economic Studies* 41(2): 103.

Haas, P.M. (1992). 'Banning Chlorofluorocarbons: Epistemic Community Efforts to Protect Stratospheric Ozone', *International Organization* 46(1): 187–224.

Hadfield, A. (2008). 'Energy and Foreign Policy: EU-Russia Energy Dynamics', in Smith, S. *et al.* (eds.), *Foreign Policy: Theories, Actors, Cases*. Oxford: Oxford University Press.

Hall, D. (2007). *Energy Privatisation and Reform in East Africa*. University of Greenwich: PSIRU.

Hall, P. (1993). 'Policy Paradigms, Social Learning, and the State: The Case of Economic Policymaking in Britain', *Comparative Politics* 25(3): 275–96.

Hamilton, A. (1791). *Report on the Subject of Manufactures*. 2007 edition. New York: Cosimo.

Harks, E. (2010). 'The International Energy Forum and the Mitigation of Oil Market Risks', in Goldthau, A. and Witte, J.M. (eds.), *Global Energy Governance: The New Rules of the Game*. Washington, DC: Brookings Institution Press.

Harvey, D. (2005). *A Brief History of Neoliberalism*. Oxford: Oxford University Press.

Hayes, M.H. and Victor, D.G. (2006) 'Politics, Markets, and the Shift to Gas: Insights from the Seven Historical Cases', in Victor, D.G. *et al.* (eds.), *Natural Gas and Geopolitics: From 1970 to 2040*. Cambridge: Cambridge University Press.

Helm, D., Kay, J. and Thompson, D. (1989). *The Market for Energy*. Oxford: Oxford University Press.

Heynen, N., McCarthy, J., Prudham, S. and Robbins, P. (eds.) (2007). *Neoliberal Environments: False Promises and Unnatural Consequences*. Oxford: Routledge.

Hobbes, T. (1651). *Leviathan*. 1996 edition. Oxford: Oxford University Press.

Hoggett, R., Eyre, N. and Keay, M. (2013). 'Demand and Energy Security', in Mitchell, C. *et al.* (eds.), *New Challenges in Energy Security: The UK in a Multipolar World*. Basingstoke and New York: Palgrave Macmillan.

International Energy Agency (IEA) (2009). *Global Gaps in Clean Energy Research, Development, and Demonstration*. Paris: OECD/IEA.

International Energy Agency (IEA) (2012). *World Energy Outlook 2012*. Paris: OECD.

International Energy Agency (IEA) (2013). *World Energy Outlook 2013*. Paris: OECD.

International Energy Agency (IEA) (2014). *World Energy Outlook 2014*. Paris: OECD.

IEF (International Energy Forum) (2012). 'The IEA/IEF/OPEC Areas for Cooperation', a *Report for the 13th IEF Ministerial, Kuwait 12–14 March 2012*. Riyadh: IEF.

Inglehart, R. (1981). 'Post-Materialism in an Environment of Insecurity', *American Political Science Review* 75: 880–900.

International Energy Agency (IEA) (2007). *World Energy Outlook 2007: China and India Insights*. Paris: OECD.

International Energy Agency (IEA) (2008). *Energy Policy Review of Indonesia*. Paris: OECD.

International Energy Agency (IEA) (2010). *Energy Poverty: How to Make Modern Energy Access Universal?* Paris: OECD.

International Energy Agency (IEA) (2011). *World Energy Outlook 2011*. Paris: OECD.

International Energy Agency (IEA) (2013a). *Key World Energy Statistics*. Paris: OECD.

International Energy Agency/Organisation for Economic Cooperation and Development (IEA/OECD) (2010). *Analysis of the Scope of Energy Subsidies and Suggestions for the G-20 Initiative*. Joint Report (IEA/OECD/OPEC/World Bank) prepared 16 June 2010 for submission to the G-20 Summit Meeting, Toronto (Canada), 26–27 June 2010. World Bank.

IPCC (2007). *Climate Change 2007: Synthesis Report: Adaptation and Mitigation Options*. Geneva: IPCC. Available at: http://www.ipcc.ch/publications_and_data/ar4/syr/en/spms4.html (Last Accessed 29 April 2015).

IPCC (2013). *Climate Change 2013: The Physical Science Basis. Summary for Policymakers*. Available at: http://www.ipcc.ch/report/ar5/wg1/ (Last Accessed 29 April 2015).

IRENA (2014). *Renewable Energy and Jobs – Annual Report 2014*. Abu Dhabi, UAE: IRENA.

Irving, S. (2010). 'The Desertec Mirage: The Validity of DII Skepticism', *Human Security* 6: Spring.

ITPOES (2010). 'The Oil Crunch: a Wake-up Call for the UK Economy', Second report of the *UK Industry Taskforce on Peak Oil & Energy Security*. London: ITPOES.

Jarvis, D. (2010). 'Regulatory States in the South: Can They Exist and Do We Want Them? The Case of the Indonesia Power Sector', *Lee Kuan Yew School of Public Policy Working Paper Series*, Working Paper No.: SPP10-11, December.

Juma, C. and Yee-Cheong, L. (2005). *Innovation: Applying Knowledge to Development*. London: UNDP/Earthscan.

Junne, G. (1997). 'The End of Dinosaurs? Do New Technologies Lead to the Decline of Multinational?', in Talalay, M. *et al.* (eds.), *Technology, Culture and Competitiveness: Change and the World Political Economy*. London: Routledge.

Kant, I. (1795). *Perpetual Peace*. 2005 edition. New York: Cosimo.

Keating, M.F. (2011). 'Can Democratization Undermine Democracy? Economic and Political Reform in Uganda', *Democratization* 18(2): 415–42.

Keating, M.F. (2012a). 'Re-Thinking EU Energy Security: The Utility of Global Best Practices for Successful Transnational Energy Governance', in Kuzemko, C. *et al.* (eds.), *Dynamics of Energy Governance in Europe and Russia*. London: Palgrave Macmillan.

Keating, M.F. (2012b). 'Global Best Practices, National Innovation Systems, and Tertiary Education: A Critique of the World Bank's Accelerating Catch–up (2009)', *International Journal of Public Policy* 8(4): 251–65.

Keating, M.F., Kuzemko, C., Belyi, A.V. and Goldthau, A. (2012). 'Introduction: Bringing Energy into International Political Economy' in Kuzemko, C. *et al.* (eds.), *Dynamics of Energy Governance in Europe and Russia*. London: Palgrave Macmillan.

Keohane, R. (1984). *After Hegemony: Cooperation and Discord in the World Political Economy*. Princeton: Princeton University Press.

Keohane, R. (1990). 'Multilateralism: An Agenda for Research', *International Journal* 45: 731–64.

Keohane, R. and Nye, J. Jr. (1977). *Power and Interdependence*, 2nd ed. Boston: Little and Brown.

Keynes, J.M. (1936). *General Theory of Employment, Interest and Money*. 2007 edition. London: Palgrave Macmillan.

Klare, M. (2008). *Rising Powers, Shrinking Planet: How Scarce Energy is creating a New World Order*. Oxford: One World Publications.

Kline, S.J. and Rosenberg, N. (1986). 'An Overview of Innovation', in Landau, R. and Rosenberg, N. (eds.), *The Positive Sum Strategy: Harnessing Technology for Economic Growth*. Washington, DC: National Academies Press.

Krasner, S.D. (1983). 'Structural Causes and Regime Consequences: Regimes as Intervening Variables', in Krasner S.D. (ed.), *International Regimes*. Ithaca, NY: Cornell University Press.

Kuhn, T. (1962). *The Structure of Scientific Revolutions*. Chicago: University of Chicago Press.

Kuzemko, C. (2014a). 'Politicising UK Energy: What Speaking Energy Security Can Do', *Policy & Politics* 42(2): 259–74.

Kuzemko, C. (2014b). 'Ideas, Power and Change: Explaining EU-Russia Energy Relations', *Journal of European Public Policy* 21(1): 58–75.

Lee, B., Preston, F., Kooroshy, J., Bailey, R. and Lahn, G. (2013). 'Resources Futures', *A Chatham House Report, December 2012*. Available at: http://www.chathamhouse .org/sites/files/chathamhouse/public/Research/Energy,%20Environment%20 and%20Development/1212r_resourcesfutures.pdf (Last Accessed 29 April 2015).

Leftwich, A. (2000). *States of Development: On the Primacy of Politics in Development*. Cambridge: Polity.

Lenin, V.I. (1917). *Imperialism: The Highest Stage of Capitalism*. 1963 edition. Moscow: Progress Publishers.

Light, M (2006). 'Russia's Political Engagement with the EU', in Allison, R. *et al.* (eds.), *Putin's Russia and the Enlarged Europe*. Oxford: Blackwell Publishing.

Lipsey, R. and Chrystal, A. (2011). *Economics*. 12th ed. Oxford: Oxford University Press.

List, F. (1841). *The National System of Political Economy*. 2005 edition, Volumes 1-3. New York: Cosimo.

Litvinoff, M. (2012). 'Oil Extraction in Lake Albert'. *Briefing Booklet: Action for Better Governance Programme*. February. CAFOD/TROCAIRE

Locke J. (1689). *Second Treatise of Government*. 1980 edition. Indianapolis: Hackett.

Lockwood, M. (2013). 'The Political Economy of Low Carbon Development', in Urban, F. and Nordensvard, J. (eds.), *Low Carbon Development: Key Issues*. Oxford and New York: Earthscan from Routledge.

Löschel, A., Moslener, U. and Rübbelke, D. (2010). 'Energy Security – Concepts and Indicators', *Energy Policy* 38: 1607–8.

Lund, H. and Muenster, E. (2003). 'Management of Surplus Electricity-Production from a Fluctuating Energy Source', *Applied Energy* 76(1–3): 65–74.

Machiavelli, N. (1532). *The Prince*. 2005 edition. Oxford: Oxford University Press.

Mackinder, H. (1919). *Democratic Ideals and Reality: A Study in the Politics of Reconstruction*. 2009 edition. London: Faber and Faber.

Malthus, T. (1798). *An Essay on the Principles of Population*. 2008 edition. Oxford: Oxford University Press.

Markard, J., Raven, R. and Truffer, B. (2012). 'Sustainability Transitions: An Emerging Field of Research and its Prospects', *Research Policy* 41: 955–67.

Marx, K. (1867). *Capital (Volume 1)*. 1990 edition. London: Penguin.

Marx, K. and Engels, F. (1848). *The Communist Manifesto*. 2004 edition. London: Penguin.

Mazzucato, M. (2013). *The Entrepreneurial State: Debunking Public vs. Private Sector Myths*. London: Anthem Press.

Meadows, D.H., Goldsmith, E.I. and Meadow, P. (1972). *The Limits to Growth*. London: Earth Island Limited.

Medvedev, D. (2009). 'Conceptual Approach to the New Legal Framework for Energy Cooperation (Goals and Principles)', Moscow: President of Russia, April 21. Available at: http://en.kremlin.ru/supplement/258 (Last Accessed 29 April 2015).

Meeus, M. and Hage, J. (2006). 'Product and Process Innovation, Scientific Research, Knowledge Dynamics, and Institutional Change: An Introduction', in Hage, J. and Meeus, M. (eds.), *Innovation, Science and Institutional Change*. Oxford: Oxford University Press.

Meierding, E. (2011). 'Energy Security and Sub-Saharan Africa', *International Development Policy / Revue Internationale de Politique de Développement*, 2.

Menz, F.C. and Seip, H.M. (2004). 'Acid Rain in Europe and the United States', *Environmental Science and Policy* 7(4): 235–65.

Metcalfe, J.S. (1995). 'The Economic Foundations of Technology Policy: Equilibrium and Evolutionary Perspectives', in Stoneman, P. (ed.), *Handbook of the Economics of Innovation and Technological Change*. Oxford: Blackwell.

Metcalfe, J.S. (2006). 'Innovation, Competition, and Enterprise: Foundations for Economic Evolution in Learning Economies', in Hage, J. and Meeus, M. (eds.), *Innovation, Science and Institutional Change*. Oxford: Oxford University Press.

Mill, J.S. (1859). *On Liberty*. 2006 edition. London: Penguin.

Ministry of Energy of the Russian Federation (2010). *Energy Strategy of Russia: for the Period up to 2030*. Moscow: Institute of Energy Strategy.

Mitchell, C. (2008). *The Political Economy of Sustainable Energy*. Basingstoke and New York: Palgrave Macmillan.

Mitchell, C., Watson, J. and Whiting, J. (2013). *New Challenges in Energy Security: the UK in a Multipolar World*. Basingstoke and New York: Palgrave Macmillan.

Mitchell, J. with Morita, K., Selley, N. and Stern, J. (2001). 'Energy Security', in Mitchell, J.V. et al. (eds.) *The New Economy of Oil: Impacts on Business, Geopolitics and Society*. London: Royal Institute of International Affairs.

Mitchell, J., Morita, N., Selley, N. and Stern, J. (eds.) (2001). *The New Economy of Oil: Impacts on Business, Geopolitics and Society*. London: Royal Institute for International Affairs.

Mitchell, J.V. (2005). *Producer-Consumer Dialogue: What can Energy Ministers say to Each Other?* London: Chatham House.

Monbiot, G. (2007). *Heat: How we can Stop the Planet Burning*. London: Penguin.

Müller-Jentsch, D. (2001). 'The Development of Electricity Markets in the Euro-Mediterranean Area – Trends and Prospects for Liberalization and Regional Integration', World Bank Technical Paper No. 491. Washington, DC: World Bank/European Commission on Private Participation in Mediterranean Infrastructure (PPMI).

Newberry, D. (1990). 'Acid Rain', *Economic Policy* 5(11): 297–346.

Newell, P. (2011). 'The Governance of Energy Finance: The Public, the Private and the Hybrid', *Global Policy* 2(September): 94–105.

Nonaka, I. and Peltokorpi, V. (2006). 'Knowledge-Based View of Radical Innovation: Toyota Prius Case', in Hage, J. and Meeus, M. (eds.), *Innovation, Science and Institutional Change*. Oxford: Oxford University Press.

OPEC (2012). *Statute 2012*. Vienna: Organization of the Petroleum Exporting Countries (OPEC).

O'Sullivan, M. (2013). 'The Entanglement of Energy, Grand Strategy, and International Security', in Goldthau, A. (ed.) *Wiley Handbook of Global Energy Policy*. London: Wiley Blackwell.

Owen, R. (1813-16). *A New View of Society*. 1991 edition. London: Penguin.

Perez, C. (2002). *Technological Revolutions and Financial Capital: The Dynamics of Bubbles and Golden Ages*. Cheltenham: Edward Elgar.

Pirani, S., Stern, J.P. and Yafimava, K. (2009). *The Russo-Ukrainian Gas Dispute of January 2009: A Comprehensive Assessment*. Oxford: Oxford Institute for Energy Studies.

Polanyi, K. (1944). *The Great Transformation*. 2001 edition. Boston: Beacon Press.

Pricewaterhousecoopers (2013). *Decarbonisation and the Economy: An Empirical Analysis of the Economic Impact of Energy and Climate Change Policies in Denmark, Sweden, Germany, UK and the Netherlands*. Pricewaterhousecoopers, October.

REN21 (The Renewable Energy Policy Network for the 21st Century) (2014). http://www.ren21.net/Portals/0/documents/Resources/GSR/2014/GSR2014_ KeyFindings_low%20res.pdf (Last Accessed 29 April 2015).

Ricardo, D. (1817). *On the Principles of Political Economy and Taxation*. 1973 edition. London: Cambridge University Press.

Rifkin, J. (2011). *The Third Industrial Revolution: How Lateral Power is transforming Energy, the Economy, and the World*. New York: Palgrave Macmillan.

Roberts, B. and McDowall, J. (2005). 'Commercial Successes in Power Storage', *Power and Energy Magazine, IEEE* 3(2): 24–30.

Rosenau, J.N. (1990). *Turbulence in World Politics*. London: Harvester-Wheatsheaf.

Rosser, A. (2006). 'The Political Economy of the Resource Curse: A Literature Survey'. *Institute of Development Studies Working Paper 268*. Brighton, UK: Institute of Development Studies.

Rubin, E.S., Taylor, M.R., Yeh, S. and Hounshell, D.A. (2004). 'Learning Curves for Environmental Technology and their Importance for Climate Policy Analysis', *Energy* 29: 1551–9.

Rudd, K. (2009). 'The Global Financial Crisis', *The Monthly*. February 20.

Sachs, J.D. and Warner, A.M. (1995). 'Natural Resource Abundance and Economic Growth', *National Bureau of Economic Research Working paper No. 5398*, Cambridge, MA. Revised 1997, 1999.

Sachs, J.D. and Warner, A.M. (2001). 'Natural Resources and Economic Development: The Curse of Natural Resources', *European Economic Review* 45: 827–38.

Schneider, M., Froggatt, A. and Thomas, S. (2011). *Nuclear Power in a Post-Fukushima World: 25 Years after the Chernobyl Accident*. Washington, DC: World Watch Institute.

Schobart, H. (2014). *Energy: The Basics*. London and New York: Routledge.

Schumacher, E.F. (1973). *Small is Beautiful: Economics as if People Mattered*. New York: Harper Perennial.

Schumpeter, J. (1912). *The Theory of Economic Development: An Inquiry into Profits, Capital, Credit, Interest and the Business Cycle*. Cambridge: Harvard University Press.

Schumpeter, J. (1942). *Capitalism, Socialism and Democracy*. New York: Harper.

Selivanova, Y. (2010). 'Managing the Patchwork of Agreements in Trade and Investment', in Goldthau, A. and Witte, J.M. (eds.) *Global Energy Governance: The New Rules of the Game*. Washington, DC: Brookings Press.

Sen, A. (1999). *Development as Freedom*. New York: Random House.

Shell (2008). *Shell Energy Scenarios to 2050*. The Hague, Netherlands: Shell International BV.

Shi, X. and Malik, C. (2013). 'Assessment of ASEAN Energy Cooperation within the ASAN Economic Community', *ERIA Discussion Paper 2013-37*, ERIA-DP-2013-37, Jakarta, Indonesia: Economic Research Institute for ASEAN and East Asia (ERIA).

Sims, R.E.H., Schock, R.N., Adegbululgbe, A., Fenhann, J., Konstantinavicuite, I., Moomaw, W., Nimir, H.B., Schlamadinger, B., Torres-Martínez, J., Turner, C., Uchiyama, Y., Vuori, S.J.V., Wamukonya, N. and Zhang, X. (2007). 'Energy Supply', in Mietz, B. *et al.* (eds.), *Climate Change 2007: Contribution of Working Group III to the Fourth Assessment Report of the Intergovernmental Panel on Climate Change*. Cambridge and New York: Cambridge University Press.

Smil, V. (2010). *Prime Movers of Globalization: The History and Impact of Diesel Engines and Gas Turbines*. Cambridge, MA: MIT Press.

Smith, A. (1776). *The Wealth of Nations*. 2008 edition. Oxford: Oxford University Press.

Sørensen, B. (2012). *A History of Energy: Northern Europe from the Stone Age to the Present Day*. Oxford and New York: Earthscan from Routledge.

Sovacool, B. (2011). *The Routledge Handbook of Energy Security*. London and New York: Routledge.

Sovacool, B. (2012). 'The Political Economy of Energy Poverty: A Review of Key Challenges', *Energy for Sustainable Development* 16: 272–82.

Sovacool, B.K., Sidortsov, R.V. and Jones, B.J. (2014). *Energy Security, Equality, and Justice*. Oxford and New York: Earthscan from Routledge.

Spero, J.E. and Hart, J.A. (1997). *The Politics of International Economic Relations*, 5th ed. London: Routledge.

Stanislaw, J. (2004). 'Energy Competition or Co-operation: Shifting the Paradigm', *Economic Perspectives* 9(2): 17–20.

Stern, N. (2006). *Stern Review on the Economics of Climate Change*. London: HM Government.

Strange, S. (1988). *States and Markets*. London and New York: Continuum.

Thompson, A. (2010). *An Introduction to African Politics*. 3rd ed. London: Routledge.

Thucydides (431 BCE). *The Peloponnesian War*. 2009 edition. Oxford: Oxford University Press.

Trotsky, L. (1930). *The History of the Russian Revolution*. 2008 edition. Chicago: Haymarket.

UK Department for Business Innovation and Skills (BIS) (2012). *Low Carbon Environmental Goods and Services (LCEGS)*. London: BIS.

United Nations Industrial Development Organization (UNIDO) (2011). *Industrial Development Report: Industrial Energy Efficiency for Sustainable Wealth Creation*. Vienna: UNIDO. Available at: http://www.unido.org/fileadmin/user_media/Publications/IDR/2011/UNIDO_FULL_REPORT_EBOOK.pdf (Last Accessed 29 April 2015).

United Nations Commission on Environment and Development (UNCED) (1987). *Our Common Future* (the Brundtland Report). Oxford: Oxford University Press.

United Nations Department of Economic and Social Affairs (2010). *The World's Women 2010: Trends and Statistics*. New York: UN DESA.

United Nations Development Program (UNDP) (2000). *World Energy Assessment: Energy and the Challenge of Sustainability*. New York: UNDP.

United Nations Development Program (UNDP) (2009). *Contribution of Energy Services to the Millennium Development Goals and to Poverty Alleviation in Latin America and the Caribbean*. Santiago, Chile: UNDP.

United Nations Development Program (UNDP) (2010). *Human Development Report 2010 – 20th Anniversary Edition. The Real Wealth of Nations: Pathways to Human Development*. New York: UNDP.

United Nations Development Program (UNDP) (2013). *Human Development Report 2013. The Rise of the South: Human Progress in a Diverse World*. New York: UNDP.

Unruh, G.C. (2000). 'Understanding Carbon Lock-in', *Energy Policy* 28(12): 817–30.

Urban, F. and Nordensvärd, J. (2013). 'Low Carbon Development: Origins, Concepts and Key Issues', in Urban, F. and Nordensvärd, J. (eds.), *Low Carbon Development: Key Issues*. Oxford and New York: Earthscan from Routledge.

Valencia, M.J. (1986). 'Taming Troubled Waters: Joint Development of Oil and Mineral Resources in Overlapping Claim Areas', *San Diego Law Review* 23(3): 661–84.

Victor, D. and Yueh, L. (2010). 'The New Energy Order: Managing Insecurities in the Twenty-first Century', *Foreign Affairs* 89(1): 61–73.

Victor, D. and Heller, T.C. (eds.) (2007). *The Political Economy of Power Sector Reform: The Experiences of Five Major Developing Countries*. Cambridge: Cambridge University Press.

Vie, O.E. (2012). 'The Need for Knowledge Integration in Renewable Energy Innovation Projects', *Energy Procedia* 20: 364–76.

Von Clausewitz, C. (1832). *On War*. 1997 edition. London: Wordsworth Editions.

von Hayek, F. (1944). *The Road to Serfdom*. 2001 edition. London: Routledge.

Waltz, K. (1959). *Man, the State, and War*. New York: Columbia University Press.

Weber, M. (2009). *From Max Weber: Essays in Sociology*. London: Routledge.

Which? (2013). The (Im)balance of Power: Wholesale Costs and Retail Pricing, July 2013. Available at: http://press.which.co.uk/wp-content/uploads/2013/08/The-Imbalance-of-Power-Wholesale-Costs-and-Retail-Prices-LOW-RES-July-2013.pdf (Last Accessed 29 April 2015).

World Bank (1996). *Rural Energy and Development: Improving Energy Supplies for Two Billion People*. Washington, DC: World Bank.

World Bank (2010). *Meeting the Electricity Supply/Demand Balance in Latin America & the Caribbean*. Washington, DC: World Bank/ESMAP.

World Health Organisation (WHO) (2006). *Fuel for Life: Household Energy and Health*. Geneva: WHO.

World Health Organisation (WHO) (2011). *World Health Statistics* 2011. Geneva: WHO.

Yergin, D. (2007). 'The Fundamentals of Energy Security', a Testimonial before the U.S. House of Representatives' Committee on Foreign Policy and National Security Implications of Oil Dependence, March 22 2007. Washington, DC: US House of Representatives. Available at: http://democrats.foreignaffairs.house.gov/110/yer032207.htm (Last Accessed 29 April 2015).

Yergin, D. (1990). *The Prize: The Epic Quest for Oil, Money & Power*. London: Simon and Schuster.

Yergin, D. and Stanislaw, J. (1998). *The Commanding Heights: The Battle between Government and the Marketplace that is Remaking the Modern World*. London: Simon and Schuster.

Yergin, D. (2006). 'Ensuring Energy Security', *Foreign Affairs* 85(2): 69–82.

Youngs, R. (2009). *Energy Security: Europe's New Foreign Policy Challenge*. Abingdon and New York: Routledge.

Zysman, J. (1996). 'The Myth of a 'Global Economy': Enduring National Foundations and Emerging Regional Realities', *New Political Economy* 1(2): 157–84.

Index

Note: Page numbers with b indicate boxes; those with f indicate figures.

235